The Inner Circle

Guide to Foundational Knowledge of All Things Direct Sales

By Sydney Brown

The Inner Circle

GUIDE TO FOUNDATIONAL KNOWLEDGE OF ALL THINGS DIRECT SALES

by Sydney Brown

Published by TLM Publishing House

5905 Atlanta Highway, Alpharetta GA.
https://www.ttpublishinghouse.com
Copyright © 2023 TLM Publishing House

All rights reserved. No portion of this book may be reproduced in any form without permission from the publisher except as permitted by U.S. copyright law. For permissions, contact: info@tlmpublishinghouse.com

Legal Disclaimer: We utilized ChatGPT for help with research. We are making no claims, whether medical, financial, or otherwise.

Contents

Section 1: 1

Discovering Your "Why" and Developing Passion 1

Understanding the Importance of Your "Why" in Life and Decision-Making 2

    Defining Your "Why" 2

    The Power of Purpose 2

    Identifying Your "Why" 3

    Applying Your "Why" 4

    Reviewing and Adapting 4

Reflecting on Your Personal Values and Beliefs: A Path to Self-Discovery and Fulfillment 7

    Understanding Personal Values 7

    Common examples of personal values include: 7

    Identifying Your Beliefs 8

    Examples of personal beliefs might include: 8

    The Importance of Reflecting on Values and Beliefs 8

    The Reflective Process 9

Discovering Your Passion: A Comprehensive Guide to Identifying Your Passions and Interests 11

    The Significance of Identifying Your Passions and Interests 11

    How to Identify Your Passions and Interests 12

    Overcoming Challenges in Identifying Your Passions 12

    Incorporating Passions into Your Life 13

The Synergy of Purpose: Connecting Your "Why" to Your Passions 15

    Understanding Your "Why" 15

    Identifying Your Passions 15

    The Synergy of Purpose 16

    Steps to Connect Your "Why" to Your Passions 16

The North Star of Success: The Role of Purpose in Business Decisions 19

The Concept of Purpose in Business 19

The Role of Purpose in Business Decisions 19

Impact on Sustainability and Corporate Responsibility 20

Case Studies: Successful Purpose-Driven Companies 21

Steps to Integrate Purpose into Business Decisions 21

Pursuing Passion and Profit: Researching Industries Aligned with Your Passions 23

Why Align Your Career or Business with Your Passions 23

Researching Industries Aligned with Your Passions 24

Case Studies: Real-world Examples 24

Overcoming Challenges 25

Steps to Pursuing Your Passion-Driven Career 25

Navigating Success: Analyzing Market Trends and Opportunities 27

The Significance of Analyzing Market Trends 27

The Process of Analyzing Market Trends and Opportunities 28

Tools and Resources for Analyzing Market Trends 28

Navigating Through Industry Disruption 29

Case Studies: Examples of Successful Market Trend Analysis 29

The Art of Opportunity Identification 30

Strategic Planning 30

Uncovering Opportunities: Identifying Gaps in the Market 31

The Significance of Identifying Market Gaps 31

The Process of Identifying Market Gaps 32

Tools and Resources for Identifying Market Gaps 32

Analyzing Market Gaps 33

Case Studies: Examples of Identifying Market Gaps 33

The Art of Opportunity Identification 34

Implementing Strategies 34

Evaluating Your Skills and Expertise: A Comprehensive Guide 35

  Self-Assessment 35

  Goal Setting 36

  Skill Gap Analysis 36

  Seek Professional Advice 37

  Continuous Learning 37

  Monitor Progress 38

Choosing Industries That Align with Your "Why": A Comprehensive Guide 39

  Define Your "Why" 39

  Research and Explore 40

  Assess Career Fit 40

  Education and Skill Development 41

  Take Action 41

  Adapt and Evolve 42

Researching Potential Network Marketing Companies: A Comprehensive Guide 43

  Understand the Basics of Network Marketing 43

  Check the Company's Background 44

  Product or Service Quality 44

  Compensation Plan Analysis 45

  Company Reputation and Reviews 45

  Training and Support 46

  Assess Your Fit 46

Assessing a Company's Mission and Values: A Comprehensive Guide 49

  Understanding the Significance 49

  Start with the Company's Mission Statement 50

  Analyze the Company's Core Values 50

  Corporate Social Responsibility (CSR) Initiatives 51

  Investigate Ethical and Legal Issues 52

Seek Third-Party Evaluations 52

Company Culture and Employee Feedback 52

Assessing Your Personal Alignment 53

Evaluating the Product or Service Offered: A Comprehensive Guide ... 55

Define Your Objectives 55

Research and Gather Information 56

Quality and Performance 56

Suitability and Compatibility 57

Customer Support and Reliability 57

Cost and Value 58

Risk Assessment 58

Trial Period or Pilot Testing 59

Understanding Compensation Plans: A Comprehensive Guide 61

What Is a Compensation Plan? 61

Components of a Compensation Plan 62

Employee Compensation Plans 62

Sales Compensation Plans 63

MLM Compensation Plans 64

Investment Compensation Plans 65

Tax Considerations 65

Connecting Your "Why" with a Network Marketing Opportunity: A Comprehensive Guide 67

Define Your "Why" 67

Understand Network Marketing 68

Assess the Product or Service 68

Determine Your Unique Selling Proposition (USP) 69

Evaluate the Company Culture 69

Set Clear Goals 70

Align Your "Why" with Your Team 70

The Importance of Personal Alignment in Business: Achieving Success and Fulfillment 73
    Personal Alignment Defined 73
    Personal Alignment and Career Satisfaction 74
    Building an Aligned Career 74
    Business Success Through Personal Alignment 75
    Case Studies: Personal Alignment in Business 76
    Challenges and Strategies 76

Strategies for Staying Passionate About Your Business: Keys to Long-Term Success 79
    Reconnect with Your "Why" 79
    Set Clear and Inspiring Goals 80
    Embrace Continuous Learning 80
    Surround Yourself with Passionate People 81
    Reevaluate and Evolve 81
    Practice Self-Care 81
    Celebrate Milestones and Achievements 82
    Reignite Your Creativity 82
    Delegate and Collaborate 83
    Stay Adaptable 83

Setting Long-Term Business Goals: A Comprehensive Guide to Sustainable Success 85
    Why Long-Term Business Goals Matter 85
    Types of Long-Term Business Goals 86
    The SMART Approach 86
    Steps to Setting Long-Term Business Goals 87
    Long-Term Goal Examples 88
    Maintaining Focus and Motivation 89

Identifying Potential Obstacles and Challenges: A Comprehensive Guide to Effective Problem-Solving 91

- The Significance of Identifying Obstacles and Challenges 91
- Strategies for Identifying Potential Obstacles and Challenges 92
- Common Obstacles and Challenges in Various Fields 92
- Effective Problem-Solving Strategies 93
- Emotional Resilience and Attitude 94
- Case Studies: Learning from Obstacles 95

Building a Support Network for Motivation: A Comprehensive Guide to Achieving Your Goals 97
- The Role of a Support Network in Motivation 97
- Types of Support Network Members 98
- Strategies for Building a Support Network 98
- Maintaining Your Support Network 99
- Virtual and Online Support Networks 100
- Case Studies: The Power of Support Networks 101

Crafting a Personal Mission Statement: A Guiding Light to a Purposeful Life 103
- Understanding the Purpose of a Personal Mission Statement 103
- Steps to Crafting Your Personal Mission Statement 104
- Key Elements of a Personal Mission Statement 105
- Examples of Personal Mission Statements 106
- Implementing Your Personal Mission Statement 106
- The Impact of a Personal Mission Statement 107

Defining Your Unique Selling Proposition (USP): Unleashing Your Competitive Advantage 109
- Understanding the Unique Selling Proposition (USP) 109
- The Importance of a Strong USP 109
- Steps to Define Your Unique Selling Proposition (USP) 110
- Types of USP 111
- Examples of Successful USPs 112
- Implementing Your USP 112

- Measuring the Success of Your USP 113
- Setting Personal Development Goals: A Path to Self-Improvement and Fulfillment 115
  - Why Set Personal Development Goals? 115
  - The SMART Goal Setting Framework 116
  - The Steps to Setting Personal Development Goals 116
  - Common Areas for Personal Development Goals 117
  - Tips for Achieving Personal Development Goals 118
- Developing a Growth Mindset: Unlocking Your Potential for Success 121
  - Understanding the Growth Mindset 121
  - The Importance of a Growth Mindset 121
  - Steps to Develop a Growth Mindset 122
  - The Impact of a Growth Mindset 123
  - Cultivating a Growth Mindset in Different Areas of Life 124
  - Overcoming Challenges in Developing a Growth Mindset 124
  - Case Studies: Real-Life Examples of a Growth Mindset 125
- Leveraging Your "Why" in Marketing: Building Authentic Connections with Your Audience 127
  - Understanding Your "Why" in Marketing 127
  - The Importance of Leveraging Your "Why" 127
  - Steps to Leverage Your "Why" in Marketing 128
  - Real-Life Examples of Brands Leveraging Their "Why" 129
  - Measuring the Impact of Leveraging Your "Why" 130
- Creating a Brand Story that Resonates: The Art of Authentic Branding 131
  - The Power of a Resonating Brand Story 131
  - Steps to Create a Resonating Brand Story 132
  - Real-Life Examples of Resonating Brand Stories 133
  - Measuring the Impact of Your Brand Story 133

Building a Strong Online Presence: Strategies for Success 135

    Understanding the Importance of an Online Presence 135

    Strategies to Build a Strong Online Presence 136

    Tools to Help Build Your Online Presence 137

    Common Pitfalls to Avoid 138

    Measuring the Success of Your Online Presence 138

The Power of Storytelling in Business Communication 141

    The Significance of Storytelling in Business Communication 141

    Strategies for Effective Storytelling in Business Communication ... 142

    Real-World Examples of Storytelling in Business 143

    Measuring the Impact of Storytelling 144

Incorporating Your "Why" into Your Brand: Creating Authentic Connections 145

    The Significance of Your "Why" in Your Brand 145

    Steps to Incorporate Your "Why" into Your Brand 146

    Real-Life Examples of Brands Incorporating Their "Why" 147

    Measuring the Impact of Incorporating Your "Why" 147

Section 2: 149

Progression to Finding Your Ideal Customer 149

Monitoring and Adjusting Your Business Alignment for Success 151

    The Significance of Monitoring Business Alignment 151

    Key Areas to Monitor for Business Alignment 152

    Strategies for Monitoring and Adjusting Business Alignment 153

    Real-World Examples of Monitoring and Adjusting Business Alignment 154

    Measuring the Impact of Monitoring and Adjusting Business Alignment 154

Understanding the Concept of an Ideal Customer 157

    What is an Ideal Customer? 157

    Why is Defining Your Ideal Customer Important? 157

How to Define Your Ideal Customer 158

Benefits of Catering to Your Ideal Customer 159

Real-World Examples of Defining Ideal Customers 159

Defining Demographic and Psychographic Characteristics 161

Demographic Characteristics 161

Psychographic Characteristics 162

The Significance of Demographic and Psychographic Characteristics 163

Methods to Define Demographic and Psychographic Characteristics 164

Practical Applications in Business and Marketing 164

Conducting Market Research to Identify Your Target Audience 167

The Significance of Identifying Your Target Audience 167

Key Steps in Conducting Market Research 168

Tools and Techniques for Market Research 169

The Role of Buyer Personas 169

Benefits of Target Audience Identification 170

Conclusion 171

Creating Customer Personas: A Guide to Understanding Your Audience 173

The Significance of Creating Customer Personas 173

Steps to Create Customer Personas 174

Elements of a Customer Persona 174

Real-World Examples of Customer Personas 175

Benefits of Customer Personas 176

Analyzing Your Existing Customer Base: A Guide to Informed Business Growth 177

The Significance of Analyzing Your Existing Customer Base 177

Key Steps in Analyzing Your Existing Customer Base 178

Methods and Tools for Analyzing Your Customer Base 179

Practical Applications for Informed Business Growth 179

Real-World Examples of Customer Base Analysis 180

Segmenting Your Audience for Tailored Marketing: A Comprehensive Guide 183

The Significance of Audience Segmentation 183

Key Steps in Audience Segmentation 184

Segmentation Criteria 184

Practical Applications in Marketing 185

Real-World Examples of Audience Segmentation 186

Identifying Your Audience's Pain Points: A Comprehensive Guide 189

The Significance of Identifying Your Audience's Pain Points 189

Key Steps in Identifying Pain Points 190

Methods for Identifying Pain Points 190

Practical Applications for Addressing Pain Points 191

Real-World Examples of Addressing Pain Points 192

Conducting Surveys and Interviews for Insights: A Comprehensive Guide 193

The Significance of Conducting Surveys and Interviews 193

Key Steps in Conducting Surveys and Interviews 194

Best Practices for Effective Surveys and Interviews 195

Practical Applications for Gaining Insights 195

Real-World Examples of Surveys and Interviews 196

Using Social Listening to Understand Customer Needs: A Comprehensive Guide 199

The Significance of Using Social Listening 199

Key Steps in Using Social Listening 200

Best Practices for Effective Social Listening 200

Practical Applications for Understanding Customer Needs 201

Real-World Examples of Successful Social Listening 202

Exploring Customer Journey Mapping: A Comprehensive Guide 203

- The Significance of Customer Journey Mapping 203
- Key Steps in Customer Journey Mapping 204
- Best Practices for Effective Customer Journey Mapping 204
- Practical Applications of Customer Journey Mapping 205
- Real-World Examples of Successful Customer Journey Mapping 206

Analyzing Customer Feedback for Improvement: A Comprehensive Guide 209

- The Significance of Analyzing Customer Feedback 209
- Key Steps in Analyzing Customer Feedback 210
- Best Practices for Effective Customer Feedback Analysis 210
- Practical Applications for Improvement 211
- Real-World Examples of Successful Customer Feedback Analysis . 212

Creating Empathy Maps to Understand Your Audience: A Comprehensive Guide 213

- The Significance of Creating Empathy Maps 213
- Key Steps in Creating Empathy Maps 214
- Best Practices for Effective Empathy Maps 214
- Practical Applications for Understanding Your Audience 215
- Real-World Examples of Successful Empathy Mapping 215

Identifying Common Challenges Your Audience Faces: A Comprehensive Guide 217

- The Significance of Identifying Common Challenges 217
- Key Steps in Identifying Common Challenges 218
- Best Practices for Identifying Common Challenges 218
- Practical Applications for Addressing Common Challenges 219
- Real-World Examples of Identifying Common Challenges 220

Understanding the Emotional Aspect of Pain Points: A Comprehensive Guide 221

- The Significance of Understanding Emotional Pain Points 221
- Identifying Emotional Pain Points 222

- Best Practices for Addressing Emotional Pain Points 223
- Examples of Emotional Pain Points 223
- Addressing Emotional Pain Points in Different Contexts 224

Prioritizing Pain Points for Addressing: A Comprehensive Guide 227
- The Significance of Prioritizing Pain Points 227
- Key Steps in Prioritizing Pain Points 228
- Best Practices for Prioritizing Pain Points 229
- Practical Applications for Prioritization 229
- Real-World Examples of Prioritizing Pain Points 230

Using Data Analysis to Pinpoint Critical Issues: A Comprehensive Guide 231
- The Significance of Using Data Analysis 231
- Key Steps in Using Data Analysis 232
- Best Practices for Data Analysis 233
- Practical Applications for Data Analysis 233
- Real-World Examples of Using Data Analysis 234

Assessing the Impact of Pain Points on Decision-Making: A Comprehensive Guide 235
- The Significance of Assessing the Impact of Pain Points 235
- Key Steps in Assessing the Impact of Pain Points 236
- Best Practices for Assessing the Impact of Pain Points 237
- Practical Applications for Assessment 237
- Real-World Examples of Impact Assessment 238

Creating a Pain Point Scorecard: A Comprehensive Guide 241
- The Significance of Creating a Pain Point Scorecard 241
- Key Steps in Creating a Pain Point Scorecard 242
- Best Practices for Creating a Pain Point Scorecard 243
- Practical Applications for a Pain Point Scorecard 243
- Real-World Examples of Pain Point Scorecards 244

Crafting Messaging that Resonates with Pain Points: A Comprehensive Guide 247

    The Significance of Crafting Messaging that Resonates with Pain Points 247

    Key Steps in Crafting Messaging that Resonates with Pain Points . 248

    Best Practices for Crafting Messaging 249

    Practical Applications for Crafting Messaging 250

    Real-World Examples of Pain Point Messaging 250

Developing Solutions to Address Customer Pain Points: A Comprehensive Guide 253

    The Significance of Addressing Customer Pain Points 253

    Key Steps in Developing Solutions for Customer Pain Points 254

    Best Practices for Developing Solutions 255

    Practical Applications for Developing Solutions 256

    Real-World Examples of Pain Point Solutions 256

Personalizing Your Approach for Each Customer: A Comprehensive Guide 259

    The Significance of Personalizing Your Approach 259

    Key Steps in Personalizing Your Approach 260

    Best Practices for Personalization 261

    Practical Applications for Personalization 261

    Real-World Examples of Personalization 262

Mapping Pain Point Solutions to Your Product/Service: A Comprehensive Guide 263

    The Significance of Mapping Pain Point Solutions 263

    Key Steps in Mapping Pain Point Solutions 264

    Best Practices for Mapping Pain Point Solutions 265

    Practical Applications for Mapping Pain Point Solutions 265

    Real-World Examples of Pain Point Solutions 266

Building Trust Through Addressing Pain Points 269

- Understanding Pain Points 269
- Addressing Pain Points 270
- Case Study: Amazon's Approach to Addressing Pain Points 271
- Maintaining Trust 271

Measuring the Effectiveness of Your Solutions 273
- Define Clear Objectives and Metrics 273
- Pre-Implementation Baseline Data 273
- Key Performance Indicators (KPIs) 274
- Surveys and Feedback 274
- Comparative Analysis 274
- Cost-Benefit Analysis 274
- A/B Testing 275
- Post-Implementation Data 275
- Feedback Loops 275
- Reporting and Visualization 275

The Power of Testimonials and Success Stories 277
- The Significance of Testimonials and Success Stories 277
- Gathering Testimonials 278
- Creating Compelling Success Stories 279
- Leveraging Testimonials and Success Stories 279

Section 3: Effective Communication Without Being Salesy 281

The Psychology of Sales and Persuasion 283
- The Psychology of Persuasion 283
- The Psychology of Sales 284
- Persuasion Techniques 285

Building Rapport with Potential Customers 287
- The Importance of Building Rapport 287
- The Psychology of Rapport Building 288
- Practical Strategies for Building Rapport 289

Creating a Genuine Connection with Your Audience 291
- The Importance of Creating a Genuine Connection 291
- The Psychology of Creating a Connection 292
- Practical Strategies for Creating a Genuine Connection 293
- Engage in Conversations 293

The Art of Active Listening: A Comprehensive Guide 295
- Understanding Active Listening 295
- The Psychology of Active Listening 296
- Practical Techniques for Active Listening 296

The Art of Asking Open-Ended Questions to Uncover Needs: A Comprehensive Guide 299
- Understanding Open-Ended Questions 299
- The Psychology of Open-Ended Questions 300
- Practical Techniques for Asking Open-Ended Questions 300

Avoiding Common Sales Pitfalls 303
- The Common Sales Pitfalls 303
- The Consequences of Sales Pitfalls 304
- Practical Strategies to Avoid Common Sales Pitfalls 305

Mastering Consultative Selling Techniques 307
- Understanding Consultative Selling 307
- The Psychology of Consultative Selling 308
- Practical Techniques for Consultative Selling 308

Demonstrating Empathy in Sales Conversations 311
- Understanding the Importance of Empathy in Sales 311
- The Psychology of Empathy 312
- Practical Strategies for Demonstrating Empathy 313

Handling Objections with Grace and Professionalism 315
- Understanding the Importance of Objection Handling 315
- The Psychology of Objection Handling 316

Practical Strategies for Handling Objections with Grace and Professionalism 317

Crafting Compelling Sales Pitches 319
Understanding the Importance of a Compelling Sales Pitch 319
The Psychology of Crafting Compelling Sales Pitches 320
Practical Strategies for Crafting Compelling Sales Pitches 321

Creating Value-Driven Proposals 323
Know Your Audience 323
Start with a Strong Value Proposition 323
Utilize Storytelling 324
Emphasize Benefits over Features 324
Offer Proof of Concept 324
Tailor Your Proposal 324
Foster Transparency 325
Address Objections and Concerns 325
Provide a Clear Call to Action (CTA) 325
Follow Up 325

Developing trust in your relationships 327
Self-Trust: The Foundation 327
Open and Honest Communication 327
Reliability and Consistency 327
Vulnerability and Empathy 328
Mutual Respect 328
Consistency in Behavior 328
Deliver on Promises 328
Honesty and Transparency 329
Admit Mistakes and Apologize 329
Establish Boundaries 329
Time and Patience 329

- Forgiveness 330
- Weaving Narratives: Using Storytelling to Illustrate Solutions 331
  - The Power of Storytelling in Problem-Solving 331
  - Practical Tips for Using Storytelling to Illustrate Solutions 332
  - Examples of Storytelling in Problem-Solving 333
- Mastering Communication: Employing the "Feel, Felt, Found" Method 335
  - What is the "Feel, Felt, Found" Method? 335
  - How it Works 335
  - Examples of the "Feel, Felt, Found" Method in Action 336
- The Power of Social Proof and Testimonials 339
  - Understanding Social Proof 339
  - Types of Social Proof 339
  - The Significance of Testimonials 340
  - Utilizing Social Proof and Testimonials 341
- Tailored to Perfection: The Art of Offering Customized Solutions 343
  - The Significance of Customized Solutions 343
  - Steps to Offering Customized Solutions 344
  - Benefits of Offering Customized Solutions 345
- Empowering Minds: Providing Education and Valuable Insights 347
  - The Importance of Providing Education and Valuable Insights 347
  - Effectively Providing Education and Valuable Insights 348
  - Benefits of Providing Education and Valuable Insights 349
- The Pillars of Trust: Maintaining Honesty and Transparency 351
  - The Importance of Honesty and Transparency 351
  - Ways to Maintain Honesty and Transparency 352
  - The Benefits of Honesty and Transparency 353
- Selling with Integrity: The Art of Avoiding High-Pressure Sales Tactics 355

- The Consequences of High-Pressure Sales Tactics 355
- The Value of Ethical Sales Methods 356
- How to Avoid High-Pressure Sales Tactics 356
- Benefits of Avoiding High-Pressure Sales Tactics 357

Nurturing Forever Bonds: The Art of Establishing a Long-Term Relationship Mindset 359

- The Significance of a Long-Term Relationship Mindset 359
- Key Components of a Long-Term Relationship Mindset 360
- Applying a Long-Term Relationship Mindset 360
- Benefits of a Long-Term Relationship Mindset 361

The Power of Knowledge: Leveraging Content Marketing for Education 363

- The Significance of Content Marketing for Education 363
- Best Practices for Leveraging Content Marketing in Education 364
- Benefits of Leveraging Content Marketing for Education 365

The Power of Follow-Up in Sales: Turning Leads into Loyal Customers 367

- The Significance of Follow-Up in Sales 367
- Best Practices for Effective Follow-Up in Sales 368
- The Benefits of Effective Follow-Up in Sales 369

Building Authority and Expertise: Your Path to Recognition and Influence 371

- The Significance of Building Authority and Expertise 371
- Strategies for Building Authority and Expertise 372
- Benefits of Building Authority and Expertise 373

Empowering Your Customers: The Value of Offering Free Resources 375

- The Significance of Offering Free Resources 375
- Strategies for Providing Value Through Free Resources 376
- Benefits of Offering Free Resources 376

Mastering the Art of Nurturing Leads with Email Marketing 379
- The Importance of Email Marketing for Nurturing Leads 379
- Best Practices for Nurturing Leads with Email Marketing 380
- Benefits of Nurturing Leads with Email Marketing 381

Crafting Effective Sales Emails: A Guide to Persuasive Communication 383
- The Key Principles of Effective Sales Emails 383
- Best Practices for Crafting Effective Sales Emails 384
- Strategies for Success in Crafting Sales Emails 384
- Benefits of Effective Sales Emails 385

Understanding the Buyer's Journey 387
- The Three Key Stages of the Buyer's Journey 387
- Understanding the Buyer's Journey 388
- Tailoring Your Marketing Efforts to the Buyer's Journey 389
- Benefits of Understanding the Buyer's Journey 389

Building Business Success: A Comprehensive Guide to Implementing Referral Programs 391
- The Significance of Implementing Referral Programs 391
- Strategies for Successful Referral Programs 392
- Benefits of Implementing Referral Programs 393

Building a Loyal Customer Community: A Comprehensive Guide to Success 395
- The Importance of Building a Loyal Customer Community 395
- Strategies for Building a Loyal Customer Community 396
- Benefits of Building a Loyal Customer Community 397

The Power of Social Listening: How to Engage Actively and Gain Insights 399
- The Significance of Social Listening 399
- Strategies for Active Social Listening 400
- Benefits of Active Social Listening 401

Building Lasting Connections: How to Leverage Social Media for Relationship-Building 403
    The Significance of Leveraging Social Media for Relationship-Building 403
    Strategies for Leveraging Social Media for Relationship-Building .. 404
    Benefits of Leveraging Social Media for Relationship-Building 405
Hosting Webinars for Education and Connection 407
    The Significance of Hosting Webinars for Education and Connection 407
    Strategies for Successful Webinars 408
    Benefits of Hosting Webinars for Education and Connection 409
Leveraging Chatbots for Instant Support 411
    The Significance of Using Chatbots for Instant Support 411
    Strategies for Implementing Chatbots for Instant Support 412
    Benefits of Using Chatbots for Instant Support 413
Providing Exceptional Customer Service 415
    The Significance of Providing Exceptional Customer Service 415
    Key Principles of Exceptional Customer Service 416
    Strategies for Providing Exceptional Customer Service 417
    Benefits of Providing Exceptional Customer Service 418
Responding to Customer Feedback with Gratitude 419
    The Significance of Responding to Customer Feedback with Gratitude 419
    Strategies for Responding to Customer Feedback with Gratitude .. 420
    Benefits of Responding to Customer Feedback with Gratitude 421
Hosting Exclusive Customer Appreciation Events 423
    The Significance of Hosting Exclusive Customer Appreciation Events 423
    Strategies for Hosting Exclusive Customer Appreciation Events 424
    Benefits of Hosting Exclusive Customer Appreciation Events 425

Recognizing and Rewarding Customer Loyalty 427
    The Significance of Recognizing and Rewarding Customer Loyalty 427
    Strategies for Recognizing and Rewarding Customer Loyalty 428
    Benefits of Recognizing and Rewarding Customer Loyalty 429

Building a Brand Ambassador Program 431
    The Significance of Building a Brand Ambassador Program 431
    Key Steps for Building a Brand Ambassador Program 432
    Benefits of Building a Brand Ambassador Program............................ 433

Encouraging Customer Reviews and Referrals.. 435
    The Significance of Encouraging Customer Reviews and Referrals 435
    Effective Strategies for Encouraging Customer Reviews and Referrals 436
    Benefits of Encouraging Customer Reviews and Referrals................ 437

Using Feedback to Continuously Improve 439
    The Significance of Using Feedback to Continuously Improve 439
    Strategies for Using Feedback to Continuously Improve 440
    Benefits of Using Feedback to Continuously Improve 441

Staying Adaptable in a Changing Market... 443
    The Significance of Staying Adaptable in a Changing Market 443
    Strategies for Staying Adaptable in a Changing Market 444
    Benefits of Staying Adaptable in a Changing Market........................... 445

Measuring Customer Satisfaction and Loyalty... 447
    The Significance of Measuring Customer Satisfaction and Loyalty 447
    Methods and Metrics for Measuring Customer Satisfaction and Loyalty.. 448
    Benefits of Measuring Customer Satisfaction and Loyalty................ 449

Demonstrating Authenticity and Integrity.. 451
    The Significance of Demonstrating Authenticity and Integrity 451
    Strategies for Demonstrating Authenticity and Integrity 452

- Benefits of Demonstrating Authenticity and Integrity 453
- Becoming a Trusted Advisor to Your Customers 455
  - The Significance of Becoming a Trusted Advisor to Your Customers 455
  - Strategies for Becoming a Trusted Advisor to Your Customers 456
  - Benefits of Becoming a Trusted Advisor to Your Customers 457
- Building a Reputation for Exceptional Service 459
  - The Significance of Building a Reputation for Exceptional Service 459
  - Strategies for Building a Reputation for Exceptional Service 460
  - Benefits of Building a Reputation for Exceptional Service 461
- Celebrating Customer Success Stories 463
  - The Significance of Celebrating Customer Success Stories 463
  - Strategies for Celebrating Customer Success Stories 464
  - Benefits of Celebrating Customer Success Stories 465

Section 1:

Discovering Your "Why" and Developing Passion

Understanding the Importance of Your "Why" in Life and Decision-Making

Introduction

Have you ever asked yourself why you do what you do? The concept of understanding your "why" is a powerful tool for personal development and decision-making. Whether you're setting goals, pursuing a career, or making life choices, having a clear understanding of your "why" can provide motivation, direction, and a sense of purpose, Let's explore the significance of your "why" and how you can discover and leverage it to lead a more fulfilling life.

Defining Your "Why"

Your "why" is the fundamental reason or purpose behind your actions, decisions, and goals. It is the core motivation that drives you to achieve what you desire. Your "why" represents your deepest values, beliefs, and aspirations. It's not just about what you want; it's about why you want it.

The Power of Purpose

Understanding your "why" can significantly impact various aspects of your life:

a. Motivation: Your "why" serves as a powerful source of motivation. When you connect your actions to a meaningful purpose, you're more likely to stay committed and persevere through challenges.

b. Clarity: Your "why" helps you gain clarity about your goals and priorities. It allows you to distinguish between what truly matters and what doesn't, making decision-making more straightforward.

c. Resilience: In the face of setbacks and obstacles, a strong "why" can provide the resilience needed to push through difficult times and maintain a positive outlook.

d. Fulfillment: Living in alignment with your "why" can lead to a deeper sense of fulfillment and contentment in life, as you're pursuing what truly matters to you.

Identifying Your "Why"

Discovering your "why" is an introspective process that involves self-reflection and self-awareness. Here are some steps to help you identify your "why":

a. Ask yourself questions: Start by asking questions like, "What truly matters to me?" "What do I want to achieve in life?" "What values do I hold dear?" These questions can help you uncover your core motivations.

b. Reflect on past experiences: Analyze your past accomplishments, struggles, and moments of happiness. Identify common themes or values that have consistently driven your actions.

c. Seek feedback from others: Sometimes, those close to you can offer insights into your strengths, passions, and values. They might see aspects of your character that you are unaware of.

d. Visualize your ideal life: Imagine your perfect future. What does it look like, and why does it matter to you? This exercise can reveal your long-term goals and aspirations.

e. Write it down: Keep a journal to document your thoughts, feelings, and revelations about your "why." This can help you track your progress and refine your understanding over time.

Applying Your "Why"

Once you've identified your "why," it's time to apply it to various areas of your life:

a. Goal setting: Align your goals with your "why" to ensure they are truly meaningful to you. This will make it easier to stay committed and motivated throughout the journey.

b. Decision-making: Use your "why" as a guiding compass when making decisions. It will help you choose options that align with your values and long-term objectives.

c. Personal growth: Your "why" can be a catalyst for personal development. Focus on acquiring skills and knowledge that enhance your ability to live in alignment with your purpose.

d. Relationships: Understanding your "why" can improve your relationships by fostering authentic connections with people who share similar values and goals.

Reviewing and Adapting

Your "why" may evolve over time as you gain new experiences and insights. Regularly review and adapt your "why" to ensure it remains a relevant and motivating force in your life.

Conclusion

Understanding the importance of your "why" is an essential step toward living a purposeful, fulfilling, and motivated life. By uncovering your core motivations and aligning your goals and decisions with your "why," you can create a path that leads to a sense of purpose and satisfaction. Embrace this journey of self-discovery and watch as your "why" becomes a powerful force for positive change in your life.

Reflecting on Your Personal Values and Beliefs: A Path to Self-Discovery and Fulfillment

Introduction

Personal values and beliefs are the core principles that shape our attitudes, guide our decisions, and define who we are as individuals. Taking the time to reflect on these values and beliefs is a valuable journey towards self-discovery, personal growth, and living a more fulfilling life. Let's delve into the importance of reflecting on your personal values and beliefs and provide a step-by-step guide to help you in this introspective process.

Understanding Personal Values

Personal values are the fundamental principles or standards that you hold dear. They are the core convictions that influence your behavior, relationships, and decision-making. Personal values often form as a result of your upbringing, cultural influences, life experiences, and personal philosophies.

Common examples of personal values include:

- Integrity
- Family
- Honesty
- Success
- Compassion
- Freedom

- Creativity
- Respect
- Sustainability
- Growth

Identifying Your Beliefs

Beliefs are the convictions or acceptances that something is true or exists. They often stem from your values and can be related to your worldview, spirituality, or moral principles. Your beliefs shape your perceptions, attitudes, and behaviors.

Examples of personal beliefs might include:

- Belief in a higher power or spirituality
- Belief in the importance of education
- Belief in the value of hard work
- Belief in the importance of equality and justice
- Belief in environmental sustainability

The Importance of Reflecting on Values and Beliefs

a. Self-Discovery: Reflecting on your personal values and beliefs provides an opportunity to gain a deeper understanding of yourself. It allows you to uncover what truly matters to you and what motivates your choices and actions.

b. Guiding Decisions: Your values and beliefs serve as a moral compass, helping you make ethical and principled decisions in various aspects of your life, including relationships, career, and personal goals.

c. Creating Alignment: By aligning your actions and decisions with your values and beliefs, you can lead a more authentic and fulfilling life. This alignment fosters a sense of purpose and inner peace.

d. Strengthening Relationships: Reflecting on your values and beliefs can lead to better communication and understanding in your relationships. It allows you to connect with others who share similar values and beliefs while respecting differences.

The Reflective Process

a. Self-Examination: Start by setting aside time for self-reflection. This can be done through meditation, journaling, or deep contemplation. Ask yourself questions like "What do I truly value in life?" and "What do I believe about the world and my role in it?"

b. Identify Core Values: List your core values by considering what principles you hold most dear. This can be a challenging but rewarding exercise.

c. Explore Your Beliefs: Delve into your beliefs by examining your thoughts, convictions, and principles. Are there beliefs that you've held onto without questioning them? Are there beliefs you'd like to develop or change?

d. Assess Alignment: Consider whether your actions and decisions align with your values and beliefs. If you find areas of misalignment, contemplate how you can make changes to bring your life more in sync with your values.

e. Set Goals: Use your values and beliefs to set meaningful goals. These goals will be more motivating and fulfilling because they are in harmony with who you are at your core.

Conclusion

Reflecting on your personal values and beliefs is a transformative journey that can lead to self-discovery, personal growth, and a more fulfilling life. It empowers you to make decisions aligned with your core principles, fosters authenticity, and strengthens relationships. Embracing this introspective process can guide you toward a life that is true to your deepest convictions, allowing you to live with purpose and integrity.

Discovering Your Passion: A Comprehensive Guide to Identifying Your Passions and Interests

Introduction

Your passions and interests are the keys to living a fulfilling life. They drive your enthusiasm, motivate your actions, and contribute to your sense of purpose. Identifying your passions and interests can be a transformative journey of self-discovery. Let's explore the importance of understanding your passions and interests and provide a step-by-step guide to help you uncover what truly ignites your soul.

The Significance of Identifying Your Passions and Interests

a. Fulfillment and Happiness: Pursuing activities and hobbies that align with your passions and interests can lead to a sense of fulfillment and happiness. When you do what you love, it rarely feels like work.

b. Motivation and Drive: Passion and interest provide the fuel for your motivation and drive. They give you the energy to push through challenges and setbacks.

c. Improved Well-Being: Engaging in activities you are passionate about has been linked to improved mental and emotional well-being, reducing stress and enhancing overall life satisfaction.

d. Self-Discovery: Identifying your passions and interests is a valuable journey of self-discovery. It allows you to connect with your authentic self and gain a deeper understanding of who you are.

How to Identify Your Passions and Interests

a. Self-Reflection: Take time to reflect on what truly excites you. Ask yourself questions like:
  - What activities make me lose track of time?
  - What subjects or hobbies have I been curious about?
  - What are my fondest childhood memories?
  - What are the things I could talk about endlessly?

b. Explore Diverse Interests: Try out different activities, hobbies, and experiences. This exploration can help you discover new passions you may not have considered before.

c. Pay Attention to Your Emotions: Monitor your emotional responses to various activities. Activities that evoke excitement, enthusiasm, and happiness are often good indicators of your passions.

d. Listen to Feedback: Sometimes, those around you can offer insights into your strengths and interests. Ask friends and family for their observations about what they believe you are passionate about.

e. Create a Passion Journal: Keep a journal where you record your thoughts, feelings, and experiences related to different activities. Over time, patterns may emerge that reveal your true passions.

Overcoming Challenges in Identifying Your Passions

a. Fear of Failure: Don't let fear of not excelling at something immediately deter you from exploration. Passion often emerges as you become more skilled and knowledgeable in an area.

b. External Expectations: It's important to distinguish between what you are truly passionate about and what others expect you to pursue.

Your passions should reflect your authentic desires, not societal pressures.

c. Patience and Persistence: Identifying your passions can be a process that takes time. Be patient with yourself and remain open to new experiences.

d. Embracing Change: Your passions and interests may evolve over time. Embrace change and allow yourself to explore new avenues.

Incorporating Passions into Your Life

a. Set Goals: Once you've identified your passions and interests, set specific goals related to them. This will help you channel your energy and enthusiasm into meaningful actions.

b. Prioritize and Make Time: Allocate time in your schedule to engage in activities related to your passions. Prioritizing what you love will ensure you nurture your interests.

c. Share Your Passions: Consider sharing your passions with others. Teaching or discussing your interests with like-minded individuals can enhance your enthusiasm.

Conclusion

Identifying your passions and interests is an empowering journey that leads to a more fulfilling and purposeful life. By understanding what truly excites and motivates you, you can focus your energy on activities that bring you joy and satisfaction. The process of self-discovery can be transformative, guiding you toward a life filled with purpose and enthusiasm. Embrace this journey and let your passions lead you to a more fulfilling existence.

The Synergy of Purpose: Connecting Your "Why" to Your Passions

Introduction

Your "why" represents your deepest motivations and values, while your passions are the activities and interests that bring you joy and fulfillment. The connection between your "why" and your passions can be a powerful force that guides you toward a life of purpose and authenticity. Let's explore the importance of linking your "why" to your passions and provide insights on how to achieve this synergy.

Understanding Your "Why"

Your "why" is the driving force that underpins your actions and decisions. It is your core purpose, your reason for being, and often reflects your values, beliefs, and personal mission. Your "why" can be both intrinsic (focused on your personal fulfillment) and extrinsic (focused on helping others or contributing to a cause).

Examples of "why" statements might include:

- To make a positive impact on the environment.
- To provide a better life for my family.
- To create and innovate to make the world a better place.
- To inspire and empower others to achieve their goals.

Identifying Your Passions

Your passions are the activities, hobbies, or interests that ignite your enthusiasm and make you feel alive. These are the things that you enjoy doing, that bring you joy and fulfillment, and that you could lose yourself in for hours without realizing it.

Examples of passions might include:

- Painting or other forms of artistic expression.
- Playing a musical instrument.
- Writing, whether it's fiction, poetry, or non-fiction.
- Cooking and experimenting with new recipes.
- Volunteering for a social cause or charity.
- Hiking, traveling, or exploring the outdoors.

The Synergy of Purpose

a. Finding Alignment: When your "why" aligns with your passions, it creates a powerful synergy that enhances your sense of purpose. Your actions and interests are no longer separate but interconnected, giving you a clear sense of direction.

b. Enhanced Motivation: Connecting your "why" to your passions amplifies your motivation. You are naturally drawn to activities that resonate with your purpose, making it easier to stay committed and inspired.

c. Meaningful Pursuits: Pursuing your passions in line with your "why" transforms hobbies into meaningful pursuits. You understand the greater purpose behind what you love doing, which can be deeply fulfilling.

Steps to Connect Your "Why" to Your Passions

a. Self-Reflection: Start by reflecting on your "why." What is your ultimate purpose or motivation in life? Write down your "why" statement and make it clear.

b. Identify Your Passions: Make a list of activities that truly ignite your enthusiasm and bring you joy. Be as specific as possible.

c. Analyze Overlaps: Examine the list of your passions and consider how they can be aligned with your "why." Are there passions that naturally resonate with your purpose?

d. Set Goals: Create specific goals related to your passions that are in harmony with your "why." These goals become meaningful and aligned with your deeper purpose.

e. Take Action: Start taking steps to integrate your passions with your "why." It may involve volunteering, working on personal projects, or pursuing a career that resonates with your purpose.

f. Evaluate and Adapt: Regularly assess how well your passions are connected to your "why." Adapt and refine your approach as needed to maintain alignment.

Conclusion

The connection between your "why" and your passions is a transformative journey that can lead to a life of purpose and authenticity. By aligning your deepest motivations with the activities that bring you joy and fulfillment, you create a powerful synergy that drives you forward. Your life becomes a reflection of your values and beliefs, and your passions become a means to express your purpose in a meaningful way. Embrace this journey of alignment and let your "why" guide you toward a more fulfilling and passionate life.

The North Star of Success: The Role of Purpose in Business Decisions

Introduction

In the ever-evolving world of business, the role of purpose in decision-making has gained increasing significance. Purpose-driven organizations are not only achieving financial success but also making a positive impact on society and the environment. Let's explore the pivotal role of purpose in business decisions, its impact on various aspects of an organization, and how it can lead to long-term success.

The Concept of Purpose in Business

a. Defining Purpose: Purpose in business refers to the fundamental reason an organization exists beyond profit generation. It's a commitment to a broader mission or vision that guides and informs the company's actions, culture, and decisions.

b. Beyond Profit: Purpose-driven organizations aim to create value for stakeholders, including employees, customers, communities, and the environment. Profit is viewed as a means to achieve these broader goals rather than an end in itself.

The Role of Purpose in Business Decisions

a. Ethical Decision-Making: A sense of purpose encourages ethical decision-making. Organizations with a clear purpose are more likely to prioritize values and principles when faced with challenging choices.

b. Long-term Strategy: Purpose serves as a guiding force for the development of long-term business strategies. It helps organizations remain focused on their core mission, even amid market fluctuations and industry changes.

c. Employee Engagement: A well-defined purpose can boost employee engagement and satisfaction. When employees understand how their work contributes to a larger mission, they tend to be more motivated and committed.

d. Customer Loyalty: Purpose-driven organizations often build stronger customer loyalty. Customers are more likely to support businesses that align with their values and contribute positively to society.

e. Innovation: Purpose can be a catalyst for innovation. Organizations with a clear sense of purpose are often more willing to explore new ideas and technologies to fulfill their mission.

Impact on Sustainability and Corporate Responsibility

a. Environmental Responsibility: Purpose-driven organizations tend to prioritize sustainability and environmental responsibility. They take measures to reduce their environmental footprint and adopt eco-friendly practices.

b. Social Responsibility: Businesses with a clear purpose are more likely to engage in social initiatives, such as supporting local communities, education, or addressing social inequalities.

c. Stakeholder Engagement: Purpose-driven companies maintain open and constructive relationships with stakeholders, including suppliers, investors, and regulators. They are more transparent about their actions and objectives.

Case Studies: Successful Purpose-Driven Companies

a. Patagonia: The outdoor clothing company Patagonia is a renowned example of a purpose-driven organization. Its mission is to "build the best product, cause no unnecessary harm, and use business to inspire and implement solutions to the environmental crisis."

b. Toms: Toms is a well-known example of a company that has integrated purpose into its core business model. For every pair of shoes sold, Toms donates a pair to a child in need. Their "One for One" mission has driven both their business and their impact.

Steps to Integrate Purpose into Business Decisions

a. Define Your Purpose: Clearly articulate your organization's purpose and ensure it resonates with your team, customers, and stakeholders.

b. Align Business Strategy: Align your company's strategic decisions with your purpose. Ensure that your actions reflect your commitment to your mission.

c. Communicate Effectively: Transparency and effective communication are key. Share your purpose with your team, customers, and the public. This fosters trust and support.

d. Measure Impact: Regularly evaluate the impact of your purpose-driven decisions. Assess how well you are advancing toward your mission and make necessary adjustments.

Conclusion

The role of purpose in business decisions is transformative. Organizations that embrace a clear sense of purpose tend to make more ethical decisions, engage employees, build customer loyalty, and have a positive impact on society and the environment. In today's business landscape, success isn't solely defined by financial metrics but by an organization's ability to make a meaningful contribution to the world. By integrating purpose into business decisions, companies can create a more sustainable, socially responsible, and prosperous future.

Pursuing Passion and Profit: Researching Industries Aligned with Your Passions

Introduction

In the journey of choosing a career or starting a business, aligning your professional life with your passions can lead to a more fulfilling and rewarding path. Researching industries that resonate with your interests and values is a pivotal step in this process. Let's explore the importance of aligning your career or business with your passions and provide guidance on how to conduct thorough research to discover industries that match your personal preferences.

Why Align Your Career or Business with Your Passions

a. Enhanced Job Satisfaction: When you are passionate about your work, it doesn't feel like a chore. Job satisfaction tends to be higher, and you are more likely to stay engaged and motivated.

b. Long-term Commitment: Aligning your career or business with your passions encourages long-term commitment. You are less likely to switch paths and are more willing to persevere through challenges.

c. Increased Productivity: Passion often leads to increased productivity. You are naturally drawn to your work, and you become more effective at what you do.

d. Emotional and Mental Well-being: Pursuing your passions in your career or business can have a positive impact on your emotional and mental well-being. You experience less stress and greater overall happiness.

Researching Industries Aligned with Your Passions

a. Self-Assessment: Start by reflecting on your passions and interests. Make a list of activities, topics, or causes that truly excite you.

b. Identify Transferable Skills: Consider your skills, strengths, and expertise. Think about how they can be applied to various industries.

c. Market Demand: Research the market demand for the industries related to your passions. Are there opportunities for growth and sustainability in those areas?

d. Networking: Connect with professionals and experts in the industries you're interested in. Seek advice, attend conferences, or join relevant online communities to gain insights.

e. Market Trends: Study industry trends and projections. Are there emerging areas or niches within an industry that align with your passions?

f. Competitive Landscape: Analyze the competition within the industries you're considering. Are there gaps or unmet needs that you could address with your unique perspective or passion?

Case Studies: Real-world Examples

a. The Sustainability Industry: Individuals passionate about environmental sustainability can research industries related to renewable energy, eco-friendly products, or sustainable agriculture.

b. The Healthcare Industry: Those interested in healthcare can explore various healthcare professions or business opportunities that focus on improving the well-being of individuals and communities.

c. The Food and Beverage Industry: Those passionate about food and beverages can research opportunities in the culinary arts, food technology, or sustainable food production.

Overcoming Challenges

a. Addressing Financial Concerns: In some cases, aligning your career or business with your passions may require financial sacrifices or investments. Consider your financial situation and plan accordingly.

b. Adapting to Change: Be prepared to adapt and evolve as you align your career or business with your passions. Markets and industries change, so flexibility is essential.

c. Balancing Risk: Assess the level of risk associated with pursuing your passions in a given industry. Consider how you can manage and mitigate these risks.

Steps to Pursuing Your Passion-Driven Career

a. Set Clear Goals: Define specific career or business goals that reflect your passions. These goals will provide direction and motivation.

b. Gain Relevant Experience: If necessary, gain experience in the industry by volunteering, interning, or working in related positions.

c. Build a Network: Connect with professionals, mentors, and like-minded individuals in your chosen industry. Their guidance and support can be invaluable.

d. Continuous Learning: Stay updated with industry developments and trends. Continuous learning is key to staying competitive and relevant.

Conclusion

Researching industries aligned with your passions is a significant step toward creating a fulfilling career or business. It enables you to connect your professional life with your personal interests, leading to higher job satisfaction, long-term commitment, and greater productivity. By conducting thorough research and pursuing your passions, you can embark on a journey that is not only financially rewarding but also deeply meaningful and enjoyable. Your career or business can become a reflection of who you are and what truly matters to you.

Navigating Success: Analyzing Market Trends and Opportunities

Introduction

In today's dynamic and competitive business landscape, staying ahead of the curve requires a keen understanding of market trends and the ability to seize emerging opportunities. Analyzing market trends and identifying growth prospects is an essential skill for entrepreneurs, business leaders, and anyone seeking to make informed decisions in the world of commerce. Let's delve into the importance of analyzing market trends and opportunities and provide a comprehensive guide to help you make well-informed choices.

The Significance of Analyzing Market Trends

a. Anticipating Change: Market trends are like signposts that help you anticipate change. Staying informed about these trends allows you to adapt and prepare for shifts in consumer behavior, technology, and industry standards.

b. Identifying Opportunities: Market trends often highlight new opportunities for growth and innovation. They can serve as a source of inspiration for product development, market expansion, and new business ventures.

c. Reducing Risk: A thorough analysis of market trends can help mitigate risk by identifying potential pitfalls or challenges that lie ahead.

The Process of Analyzing Market Trends and Opportunities

a. Data Collection: Begin by collecting relevant data. This may include market reports, customer feedback, industry news, economic indicators, and competitor performance.

b. Categorization: Organize the collected data into categories, such as consumer behavior, technological advancements, economic factors, and regulatory changes.

c. Trend Identification: Analyze the data to identify emerging trends. These could be shifts in consumer preferences, new technologies, demographic changes, or global events that may affect the market.

d. Market Segmentation: Divide your target market into segments based on common characteristics. This enables a more focused approach to analyzing trends specific to each segment.

e. Competitive Analysis: Study your competitors to identify their strategies and responses to market trends. This can provide insights into opportunities they may have overlooked.

Tools and Resources for Analyzing Market Trends

a. Industry Reports: Industry-specific reports and publications offer valuable insights into market trends, competitive landscapes, and growth opportunities.

b. Market Research Firms: Engage the services of market research firms or agencies that specialize in collecting and analyzing data related to your industry.

c. Data Analytics Software: Data analytics tools can help you process and make sense of large datasets, making trend analysis more efficient.

d. Social Media Monitoring: Social media platforms are treasure troves of customer opinions and behavior. Monitoring social media can provide real-time insights into market trends and customer sentiment.

Navigating Through Industry Disruption

a. Disruptive Innovation: Be prepared for disruptive innovation that can significantly impact your industry. Embrace innovation as an opportunity rather than a threat.

b. Adaptability: Stay agile and adaptable. Businesses that can pivot quickly in response to changing trends are more likely to thrive.

c. Strategic Partnerships: Collaborate with other industry players or startups to leverage new technologies or emerging trends.

Case Studies: Examples of Successful Market Trend Analysis

a. Apple Inc.: Apple is known for its successful analysis of market trends. They anticipated the trend towards consumer technology convergence and introduced the iPhone, combining a phone, music player, and computer in one device.

b. Airbnb: Airbnb identified the trend of the sharing economy and harnessed it to create a global platform connecting travelers with local hosts.

The Art of Opportunity Identification

a. In-depth Research: Continuously research and stay up-to-date with industry developments, technological advancements, and changing consumer behavior.

b. Customer Feedback: Pay attention to customer feedback, suggestions, and pain points to identify areas where your business can provide solutions or improvements.

c. Creative Thinking: Foster a culture of innovation within your organization. Encourage brainstorming sessions and out-of-the-box thinking to uncover new opportunities.

Strategic Planning

a. Once you identify opportunities, develop a clear and actionable strategic plan. Define goals, objectives, timelines, and responsibilities.

b. Monitor Progress: Continuously monitor the execution of your plan and be ready to adapt it based on feedback and changing market dynamics.

Conclusion

Analyzing market trends and opportunities is a crucial aspect of business strategy. It allows organizations to anticipate change, identify growth prospects, reduce risks, and stay ahead of competitors. By following a structured process, using the right tools, and fostering a culture of innovation, businesses can effectively analyze market trends and seize opportunities that can lead to sustained success and growth. In today's ever-evolving market, staying informed and being prepared to adapt is key to thriving in any industry.

Uncovering Opportunities: Identifying Gaps in the Market

Introduction

For entrepreneurs, business leaders, and innovators, identifying gaps in the market is the key to discovering untapped opportunities and achieving success. Market gaps represent areas where consumer needs or desires are unmet or under-served, providing fertile ground for innovation and business growth. Let's explore the significance of identifying gaps in the market and provide a comprehensive guide to help you uncover these opportunities.

The Significance of Identifying Market Gaps

a. Innovation and Entrepreneurship: Identifying market gaps is a cornerstone of innovation and entrepreneurship. It empowers individuals and organizations to create products or services that address unfulfilled needs.

b. Competitive Advantage: Filling market gaps can provide a significant competitive advantage, as it allows you to offer unique and differentiated solutions.

c. Business Growth: Successful identification and exploitation of market gaps can lead to business growth and profitability.

The Process of Identifying Market Gaps

a. Market Research: Conduct thorough market research to understand current trends, consumer behaviors, and competitive landscapes. Analyze industry reports, consumer feedback, and market data.

b. Consumer Feedback: Pay attention to customer feedback, reviews, complaints, and suggestions. Often, customers highlight pain points and unmet needs that can signify market gaps.

c. Industry Analysis: Study your industry and its key players. Identify areas where competitors may not be fully addressing consumer demands or where there may be underserved segments of the market.

d. Trend Analysis: Monitor emerging trends, technologies, and demographic shifts that can create new opportunities.

e. Competitive Analysis: Evaluate the strategies and offerings of your competitors. Look for areas where they may not be providing comprehensive solutions.

Tools and Resources for Identifying Market Gaps

a. Market Research Firms: Consider leveraging the services of market research firms that specialize in analyzing market trends and identifying gaps.

b. Surveys and Questionnaires: Design surveys and questionnaires to gather direct feedback from your target audience. These tools can reveal unmet needs and potential gaps.

c. Data Analytics: Utilize data analytics software to process and interpret large datasets, uncovering patterns and trends that may indicate market gaps.

d. Online Communities: Participate in online forums, social media groups, and industry-specific communities where you can engage with potential customers and gather insights.

Analyzing Market Gaps

a. Target Audience: Define your target audience and understand their preferences, pain points, and unmet needs. This is crucial for finding market gaps specific to your potential customers.

b. Brainstorm Solutions: Once you've identified potential gaps, brainstorm innovative solutions that can address them. Be creative and open to diverse ideas.

c. Feasibility Analysis: Assess the feasibility of your ideas, considering factors such as cost, resources, and market demand.

d. Competition: Evaluate whether there are competitors in your niche and how your solutions compare. Can you offer something unique and superior?

Case Studies: Examples of Identifying Market Gaps

a. Airbnb: Airbnb identified a gap in the accommodation market by offering a platform that allowed people to rent out their homes and properties to travelers, creating an alternative to traditional hotels.

b. Uber: Uber recognized a market gap in the transportation industry by providing a convenient and affordable ride-sharing service, revolutionizing the way people travel.

The Art of Opportunity Identification

a. Continuous Learning: Stay informed about industry trends, consumer behavior, and technological advancements. Continuous learning is key to identifying market gaps.

b. Networking: Connect with industry professionals, experts, and potential customers to gain insights and uncover opportunities.

c. Creative Thinking: Foster a culture of innovation within your organization. Encourage brainstorming sessions and out-of-the-box thinking to discover new gaps and solutions.

Implementing Strategies

a. Once you've identified market gaps and potential solutions, develop a clear and actionable strategy. Define goals, objectives, timelines, and responsibilities.

b. Test and Iterate: Test your solutions in the market and gather feedback. Be ready to iterate and refine your offerings based on customer responses.

Conclusion

Identifying gaps in the market is an essential skill for entrepreneurs and businesses seeking to innovate and succeed. It opens the door to unique opportunities, competitive advantages, and business growth. By following a structured process, leveraging the right tools, and fostering a culture of creativity, you can effectively identify market gaps and seize opportunities that can lead to sustained success and growth. Embrace the journey of discovering unmet needs and providing solutions, and you'll be well on your way to creating value and making a positive impact in your industry.

Evaluating Your Skills and Expertise: A Comprehensive Guide

Introduction

Evaluating your skills and expertise is a crucial step in personal and professional development. Whether you are a student trying to decide on a career path, a professional aiming to advance in your current job, or someone looking to make a career change, understanding your strengths and weaknesses is essential. This article will provide you with a comprehensive guide on how to evaluate your skills and expertise effectively.

Self-Assessment

The first step in evaluating your skills and expertise is to conduct a thorough self-assessment. This process involves taking a closer look at your abilities, knowledge, and experience. Here are some key components of self-assessment:

   a. Identify Your Core Skills: Make a list of your core skills. These can be both hard skills (technical, job-specific) and soft skills (communication, leadership, problem-solving). Ask yourself what you excel at and what areas need improvement.

   b. Examine Your Education and Training: Reflect on your formal education, degrees, certifications, and any additional training or workshops you have completed. Consider how these have contributed to your skills and expertise.

   c. Analyze Your Work Experience: Evaluate your work history. What roles have you held, and what were your responsibilities? What accomplishments or challenges have you encountered in your career? How have these experiences shaped your skills and expertise?

   d. Solicit Feedback: Seek input from peers, supervisors, mentors, or colleagues. They can provide valuable insights into your strengths and weaknesses, offering a more objective perspective on your abilities.

Goal Setting

Once you have a clear understanding of your skills and expertise, it's time to set goals. Goals help you focus on areas where you want to improve or expand your abilities. Consider the following when setting goals:

   a. Short-term and Long-term Goals: Set both short-term goals (achievable in the near future) and long-term goals (more ambitious objectives for your career). Short-term goals can help you build the foundation for achieving long-term ones.

   b. Specific, Measurable, Achievable, Relevant, and Time-Bound (SMART) Goals: Make sure your goals meet the SMART criteria. This will help you create well-defined and actionable objectives.

   c. Prioritize Goals: Identify which skills or expertise areas are most important to your personal and professional development. Prioritizing ensures that you work on what matters most.

Skill Gap Analysis

A skill gap analysis involves comparing your current skills and expertise with the requirements of your desired career or job role. Here's how to conduct a skill gap analysis:

a. **Research Job Descriptions:** Look at job descriptions and requirements for the roles you aspire to. Identify the skills and expertise that are in high demand for those positions.

   b. **Compare with Your Skills:** Compare the skills and expertise required for the job with what you have. Note any gaps or areas where you fall short.

   c. **Develop a Plan:** Create a plan to bridge the gap. This may involve further education, training, or gaining practical experience.

Seek Professional Advice

Consulting with a career counselor, mentor, or industry expert can be immensely valuable. They can offer guidance, provide insights, and suggest strategies to enhance your skills and expertise. A fresh perspective can help you see areas for improvement that you may have missed during your self-assessment.

Continuous Learning

Evaluating your skills and expertise is not a one-time process. It's an ongoing journey. Continuous learning is essential for personal and professional growth. Consider the following:

   a. **Lifelong Learning:** Embrace a mindset of continuous improvement. Stay open to new ideas, technologies, and approaches in your field.

   b. **Professional Development:** Attend workshops, conferences, and seminars related to your industry. Seek out relevant courses and certifications to stay current in your field.

c. Stay Informed: Read books, industry publications, and research articles to stay informed about the latest trends and developments in your area of expertise.

Monitor Progress

Regularly assess your progress towards your goals. Review your skills and expertise to ensure you are making the necessary improvements. Be prepared to make adjustments to your plan as needed.

Conclusion

Evaluating your skills and expertise is a vital step in personal and professional growth. It allows you to identify your strengths, weaknesses, and areas for improvement. By following the steps outlined in this comprehensive guide, you can create a clear roadmap for developing and enhancing your skills, ultimately leading to a more successful and fulfilling career. Remember, self-assessment and goal setting are ongoing processes, so make a commitment to continuous learning and improvement.

Choosing Industries That Align with Your "Why": A Comprehensive Guide

Introduction

Selecting a career or industry that aligns with your personal values, passions, and purpose is a critical step in finding fulfillment and success in your professional life. When your work aligns with your "why," it not only leads to greater job satisfaction but also promotes longevity and excellence in your chosen field. In this article, we'll explore the process of choosing industries that resonate with your core values and provide guidance on how to pursue your purpose.

Define Your "Why"

Your "why" is your underlying motivation and the core reason you do what you do. To choose an industry that aligns with your "why," start by defining your values, interests, and passions:

   a. Self-Reflection: Take time to reflect on your life experiences, values, and the activities that truly make you come alive. Ask yourself what drives you and what makes you feel fulfilled.

   b. Core Values: Identify your core values, which are the guiding principles that shape your decisions and actions. Common values include integrity, creativity, compassion, and innovation.

   c. Passions: Determine your areas of interest and passions. What are the activities or subjects that excite you the most? What could you talk about for hours without getting tired?

d. Personal Goals: Consider your long-term aspirations and what you hope to achieve in life. Your "why" should be closely tied to your overarching life goals.

Research and Explore

Once you have a clear understanding of your "why," it's time to research industries and career paths that align with your values, interests, and passions:

   a. Industry Assessment: Research different industries and sectors to identify those that resonate with your values and interests. Look into the culture, values, and goals of these industries.

   b. Network and Gather Insights: Connect with professionals who work in your areas of interest. Attend industry events, join online forums, or engage in informational interviews to gain insights into the industry culture and opportunities.

   c. Stay Informed: Stay updated on industry trends, challenges, and opportunities. Reading industry-related news and publications will help you make informed decisions.

Assess Career Fit

After exploring various industries, assess how well each aligns with your "why." Here are some key factors to consider:

   a. Values Alignment: Evaluate whether the industry's core values align with your personal values and principles. A strong alignment can lead to greater job satisfaction.

   b. Job Roles: Consider the types of roles available in the industry. Do these roles allow you to leverage your skills and passions effectively?

c. Work Environment: Assess the work environment, culture, and atmosphere of the industry. Does it feel like a place where you can thrive?

   d. Growth and Opportunities: Investigate the growth prospects and opportunities within the industry. A thriving industry may offer better long-term prospects.

   e. Work-Life Balance: Examine the work-life balance typical in the industry. Consider whether it suits your lifestyle and personal goals.

Education and Skill Development

If you find an industry that aligns with your "why," it's essential to equip yourself with the necessary skills and knowledge. This might involve:

   a. Formal Education: Pursuing relevant academic programs, degrees, or certifications to gain the knowledge required for your chosen industry.

   b. Skill Development: Identify the specific skills that are in demand within the industry and work on acquiring or improving them.

   c. Networking: Build connections and relationships within the industry to learn from professionals and gain insights into best practices.

Take Action

To fully align your career with your "why," you'll need to take actionable steps:

   a. Set Goals: Define specific career goals and objectives that reflect your desire to work in this industry.

b. Create a Plan: Develop a detailed plan outlining the steps you need to take to enter or transition within your chosen industry.

c. Leverage Experience: Use your existing skills and experience to make a compelling case for your fit within the industry.

Adapt and Evolve

The process of aligning your career with your "why" is dynamic. Be prepared to adapt, learn, and grow as you pursue your passion and purpose. Regularly assess your progress and make necessary adjustments to ensure you remain on the right path.

Conclusion

Choosing industries that align with your "why" is a journey of self-discovery and purposeful decision-making. When your career resonates with your core values, passions, and interests, it can lead to a more fulfilling and successful professional life. By following the steps outlined in this comprehensive guide, you can make informed choices and work towards a career that not only pays the bills but also fuels your sense of purpose and happiness. Remember that the journey may have challenges, but the rewards of aligning your "why" with your career are well worth the effort.

Researching Potential Network Marketing Companies: A Comprehensive Guide

Introduction

Network marketing, also known as multi-level marketing (MLM), offers an opportunity for individuals to build a business by marketing and selling products or services through a network of independent distributors. It's crucial to conduct thorough research before joining any network marketing company to ensure you're making an informed decision. In this comprehensive guide, we'll walk you through the process of researching potential network marketing companies and provide tips for making a well-informed choice.

Understand the Basics of Network Marketing

Before delving into the research process, it's essential to have a clear understanding of what network marketing is and how it operates:

   a. Pyramid Schemes vs. Legitimate MLM: Learn to differentiate between legitimate network marketing companies and pyramid schemes, which are illegal in many countries. Pyramid schemes primarily focus on recruitment, while MLM companies emphasize product sales.

   b. Compensation Structure: Understand how you'll be compensated in the MLM company. Most MLMs offer commissions on product sales and bonuses for building and managing a team.

c. Product or Service: Familiarize yourself with the company's product or service. Ensure it's something you believe in and are comfortable promoting.

d. Distributor Responsibilities: Know your roles and responsibilities as a distributor, which may include selling products, recruiting new members, and training your team.

Check the Company's Background

Researching the company's background is crucial to determine its credibility and stability. Here's what to look for:

a. Company History: Investigate how long the company has been in business. A well-established company is often more reliable.

b. Leadership Team: Examine the qualifications and experience of the company's founders and leadership team. A strong leadership team can be an indicator of a legitimate company.

c. Legal Compliance: Ensure the company adheres to all legal and regulatory requirements in your country. Check for any past legal issues or controversies.

d. Financial Stability: Look for financial reports, if available, to gauge the company's financial health. A stable company is more likely to provide a reliable income.

Product or Service Quality

Assess the quality of the product or service offered by the MLM company. This is crucial for your success as a distributor and for building a reputable business:

a. Product Research: Use the product or service yourself and gather feedback from current customers or distributors. High-quality products are easier to market and result in more satisfied customers.

b. Market Demand: Evaluate whether there's a real demand for the product or service. A niche market with limited appeal can be challenging to sell in.

c. Competitive Analysis: Compare the MLM company's product or service with similar offerings in the market. Assess pricing, features, and unique selling points.

Compensation Plan Analysis

The compensation plan is the backbone of any network marketing opportunity. Scrutinize the plan to ensure it is fair, transparent, and aligns with your financial goals:

a. Commissions and Bonuses: Understand how you'll earn commissions on product sales and bonuses for recruiting and managing a team.

b. Rank Advancement: Investigate the requirements for moving up the ranks within the company. Advancement should be based on sales and leadership, not just recruitment.

c. Fine Print: Pay attention to the fine print in the compensation plan, including any quotas, restrictions, or conditions that may affect your earnings.

Company Reputation and Reviews

Gather information about the company's reputation and what current and former distributors have to say:

a. **Online Reviews:** Look for reviews and testimonials from distributors and customers online. Check reputable sources to gauge the company's reputation.

b. **Better Business Bureau (BBB):** Check if the company is accredited by the BBB and review any complaints or ratings.

c. **Distributor Feedback:** Speak with current and former distributors to gain insights into their experiences with the company.

Training and Support

Evaluate the training and support provided by the MLM company:

a. **Training Programs:** Determine if the company offers comprehensive training programs to help you succeed in your role as a distributor.

b. **Mentorship:** Assess whether you will have access to a mentor or upline sponsor who can provide guidance and support.

c. **Marketing Materials:** Check if the company provides marketing materials, tools, and resources to help you promote the products or services effectively.

Assess Your Fit

Consider whether the network marketing opportunity aligns with your personal and professional goals:

a. **Personal Values:** Ensure the company's values align with your own and that you're comfortable representing the products or services.

b. Time Commitment: Evaluate the time and effort required to build a successful network marketing business and whether it fits your lifestyle.

c. Financial Expectations: Set realistic financial expectations based on the compensation plan and your willingness to put in the work.

Conclusion

Researching potential network marketing companies is a crucial step in determining if a specific MLM opportunity is the right fit for you. Take your time to thoroughly investigate the company's background, product or service quality, compensation plan, reputation, and support systems. By making an informed decision, you can increase your chances of building a successful and fulfilling network marketing business that aligns with your personal and professional goals. Remember that success in network marketing, like any business, requires dedication, hard work, and ethical practices.

Assessing a Company's Mission and Values: A Comprehensive Guide

Introduction

A company's mission and values serve as its guiding principles, reflecting its purpose and the core beliefs that drive its operations. As a conscious consumer, investor, or potential employee, assessing a company's mission and values is crucial in understanding its commitment to ethical practices and its alignment with your own values. In this comprehensive guide, we will explore the importance of evaluating a company's mission and values, how to do it effectively, and the benefits of making informed assessments.

Understanding the Significance

Before diving into the process of assessing a company's mission and values, it's important to recognize why this step is crucial:

   a. Ethical Alignment: By assessing a company's mission and values, you can determine if the organization operates in a way that aligns with your own ethical beliefs and principles.

   b. Employee Engagement: For job seekers, understanding a company's values can help ensure alignment with your own values, leading to greater job satisfaction and fulfillment.

   c. Investment Decisions: Investors can gauge whether a company's values align with their ethical investment criteria, supporting businesses that share their principles.

d. Informed Consumer Choices: As a consumer, you can make informed choices by supporting companies whose values and missions resonate with your own.

Start with the Company's Mission Statement

A mission statement is a concise declaration of a company's purpose and the impact it seeks to create in the world. Begin your assessment with the mission statement:

   a. Clarity: A well-crafted mission statement should be clear and succinct. It should articulate the company's primary objectives and the value it intends to provide.

   b. Impact: Evaluate whether the mission statement emphasizes the positive impact the company aims to make on society, its customers, or its industry.

   c. Alignment with Your Values: Assess whether the company's mission resonates with your personal or ethical values. Consider whether it reflects a commitment to social responsibility, sustainability, or other important causes.

   d. Consistency: Ensure that the mission statement aligns with the company's actions and practices. A disconnect between words and deeds can be a red flag.

Analyze the Company's Core Values

A company's core values are the fundamental principles that guide its decision-making, culture, and behavior. Here's how to assess a company's core values:

a. Transparency: Look for transparency regarding the company's core values. They should be clearly defined and publicly accessible.

   b. Consistency: Examine whether the company consistently upholds its core values in its practices, policies, and interactions with stakeholders.

   c. Alignment with Ethical Principles: Evaluate the core values in relation to your own ethical principles. Are they consistent with your beliefs? Do they reflect a commitment to integrity, social responsibility, diversity, or other key values?

   d. Employee Perspective: Consider seeking the perspectives of current or former employees to understand how well the company's core values are upheld in the workplace.

Corporate Social Responsibility (CSR) Initiatives

Assess a company's commitment to corporate social responsibility, which encompasses efforts to minimize its environmental impact and contribute positively to society:

   a. Sustainability Efforts: Research the company's sustainability initiatives, including environmental practices and efforts to reduce its carbon footprint.

   b. Philanthropy and Community Engagement: Explore the company's involvement in charitable activities, partnerships, and community engagement.

   c. Ethical Supply Chain: Assess the company's commitment to ethical sourcing and labor practices within its supply chain.

Investigate Ethical and Legal Issues

Scrutinize the company's history for any ethical or legal issues that may have arisen. Look for past controversies or legal violations that could indicate a misalignment with its stated values:

   a. News and Media Reports: Search for news articles or reports about the company's involvement in any legal disputes, controversies, or ethical violations.

   b. Industry Regulations: Ensure the company complies with industry regulations and standards, as well as any applicable international laws.

Seek Third-Party Evaluations

Several organizations and platforms assess and rank companies based on their environmental, social, and governance (ESG) performance. Utilize these resources to gain an independent perspective:

   a. ESG Ratings: Explore ESG rating platforms like MSCI, Sustainalytics, or the Dow Jones Sustainability Index to assess the company's ESG performance.

   b. CSR Reports: Review corporate social responsibility reports, if available, to gauge the company's commitment to sustainability and ethical practices.

Company Culture and Employee Feedback

Company culture is a crucial aspect of assessing a company's values. Employee feedback and reviews can offer valuable insights into the internal workings of the organization:

a. Employee Reviews: Visit websites like Glassdoor or Indeed to read reviews and comments from current and former employees. This can shed light on the company's culture and values.

b. Employee Satisfaction: Consider the company's employee satisfaction scores, which reflect its commitment to creating a positive and supportive work environment.

Assessing Your Personal Alignment

After collecting and analyzing information about the company's mission and values, it's essential to assess your own alignment with the organization:

a. Personal Values: Reflect on your personal values and ethical principles. Do they align with the company's mission and values?

b. Long-Term Compatibility: Consider whether you can see yourself supporting the company, working for it, or investing in it over the long term, based on your alignment with its values.

c. Ethical Consumption: As a consumer, evaluate whether you are willing to support the company's products or services based on your assessment of its mission and values.

Conclusion

Assessing a company's mission and values is a critical step in making informed decisions as a consumer, investor, or job seeker. By thoroughly researching a company's mission statement, core values, ethical practices, and alignment with your personal values, you can ensure that you support organizations that share your principles and promote responsible and ethical business practices. Making these assessments empowers individuals to be more conscious and discerning in their choices, contributing to a more ethical and responsible corporate landscape.

Evaluating the Product or Service Offered: A Comprehensive Guide

Introduction

Evaluating a product or service is a critical skill that can help you make informed decisions as a consumer, investor, or business professional. Whether you're considering a purchase, investment, or collaboration, understanding how to assess the quality, value, and suitability of a product or service is essential. In this comprehensive guide, we'll explore the step-by-step process of evaluating a product or service offered, ensuring you make choices that align with your needs and objectives.

Define Your Objectives

Before you begin evaluating a product or service, it's important to clarify your objectives and what you hope to achieve. Consider the following:

   a. Identify Your Needs: Determine what you require from the product or service. Are you looking for a solution to a specific problem, a tool to enhance productivity, or a source of entertainment?

   b. Set Goals: Define your goals and expectations. What outcomes do you hope to achieve by using the product or service?

   c. Budget Constraints: Establish your budget limitations. How much are you willing to spend on the product or service?

   d. Timeframe: Consider the timeframe within which you need the product or service. Is it for a short-term project, a long-term commitment, or a one-time use?

Research and Gather Information

Effective evaluation begins with thorough research and gathering information about the product or service:

　a. Product/Service Description: Start by understanding what the product or service offers. Read the description, features, and specifications provided by the company.

　b. Reviews and Testimonials: Look for reviews and testimonials from other users or clients. This can provide insights into real-world experiences and satisfaction levels.

　c. Company Reputation: Assess the reputation of the company or provider offering the product or service. Investigate their history, customer feedback, and track record.

　d. Industry Standards: Research industry standards and best practices to establish benchmarks for the product or service's quality and performance.

　e. Competitive Analysis: Compare the product or service with similar offerings in the market. Evaluate pricing, features, and value propositions.

Quality and Performance

Assess the quality and performance of the product or service:

　a. Reliability: Examine the reliability of the product or service. Does it consistently perform its intended function without unexpected failures or errors?

　b. Durability: Consider the lifespan of the product or service. Is it built to last, or does it require frequent replacements or maintenance?

c. Efficiency: Evaluate the efficiency and effectiveness of the product or service in meeting your goals and expectations.

   d. Performance Metrics: If applicable, review performance metrics or key performance indicators (KPIs) to gauge the product or service's effectiveness.

Suitability and Compatibility

Determine if the product or service is suitable and compatible with your specific needs and requirements:

   a. Compatibility: Ensure the product or service is compatible with your existing tools, systems, or infrastructure.

   b. Customization: Assess whether the product or service can be tailored or customized to meet your unique needs and preferences.

   c. Scalability: Consider whether the product or service can accommodate your future growth or changing demands.

   d. User-Friendly: Evaluate the user-friendliness of the product or service. Is it intuitive, easy to learn, and accessible to your intended users or audience?

Customer Support and Reliability

Customer support and reliability are essential factors in evaluating a product or service:

   a. Customer Support: Research the quality of customer support provided by the company. Assess their responsiveness, availability, and helpfulness.

b. Warranties and Guarantees: Investigate any warranties or guarantees offered with the product or service. These can provide additional peace of mind.

c. Maintenance and Updates: Understand the company's approach to maintenance and updates. Regular updates can ensure ongoing performance and security.

Cost and Value

Evaluate the cost and overall value of the product or service:

a. Price Analysis: Assess the cost of the product or service in relation to your budget and objectives. Is it a cost-effective solution?

b. Total Cost of Ownership: Consider the total cost of ownership, which includes initial purchase costs, ongoing maintenance, and any associated fees.

c. Return on Investment (ROI): Calculate the potential ROI by comparing the benefits and outcomes to the cost of the product or service.

Risk Assessment

Every decision involves some level of risk. Evaluate the potential risks associated with the product or service:

a. Security and Privacy: Assess the product or service's security measures and how it handles sensitive data or information.

b. Vendor Lock-In: Consider whether using the product or service might lead to vendor lock-in, making it difficult to switch to an alternative.

c. Data Loss or Downtime: Evaluate the potential risks of data loss or service downtime and whether the company has contingency plans in place.

Trial Period or Pilot Testing

Whenever possible, take advantage of trial periods or pilot testing options offered by the provider. This allows you to experience the product or service firsthand and evaluate its performance in your specific context.

Conclusion

Evaluating a product or service offered is a systematic process that empowers you to make informed decisions that align with your needs, objectives, and values. By following the steps outlined in this comprehensive guide, you can ensure that the product or service you choose meets your expectations and contributes to your success. Making thoughtful assessments helps consumers, investors, and professionals make the most of their resources and enhance their overall experiences.

Understanding Compensation Plans: A Comprehensive Guide

Introduction

Compensation plans are essential components of various aspects of our lives, from our jobs to investment strategies. Whether you're an employee, an entrepreneur, or an investor, understanding compensation plans is crucial for making informed decisions about your income and financial future. This comprehensive guide will provide you with an in-depth understanding of compensation plans, how they work, and how they affect your financial well-being.

What Is a Compensation Plan?

A compensation plan is a structured framework that outlines how individuals or entities will be rewarded or compensated for their work, sales, services, or investments. Compensation plans serve various purposes, and they come in many forms, including:

   a. Employee Compensation Plans: These are designed for employees and determine how they are paid, including salaries, bonuses, commissions, and benefits.

   b. Sales Compensation Plans: Common in sales and marketing, these plans outline how sales representatives earn commissions or bonuses based on sales performance.

   c. Multi-Level Marketing (MLM) Compensation Plans: MLM companies use complex compensation plans that reward both product sales and recruiting new members.

d. Investment Compensation Plans: Investors may use various compensation plans to manage their portfolios and determine how they are compensated, including performance fees and dividend distributions.

Components of a Compensation Plan

A typical compensation plan comprises several key components:

a. Base Salary: The fixed amount an employee receives regularly, often on a weekly, bi-weekly, or monthly basis.

b. Bonuses: Additional payments provided to employees based on performance, company profitability, or other factors.

c. Commissions: A percentage of sales or revenue earned by a salesperson, typically tied to individual performance.

d. Benefits: Non-monetary perks such as health insurance, retirement plans, paid time off, and stock options.

e. Incentives: Special rewards, promotions, or prizes given to encourage specific behaviors or achievements.

f. Vesting Schedules: Pertaining to stock options and retirement plans, vesting schedules determine when an employee becomes eligible to access these benefits.

Employee Compensation Plans

Employee compensation plans play a crucial role in attracting and retaining talented professionals. They come in various forms, such as:

a. Salary-Based Plans: These provide employees with a fixed salary, which can be annual, monthly, or bi-weekly. Salary-based plans offer financial stability but may lack the incentive for high performers.

b. Hourly Wage Plans: Hourly employees are compensated for the number of hours worked. These plans are common in industries where hours vary, such as retail or hospitality.

c. Commission-Based Plans: Salespeople, often in industries like real estate or retail, receive a percentage of the revenue they generate. This provides a strong incentive for higher sales performance.

d. Performance-Based Plans: These tie compensation to individual or team performance, with bonuses or profit-sharing arrangements. Performance-based plans encourage employees to strive for excellence.

e. Stock Options and Equity Plans: Some companies offer stock options or equity in the company as part of the compensation package, allowing employees to benefit from the company's growth.

Sales Compensation Plans

Sales compensation plans are designed to motivate and reward sales teams and can take various forms:

a. Straight Commission: Sales representatives earn a percentage of the sales revenue they generate, but they may not receive a base salary.

b. Salary Plus Commission: Sales reps receive a base salary plus a commission on sales, providing financial stability while incentivizing high performance.

c. Tiered Commission: Salespeople receive different commission rates based on their performance levels. Higher sales volumes result in higher commission percentages.

d. Bonus Plans: Companies may offer bonuses for achieving specific sales targets or milestones. This provides extra motivation to exceed goals.

e. Residual Commissions: In industries with subscription models, sales reps earn ongoing commissions on customer renewals or recurring sales.

MLM Compensation Plans

MLM companies employ complex compensation plans that reward both product sales and recruitment efforts. Common MLM compensation structures include:

a. Unilevel Plan: Distributors can recruit an unlimited number of people on their front-line and earn commissions on the sales made by their recruits.

b. Binary Plan: Distributors can only recruit two people on their front-line, creating a "binary" structure. Commissions are based on the sales of these two recruits and their downlines.

c. Matrix Plan: Distributors have a limited number of recruits they can sponsor, and the structure is typically organized as a matrix, such as 3x7 or 5x7. Commissions are earned on a set number of levels.

d. Stair-Step Plan: Distributors advance through ranks by meeting sales and recruitment goals. As they progress, they earn higher commissions and bonuses.

e. Breakaway Plan: Distributors break away from their upline when they reach a certain rank, becoming leaders of their own teams. They earn commissions on their team's sales.

Investment Compensation Plans

Investment compensation plans relate to how investors receive returns on their investments. Key aspects include:

a. Dividends: Investors in stocks or dividend-paying funds receive periodic payments based on the profits of the underlying companies.

b. Capital Gains: Investors benefit from capital gains when the value of their investments increases. They can realize these gains by selling the investments.

c. Performance Fees: Hedge funds and some investment funds charge a performance fee, typically a percentage of profits, as compensation for the fund manager's success.

d. Distributions: Real estate investment trusts (REITs) and other investment vehicles may provide regular distributions of income or profits to investors.

Tax Considerations

It's essential to consider the tax implications of your compensation plan. Different forms of compensation may be subject to varying tax rates, deductions, or exemptions. Consult with a tax professional to understand how your compensation affects your tax liability.

Conclusion

Understanding compensation plans is essential for making informed decisions in various aspects of your life, whether you're an employee, a salesperson, an entrepreneur, or an investor. By comprehending the different types of compensation plans and their components, you can make choices that align with your financial goals, values, and circumstances. Make sure to carefully review any compensation plan agreements and, if necessary, seek professional advice to maximize the benefits and minimize potential risks.

Connecting Your "Why" with a Network Marketing Opportunity: A Comprehensive Guide

Introduction

Network marketing, also known as multi-level marketing (MLM), offers a unique entrepreneurial path where individuals can build their own businesses by marketing and selling products or services through a network of distributors. To find success and fulfillment in network marketing, it is crucial to connect your "why" – your core purpose, values, and motivations – with the opportunity at hand. This article provides a comprehensive guide on how to align your "why" with a network marketing opportunity to create a meaningful and successful venture.

Define Your "Why"

Your "why" is your underlying motivation and the core reason you do what you do. It is essential to start by defining your "why" before considering a network marketing opportunity:

   a. Self-Reflection: Take time to reflect on your life experiences, values, and passions. What drives you? What are your core values and principles?

   b. Personal Goals: Consider your long-term aspirations and what you hope to achieve in life. How can a network marketing opportunity help you achieve these goals?

   c. Financial Objectives: Determine your financial goals and how additional income or financial independence align with your "why."

Understand Network Marketing

Before connecting your "why" with a network marketing opportunity, it's important to understand how network marketing works:

   a. Business Model: Network marketing involves building a distribution network to sell products or services. Distributors earn commissions on their sales and the sales of their recruited team members.

   b. Product or Service: Network marketing companies offer a range of products or services. It's essential to evaluate the relevance and quality of these offerings to ensure they align with your "why."

   c. Compensation Plan: Each network marketing company has its own compensation plan, detailing how you will be compensated for sales and team building efforts.

   d. Independent Business: In network marketing, you are essentially building your own business within the framework of the company. This business model allows you to leverage your "why" effectively.

Assess the Product or Service

Connecting your "why" with a network marketing opportunity starts with assessing the product or service offered:

   a. Relevance: Evaluate whether the product or service resonates with your core values and interests. It should be something you genuinely believe in and can promote enthusiastically.

   b. Quality: Examine the quality of the product or service. It's essential that the offerings meet or exceed industry standards and consumer expectations.

c. Market Demand: Consider the demand for the product or service in the market. Is there a growing customer base, or is it a niche offering?

   d. Competitive Analysis: Compare the network marketing company's product or service with similar offerings in the market. Assess pricing, features, and unique selling points.

Determine Your Unique Selling Proposition (USP)

In network marketing, your "why" and your unique selling proposition (USP) should align. Your USP is what sets you apart from other distributors and makes your approach compelling. Consider how your "why" can be woven into your USP to create an authentic and appealing message.

   a. Authenticity: Be genuine in your approach. Your "why" should resonate with your audience and reflect your passion and values.

   b. Storytelling: Share your personal story and how the product or service aligns with your "why." Authentic storytelling can connect with potential customers and team members on a deeper level.

   c. Niche Focus: If your "why" centers on a particular niche or area of expertise, focus on products or services related to that niche within the network marketing company.

Evaluate the Company Culture

The culture and values of the network marketing company can significantly impact how well your "why" aligns with the opportunity:

a. Company Values: Research the company's core values, mission statement, and culture. Ensure they align with your personal values and principles.

b. Supportive Environment: Seek a network marketing company that provides a supportive and collaborative environment. A strong team culture can enhance your sense of purpose.

c. Training and Development: Assess the company's training and development programs to determine whether they will help you align your "why" with the opportunity effectively.

Set Clear Goals

Connect your "why" with specific goals for your network marketing venture:

a. Short-term Goals: Set short-term objectives that can be achieved in the near future, such as reaching a specific sales target or recruiting team members.

b. Long-term Goals: Define long-term goals that align with your broader "why" and personal aspirations. These might include financial independence or a particular lifestyle.

c. SMART Goals: Ensure that your goals are Specific, Measurable, Achievable, Relevant, and Time-bound (SMART). This clarity makes it easier to track your progress.

Align Your "Why" with Your Team

As you build your network marketing team, help your team members connect their "why" with the opportunity. This can create a cohesive and motivated group with a shared purpose:

a. Leadership: Lead by example and demonstrate how your "why" drives your actions. Encourage team members to do the same.

b. Personal Connection: Foster a personal connection with your team members, understanding their "whys" and helping them integrate their motivations into their network marketing efforts.

c. Team Goals: Create team goals that align with your collective "whys." Working towards shared objectives can enhance motivation and success.

Conclusion

Connecting your "why" with a network marketing opportunity can be a fulfilling and rewarding journey. By assessing the product or service, considering your unique selling proposition, and evaluating the company culture, you can align your personal motivations and values with the network marketing venture. This alignment enhances your sense of purpose, drives your success, and empowers you to inspire and lead your team effectively. Remember that network marketing is a long-term commitment, so it's essential to regularly reassess your "why" and adjust your strategies as needed to stay aligned with your goals and values.

The Importance of Personal Alignment in Business: Achieving Success and Fulfillment

Introduction

Personal alignment in business refers to the harmonious integration of an individual's values, goals, and motivations with their professional endeavors. When your personal values and aspirations are in sync with your business pursuits, it can lead to a sense of fulfillment, heightened motivation, and ultimately, greater success. In this comprehensive guide, we will explore the crucial importance of personal alignment in business and how it can positively impact your career and overall life.

Personal Alignment Defined

Personal alignment involves a holistic assessment of your values, beliefs, and personal objectives, coupled with a corresponding alignment with your business goals. It goes beyond mere financial success and taps into the deeper aspects of your professional life:

   a. Values: Personal alignment involves identifying and upholding the values that are important to you, such as integrity, creativity, social responsibility, or work-life balance.

   b. Goals: Aligning personal goals with your business objectives means ensuring that your professional path supports your long-term ambitions.

   c. Motivation: Recognizing what motivates you is vital. When your work resonates with your motivations, you are more likely to be passionate and dedicated.

d. Work-Life Balance: Personal alignment also extends to maintaining a balance between your work and personal life, ensuring both are in harmony.

Personal Alignment and Career Satisfaction

Personal alignment significantly contributes to career satisfaction and overall well-being:

   a. Fulfillment: When your values and aspirations are in harmony with your work, you are more likely to find your work meaningful and fulfilling.

   b. Motivation: Personal alignment enhances motivation, as your work becomes more than just a means of earning money; it becomes an expression of your personal goals and values.

   c. Resilience: Personal alignment can boost resilience because you are more likely to persist through challenges when your work is closely tied to your values.

   d. Emotional Well-being: Achieving personal alignment often results in a higher level of overall emotional well-being and reduced stress.

Building an Aligned Career

To build an aligned career, consider the following steps:

   a. Self-Reflection: Take time to reflect on your core values, long-term objectives, and what truly motivates you in your career. This self-awareness is the foundation of personal alignment.

b. Goal Setting: Define clear, actionable career goals that reflect your personal values and aspirations. Ensure your short-term objectives lead to long-term fulfillment.

c. Values Integration: Identify how your work can integrate with your values. Seek employment or business opportunities that resonate with your personal ethics.

d. Skills and Interests: Leverage your skills and interests. Your work should allow you to apply your strengths and engage in activities you enjoy.

e. Work-Life Balance: Maintain a healthy work-life balance, ensuring that you have time for your personal life and that your work supports your overall well-being.

f. Seek Feedback: Periodically seek feedback from mentors, colleagues, or trusted advisors to assess your alignment and receive insights on potential adjustments.

Business Success Through Personal Alignment

Personal alignment can directly impact business success in several ways:

a. Improved Decision-Making: When your personal values guide your business decisions, they tend to be more aligned with ethical principles and long-term sustainability.

b. Enhanced Leadership: Aligned leaders are often more inspiring and effective, as their authentic values and motivation shine through in their leadership style.

c. Employee Satisfaction: Business owners and leaders who promote personal alignment among their employees can foster a more satisfied and motivated workforce.

d. Brand Authenticity: Consumers are increasingly drawn to authentic and socially responsible brands. Personal alignment can drive authentic branding and resonate with customers.

Case Studies: Personal Alignment in Business

Several successful business leaders and entrepreneurs have attributed their achievements to personal alignment:

a. Elon Musk: Musk's personal alignment with his vision of sustainable energy and human colonization of Mars drives his leadership at Tesla and SpaceX.

b. Patagonia: The outdoor clothing company Patagonia is known for its strong commitment to environmental and social responsibility, reflecting founder Yvon Chouinard's personal values.

c. Toms Shoes: Toms Shoes, famous for its "One for One" giving model, was founded by Blake Mycoskie, whose personal alignment with a desire to give back to those in need led to the business's success.

d. Oprah Winfrey: Media mogul Oprah Winfrey attributes her success to personal alignment with her values and a deep commitment to empowering and inspiring others.

Challenges and Strategies

Achieving personal alignment in business may pose challenges, but these challenges can be overcome:

a. Self-Doubt: You might face self-doubt or fear when pursuing an aligned career. Seek support from mentors, coaches, or counselors to address these concerns.

b. External Pressure: External expectations, societal norms, or financial pressures can lead to misalignment. Recognize the importance of staying true to your values.

c. Reevaluation: Personal alignment is not static. Regularly reevaluate your values, goals, and motivations to ensure continued alignment with your career.

d. Transition: If your current career is not aligned with your personal values, consider transitioning to a new field or position that better reflects your alignment.

Conclusion

Personal alignment in business is not only a source of fulfillment and motivation but also a driving force behind success and sustainable business practices. By connecting your values, aspirations, and motivations with your professional path, you can enjoy a more rewarding and harmonious career. Whether you are an employee, an entrepreneur, or a business leader, personal alignment can lead to better decision-making, more effective leadership, and a stronger sense of purpose, ultimately enhancing your overall well-being and success in the business world.

Strategies for Staying Passionate About Your Business: Keys to Long-Term Success

Introduction

Starting a business is often driven by passion and a strong desire to bring your vision to life. However, maintaining that passion over the long term can be challenging. The daily demands of running a business can lead to burnout and a loss of enthusiasm. In this comprehensive guide, we will explore effective strategies for staying passionate about your business, ensuring that your entrepreneurial journey remains fulfilling and successful.

Reconnect with Your "Why"

Your "why" is the driving force behind your business, representing the core purpose and motivation that led you to start it in the first place. To stay passionate, it's essential to regularly reconnect with your "why":

   a. Reflect: Take time to reflect on the original inspiration that drove you to start your business. What goals did you aim to achieve? What problems did you want to solve?

   b. Adjust Your Vision: As your business evolves, your "why" may also change. Adjust your vision and goals to ensure they align with your current passions and values.

   c. Share Your Story: Sharing your personal story and the journey behind your business can help you and your team stay connected to your "why."

Set Clear and Inspiring Goals

Setting clear and inspiring goals is a powerful way to maintain your passion for your business:

a. SMART Goals: Create Specific, Measurable, Achievable, Relevant, and Time-bound (SMART) goals that provide a clear roadmap for your business's success.

b. Long-Term Vision: Develop long-term goals that align with your "why" and keep you excited about the future of your business.

c. Break Down Goals: Divide your long-term goals into smaller, achievable milestones that you can celebrate along the way. These victories will help sustain your enthusiasm.

Embrace Continuous Learning

Learning and growing within your industry and as a business owner can reignite your passion:

a. Stay Informed: Keep up to date with industry trends, innovations, and best practices to maintain a sense of relevance and purpose.

b. Attend Workshops and Conferences: Participating in workshops, seminars, and conferences can provide fresh perspectives and inspiration.

c. Network: Engage with others in your field to share knowledge, learn from their experiences, and build a supportive community.

Surround Yourself with Passionate People

The company you keep can significantly impact your passion for your business:

   a. Collaborate: Surround yourself with like-minded individuals who share your enthusiasm for your industry or entrepreneurial journey.

   b. Seek Mentorship: Connect with mentors and advisors who can provide guidance and share their passion for business.

   c. Positive Workplace Culture: Foster a positive workplace culture that encourages passion, innovation, and creativity among your team.

Reevaluate and Evolve

Businesses evolve over time, and it's crucial to adapt and make necessary changes to stay passionate:

   a. Innovation: Embrace innovation by seeking new ways to deliver products or services, rebranding, or expanding into new markets.

   b. Pivots: Be open to pivoting your business strategy if it aligns with your "why" and can reignite your passion.

   c. Feedback: Listen to feedback from customers, employees, and advisors to guide your business's evolution.

Practice Self-Care

Staying passionate about your business requires taking care of yourself:

a. Health and Well-Being: Prioritize physical and mental health through regular exercise, a balanced diet, and relaxation techniques.

b. Work-Life Balance: Maintain a healthy work-life balance to prevent burnout and keep your enthusiasm for your business.

c. Time Off: Don't underestimate the importance of taking breaks and vacations to recharge and return to your business with renewed passion.

Celebrate Milestones and Achievements

Acknowledging and celebrating your business's milestones and achievements can keep you motivated and passionate:

a. Milestone Celebrations: Recognize and celebrate both small and significant milestones, such as anniversaries, product launches, or revenue goals.

b. Employee Recognition: Acknowledge your team's contributions and celebrate their achievements to build a positive and passionate workplace environment.

c. Reflect on Success: Regularly reflect on your accomplishments and the progress you've made since starting your business.

Reignite Your Creativity

Creativity is closely linked to passion. To reignite your creativity:

a. Change of Environment: Work in different environments or travel to gain new perspectives and stimulate creativity.

b. Creative Workshops: Attend workshops that focus on creativity and idea generation to keep your business fresh and innovative.

   c. Diverse Inputs: Consume diverse content, such as books, podcasts, and documentaries, to inspire new ideas and approaches.

Delegate and Collaborate

Don't carry the entire burden of your business on your own:

   a. Delegate Tasks: Assign tasks to trusted employees or partners to free up your time and energy for strategic and passion-driven activities.

   b. Collaborate: Partner with other businesses or individuals in joint ventures, collaborations, or projects that align with your passion.

   c. Seek Help: Don't hesitate to seek professional help for tasks that are outside your expertise or areas where you lack enthusiasm.

Stay Adaptable

The business landscape is ever-changing, and adaptability is key to staying passionate:

   a. Embrace Change: View change as an opportunity for growth and a way to continually evolve your business.

   b. Learn from Setbacks: Use setbacks and failures as opportunities to learn, improve, and come back stronger.

   c. Agility: Maintain a sense of agility in your business, making it easier to pivot and adapt when necessary.

Conclusion

Staying passionate about your business is essential for long-term success and fulfillment as an entrepreneur. By regularly reconnecting with your "why," setting inspiring goals, embracing continuous learning, surrounding yourself with passionate individuals, and practicing self-care, you can keep your enthusiasm alive. The journey of entrepreneurship is filled with challenges, but your passion and dedication can be the driving force that propels you to greater heights and achievements in your business.

Setting Long-Term Business Goals: A Comprehensive Guide to Sustainable Success

Introduction

Setting long-term business goals is a fundamental practice that guides an organization's growth, direction, and strategic decision-making. These goals provide a clear roadmap for the future, aligning the efforts of all stakeholders and helping maintain focus on a common vision. In this comprehensive guide, we will explore the importance of setting long-term business goals and provide practical steps for establishing and achieving them.

Why Long-Term Business Goals Matter

Long-term business goals play a pivotal role in an organization's success and sustainability:

   a. Strategic Direction: They provide a sense of direction and purpose, ensuring that everyone within the organization is working towards a common objective.

   b. Motivation: Long-term goals motivate employees, investors, and stakeholders, as they can see the bigger picture and the potential for growth and success.

   c. Measurement: They serve as benchmarks for evaluating performance, progress, and the success of strategies and initiatives.

d. Adaptability: Long-term goals enable organizations to be flexible while maintaining a long-term vision. They can adapt to market changes without losing sight of their primary objectives.

Types of Long-Term Business Goals

Long-term business goals can fall into various categories, each serving a different purpose:

  a. Financial Goals: These relate to revenue growth, profitability, return on investment, and financial stability.

  b. Growth Goals: Expansion objectives, including market share growth, increasing the customer base, or entering new markets.

  c. Operational Goals: Enhancements to internal processes, efficiency, or supply chain management.

  d. Innovation Goals: Promoting creativity, research, and development, and fostering a culture of innovation.

  e. Sustainability Goals: Focus on environmentally responsible practices, corporate social responsibility, and ethical business behavior.

  f. Human Resources Goals: Attracting and retaining top talent, fostering a positive work culture, and enhancing employee development.

The SMART Approach

When setting long-term business goals, it's essential to use the SMART criteria. SMART stands for Specific, Measurable, Achievable, Relevant, and Time-bound:

a. Specific: Goals should be well-defined and clear. Avoid vague objectives and use precise language to articulate what you want to achieve.

b. Measurable: Establish measurable criteria for tracking your progress. This might include quantifiable numbers, percentages, or metrics.

c. Achievable: Ensure that your goals are realistic and attainable. While ambitious objectives are important, setting unattainable goals can lead to disappointment and frustration.

d. Relevant: Goals should align with your organization's mission, vision, and values. They should make sense within the context of your business.

e. Time-bound: Set a clear timeframe for achieving your long-term goals. This helps create a sense of urgency and focus.

Steps to Setting Long-Term Business Goals

Follow these steps to set effective long-term business goals:

a. Assess the Current State: Begin by evaluating your organization's current position. What are your strengths, weaknesses, opportunities, and threats (SWOT analysis)?

b. Define Your Vision: Establish a clear and compelling vision of where you want your organization to be in the long term. This should be the driving force behind your goals.

c. Break Down the Vision: Divide your long-term vision into smaller, manageable objectives or milestones that are specific and achievable within your desired time frame.

d. Prioritize Goals: Prioritize your objectives to focus on the most critical and impactful ones. Not all goals should be given equal weight.

e. Develop Strategies: Identify the strategies and initiatives required to achieve each goal. Determine the necessary resources, timelines, and responsibilities.

f. Create a Plan: Outline a detailed plan for each goal, including key performance indicators (KPIs), timelines, and milestones. This plan should guide your organization's actions.

g. Communicate and Engage: Ensure that your employees, stakeholders, and team members understand and are aligned with your long-term goals. Encourage their commitment and engagement in achieving them.

h. Monitor and Adjust: Continuously track your progress toward your long-term goals. Regularly review and adjust your strategies as needed to stay on track.

Long-Term Goal Examples

Examples of long-term business goals in various industries may include:

a. Revenue Growth: Achieve a 50% increase in annual revenue over the next five years.

b. Market Expansion: Enter three new international markets within the next seven years.

c. Product Development: Launch a line of eco-friendly products by the end of the decade.

d. Employee Development: Provide professional development opportunities for 90% of employees within five years.

e. Sustainability: Reduce the company's carbon footprint by 20% over the next decade.

Maintaining Focus and Motivation

Maintaining motivation and focus on long-term goals is essential for success:

a. Visualize Success: Regularly visualize and remind yourself and your team of the benefits and rewards of achieving long-term goals.

b. Celebrate Milestones: Celebrate smaller milestones and achievements along the way. This can provide motivation and a sense of accomplishment.

c. Encourage Collaboration: Foster collaboration and teamwork among your employees. Share the journey and build a collective sense of purpose.

d. Stay Adaptable: Be open to adapting your goals or strategies when circumstances change. Flexibility is vital to long-term success.

e. Review and Reflect: Periodically review your progress and reflect on your goals. Ask yourself if they still align with your organization's vision and values.

Conclusion

Setting long-term business goals is a critical aspect of organizational success and sustainability. By following the SMART criteria, defining a clear vision, and breaking down your goals into manageable milestones, you can create a roadmap for your organization's future. Keep your team engaged, prioritize your goals, and regularly review and adjust your strategies to stay on the path to success. With long-term goals in place, you'll be better equipped to lead your organization toward a prosperous and fulfilling future.

Identifying Potential Obstacles and Challenges: A Comprehensive Guide to Effective Problem-Solving

Introduction

In both personal and professional pursuits, identifying potential obstacles and challenges is a crucial first step toward success. By recognizing and understanding the barriers that may stand in your way, you can develop effective strategies to overcome them. This comprehensive guide will explore the importance of identifying potential obstacles and challenges, provide strategies for recognizing them, and offer insights on how to tackle these hurdles effectively.

The Significance of Identifying Obstacles and Challenges

Identifying potential obstacles and challenges is essential for various reasons:

a. Preparedness: It allows you to anticipate and prepare for the difficulties that may arise, thereby minimizing their impact.

b. Resource Allocation: You can allocate resources more efficiently by knowing where they are needed most to overcome challenges.

c. Risk Mitigation: It enables you to develop risk mitigation strategies to reduce the likelihood and impact of potential issues.

d. Problem-Solving: Identifying challenges early in the process facilitates better problem-solving and decision-making.

Strategies for Identifying Potential Obstacles and Challenges

To effectively identify potential obstacles and challenges, consider the following strategies:

a. Risk Assessment: Conduct a comprehensive risk assessment by evaluating potential internal and external risks that could affect your project or goal.

b. SWOT Analysis: Perform a SWOT analysis, which identifies internal Strengths and Weaknesses and external Opportunities and Threats. It helps you pinpoint both advantages and vulnerabilities.

c. Brainstorming: Gather a team or engage in solo brainstorming to generate a list of possible challenges that could emerge during your project or endeavor.

d. Scenario Planning: Develop multiple scenarios that outline various challenges you may encounter. This technique prepares you for different potential outcomes.

e. Past Experience: Reflect on past experiences and challenges you've faced in similar situations. These lessons can help you anticipate future difficulties.

f. Consult Experts: Seek advice from experts, mentors, or colleagues who have experience in your field. They can provide valuable insights into potential obstacles.

Common Obstacles and Challenges in Various Fields

Recognizing potential obstacles is specific to your industry or goal. Here are some common challenges in different fields:

a. Business and Entrepreneurship: Financial constraints, competition, market volatility, and regulatory changes are common challenges.

b. Education: Challenges can include student engagement, limited resources, adapting to new technology, and curriculum development.

c. Health and Wellness: Common obstacles include lack of motivation, health-related setbacks, and difficulties in adhering to a wellness routine.

d. Project Management: Project delays, resource allocation issues, scope creep, and team coordination can be potential challenges.

e. Relationships: Communication breakdowns, misunderstandings, and personal differences can be common obstacles in personal relationships.

f. Technology: Rapid technological advancements and cybersecurity threats can pose significant challenges in the tech industry.

Effective Problem-Solving Strategies

Once you've identified potential obstacles and challenges, the next step is to develop effective problem-solving strategies:

a. Analyze: Carefully examine the challenge, breaking it down into its components. Understand the root causes and underlying issues.

b. Prioritize: Not all challenges are of equal importance. Prioritize them based on their potential impact and urgency.

c. Gather Information: Collect relevant data and information to make informed decisions. Consult experts, conduct research, or seek input from others.

d. Generate Solutions: Brainstorm potential solutions and alternatives. Encourage creative thinking and consider various approaches.

   e. Evaluate: Assess the feasibility and potential outcomes of each solution. Consider the risks and benefits associated with each option.

   f. Choose and Implement: Select the most suitable solution and put it into action. Ensure that everyone involved understands their roles and responsibilities.

   g. Monitor and Adjust: Continuously monitor the situation, evaluating the effectiveness of the chosen solution. Be prepared to adjust your approach if necessary.

   h. Learn from Experience: After overcoming a challenge, review the process and outcomes. Use this knowledge to improve future problem-solving efforts.

Emotional Resilience and Attitude

Emotional resilience is an essential aspect of dealing with obstacles and challenges. Maintaining a positive attitude and emotional fortitude can help you navigate difficulties more effectively:

   a. Stay Optimistic: A positive outlook can enhance problem-solving abilities and help you persevere through challenges.

   b. Cultivate Resilience: Develop resilience by learning from failures and setbacks, and by embracing change as an opportunity for growth.

   c. Seek Support: Don't hesitate to seek emotional support from friends, family, or colleagues during challenging times.

   d. Practice Self-Care: Prioritize self-care to ensure that you are emotionally and physically well-equipped to face obstacles.

e. Develop Adaptability: The ability to adapt to new circumstances is a key component of resilience. Be open to change and flexible in your approach.

Case Studies: Learning from Obstacles

Several famous individuals and organizations have faced and overcome significant obstacles:

a. Thomas Edison: Edison faced numerous challenges while inventing the lightbulb, but he famously stated, "I have not failed. I've just found 10,000 ways that won't work."

b. Apple Inc.: Apple experienced a period of decline in the 1990s but rebounded with innovative products like the iPod, iPhone, and iPad.

c. J.K. Rowling: The author of the Harry Potter series faced multiple rejections before achieving worldwide success.

d. NASA: NASA overcame countless obstacles to land astronauts on the moon, including technical difficulties and funding issues.

Conclusion

Identifying potential obstacles and challenges is a vital step in achieving success in any endeavor. By using a range of strategies to foresee challenges, you can develop effective problem-solving skills and stay prepared for the unexpected. A positive attitude, emotional resilience, and adaptability are also essential for navigating obstacles with grace and perseverance. Remember that obstacles are not insurmountable barriers but opportunities for growth, learning, and improvement.

Building a Support Network for Motivation: A Comprehensive Guide to Achieving Your Goals

Introduction

Motivation is a powerful force that drives individuals to pursue their goals and aspirations. However, maintaining a high level of motivation can be challenging, especially when faced with obstacles and setbacks. Building a strong support network can significantly impact your motivation, helping you stay focused, inspired, and accountable as you work toward your objectives. In this comprehensive guide, we will explore the importance of a support network for motivation and provide practical strategies for creating and maintaining one.

The Role of a Support Network in Motivation

A support network is a group of individuals who offer encouragement, guidance, and assistance to help you stay motivated and overcome challenges. Here's why such a network is essential for motivation:

   a. Accountability: Your network holds you accountable for your goals, ensuring that you remain committed to achieving them.

   b. Emotional Support: In times of self-doubt or discouragement, your support network provides emotional support and a sense of belonging.

   c. Knowledge Sharing: Network members can share their expertise, experiences, and insights to help you overcome obstacles.

   d. Positive Influence: Being around motivated and positive individuals can inspire you to maintain your own motivation.

Types of Support Network Members

Your support network can consist of various types of individuals, each offering a unique form of assistance:

  a. Family and Friends: These are the people who know you best and can provide unwavering emotional support and encouragement.

  b. Mentors: Seek mentors who can offer guidance and advice based on their experience and expertise in your field.

  c. Coaches: Professional coaches can help you set and achieve specific goals, offering valuable strategies and feedback.

  d. Peers and Colleagues: Building connections with individuals who share similar goals can create a sense of camaraderie and competition that motivates you.

  e. Online Communities: Join online forums, social media groups, or communities related to your interests or goals to connect with like-minded individuals.

  f. Support Groups: Consider joining support groups for specific challenges, such as addiction recovery, weight loss, or career development.

Strategies for Building a Support Network

Building a support network for motivation involves several key strategies:

  a. Identify Your Needs: Determine the type of support you need, such as emotional encouragement, guidance, or accountability.

  b. Reach Out to Existing Connections: Start by talking to friends, family, or colleagues who are already a part of your life.

c. Expand Your Network: Attend events, conferences, and workshops to meet potential mentors, peers, and colleagues who share your interests and goals.

   d. Join Online Communities: Explore online forums and social media groups related to your field or interests.

   e. Professional Organizations: Many fields have professional organizations that offer networking opportunities. Join and participate actively.

   f. Support Groups: If you're dealing with specific challenges, search for local or online support groups that can provide valuable encouragement.

   g. Seek Expert Guidance: Consider hiring a coach or mentor who specializes in your area of interest or goal.

   h. Foster Mutual Support: Create a reciprocal relationship within your network, offering your support and assistance in return.

Maintaining Your Support Network

After building your support network, it's essential to maintain and nurture these relationships:

   a. Regular Communication: Keep in touch with your network members through calls, meetings, or online interactions.

   b. Express Gratitude: Show appreciation for their support and let them know how their assistance has impacted your motivation and progress.

   c. Set Clear Boundaries: Define the terms of your support network relationships, ensuring that both parties understand their roles and responsibilities.

d. Share Progress: Keep your network updated on your progress and accomplishments, celebrating your successes together.

   e. Be Open to Feedback: Welcome constructive feedback from your network members, as it can help you make improvements and stay motivated.

   f. Attend Networking Events: Continue participating in networking events, workshops, and conferences to meet new people and expand your support network.

   g. Offer Your Support: Be willing to provide assistance and encouragement to others in your network when they need it.

Virtual and Online Support Networks

Online support networks have gained significant popularity in recent years and can be particularly valuable:

   a. Social Media: Join Facebook groups, Twitter chats, or LinkedIn communities relevant to your goals or interests.

   b. Online Forums: Participate in forums and discussion boards related to your field, where you can connect with people worldwide.

   c. Virtual Accountability Partners: Partner with someone who shares similar goals and maintains a virtual accountability relationship.

   d. E-Learning Platforms: Many online courses and learning platforms offer opportunities to connect with instructors and fellow learners.

Case Studies: The Power of Support Networks

Several successful individuals have attributed their achievements to their support networks:

a. Oprah Winfrey: The media mogul credits much of her success to the support and encouragement of her mentor, Maya Angelou.

b. Steve Jobs: The late Apple co-founder found inspiration and motivation in the mentorship of Mike Markkula, a close friend and early Apple investor.

c. Michelle Obama: The former First Lady has often acknowledged the essential role her mother and family played in her life, offering unwavering support.

d. Richard Branson: The Virgin Group founder has repeatedly cited the guidance and mentorship he received throughout his career.

Conclusion

Building and maintaining a support network for motivation is a vital step toward achieving your goals and staying inspired. The encouragement, guidance, and emotional support provided by your network can be a powerful force in helping you overcome obstacles and setbacks. Whether your network consists of family, friends, mentors, or online communities, these connections can significantly impact your motivation and success. Remember that while your support network is there to provide assistance, your dedication and commitment remain essential components of your journey to achieve your goals.

Crafting a Personal Mission Statement: A Guiding Light to a Purposeful Life

Introduction

A personal mission statement is a succinct declaration of your core values, beliefs, and purpose in life. It serves as a guiding compass, helping you make meaningful decisions, set clear goals, and live in alignment with your deepest values. In this comprehensive guide, we will explore the importance of crafting a personal mission statement, the steps to create one, and how it can impact your life.

Understanding the Purpose of a Personal Mission Statement

A personal mission statement is a reflection of your innermost values and aspirations. Its primary purposes include:

   a. Clarity: It provides a clear, concise statement of your purpose and values, helping you make life choices that align with your beliefs.

   b. Decision-Making: A mission statement serves as a decision-making tool, guiding you toward choices that support your life's mission.

   c. Goals and Prioritization: It helps you set and prioritize goals that are in line with your core values and long-term vision.

   d. Motivation: A personal mission statement can inspire and motivate you during challenging times by reminding you of your purpose.

e. Alignment: It encourages alignment between your personal life, career, and relationships, fostering a sense of congruence and authenticity.

Steps to Crafting Your Personal Mission Statement

Creating a personal mission statement is a thoughtful and introspective process. Follow these steps to develop your unique mission statement:

a. Self-Reflection: Set aside dedicated time for deep self-reflection. Consider your values, beliefs, and aspirations, and how they shape your decisions and actions.

b. Identify Core Values: Define your core values, the principles that matter most to you. These may include integrity, compassion, creativity, family, or personal growth.

c. Define Your Passions: Identify your passions and interests, as these are often central to your life's purpose.

d. Examine Past Experiences: Reflect on past experiences, both positive and challenging, to understand how they have influenced your values and beliefs.

e. Create a List of Personal Goals: List your short-term and long-term personal and professional goals. Consider what achievements would make your life fulfilling.

f. Write a Personal Vision Statement: Start by writing a personal vision statement that encapsulates your ideal future, including the impact you want to make in the world.

g. Write a Draft Mission Statement: Use your self-reflection, values, passions, and goals to draft a preliminary mission statement. It should be a brief, clear expression of your life's purpose.

h. Seek Feedback: Share your draft mission statement with trusted friends, mentors, or family members. Their feedback can offer valuable insights.

i. Revise and Refine: Based on feedback and personal reflection, revise and refine your mission statement until it accurately represents your values and aspirations.

j. Finalize Your Mission Statement: Once you are satisfied with your mission statement, finalize it, and consider having it professionally designed or written in an artistic format.

Key Elements of a Personal Mission Statement

A well-crafted personal mission statement typically includes the following elements:

a. Core Values: Express your foundational values and beliefs that guide your actions.

b. Long-Term Goals: Define your long-term goals, aspirations, and the impact you want to make in the world.

c. Actionable Language: Use action-oriented language that reflects your commitment to living out your mission.

d. Inspirational Tone: Make your mission statement inspirational and motivating, both for yourself and others.

e. Clarity and Brevity: Keep your statement concise and straightforward to ensure its message is easily understood.

Examples of Personal Mission Statements

Here are some examples of personal mission statements to provide inspiration:

a. "To live a life of integrity and kindness, inspiring those around me to strive for their highest potential."

b. "To empower individuals through education and mentorship, helping them achieve financial independence and personal growth."

c. "To be a loving and supportive partner, a present and caring parent, and a force for positive change in my community."

d. "To lead with courage and creativity, fostering innovation and making a lasting impact in the business world."

e. "To explore the world, embrace diverse cultures, and contribute to global understanding and peace."

Implementing Your Personal Mission Statement

Once you've crafted your mission statement, it's crucial to put it into practice:

a. Regularly Reflect: Take time for periodic reflection, evaluating how well your actions align with your mission.

b. Goal Alignment: Ensure that your personal and professional goals align with your mission statement.

c. Decision-Making: Use your mission statement as a decision-making tool, guiding you toward choices that reflect your values.

d. Share and Communicate: Share your mission statement with those close to you and use it to explain your motivations and intentions.

e. Seek Accountability: Engage with friends, mentors, or a coach who can help hold you accountable to living in accordance with your mission.

f. Embrace Adaptability: Be open to adapting your mission statement as your life and circumstances change. It should be a living document that evolves with you.

The Impact of a Personal Mission Statement

A well-defined personal mission statement can have a profound impact on your life:

a. Clarity and Direction: It provides clarity on your purpose and direction in life, making decision-making more straightforward.

b. Motivation and Inspiration: Your mission statement can serve as a source of motivation and inspiration during challenging times.

c. Goal Achievement: It helps you set and prioritize goals that are in alignment with your values, leading to a more fulfilled life.

d. Authenticity: Living according to your mission statement fosters authenticity, as your actions align with your deepest beliefs.

e. Legacy: Your mission statement can guide your actions in a way that leaves a lasting, positive impact on the world.

Conclusion

A personal mission statement is a powerful tool for shaping your life in accordance with your values and aspirations. By carefully crafting your mission statement and integrating it into your daily life, you can achieve greater clarity, motivation, and fulfillment. Your mission statement will be a guiding light on your journey, helping you make meaningful decisions and live a purposeful, authentic life.

Defining Your Unique Selling Proposition (USP): Unleashing Your Competitive Advantage

Introduction

In the competitive world of business, having a clear and compelling Unique Selling Proposition (USP) is vital to stand out from the crowd and attract customers. Your USP is what sets your product, service, or brand apart from competitors and convinces consumers to choose you over other options. In this comprehensive guide, we'll explore the importance of defining your USP, the steps to create one, and how it can boost your business's success.

Understanding the Unique Selling Proposition (USP)

Your USP is the unique and distinctive element of your product or service that differentiates it from competitors in the eyes of your target audience. It answers the fundamental question: "Why should customers choose you over other options?" Your USP is what makes your business memorable and desirable.

The Importance of a Strong USP

A well-defined USP offers several critical benefits:

   a. Competitive Advantage: It gives you a competitive edge in a crowded marketplace by highlighting your unique strengths.

b. Attraction: A compelling USP attracts and retains customers who resonate with your distinct value.

c. Brand Identity: It contributes to your brand's identity and helps you build a loyal customer base.

d. Pricing Flexibility: A strong USP allows you to command higher prices for your offerings.

e. Marketing and Messaging: It simplifies your marketing efforts by providing a clear, focused message to your audience.

Steps to Define Your Unique Selling Proposition (USP)

Creating an effective USP involves a strategic process:

a. Know Your Audience: Start by understanding your target audience's needs, preferences, and pain points. What do they value most in a product or service like yours?

b. Analyze Your Competitors: Conduct a competitive analysis to identify the strengths and weaknesses of your competitors. What are they doing well, and where are they falling short?

c. Identify Your Unique Features: Examine your product or service to pinpoint the features, qualities, or benefits that set you apart from the competition.

d. Connect to Customer Benefits: Translate these unique features into clear customer benefits. What problems do they solve, or what needs do they fulfill?

e. Highlight Emotional Appeal: Consider the emotional elements of your USP. How does your product or service make your customers feel?

f. Make It Clear and Memorable: Keep your USP concise and memorable. A strong USP should be easily communicated and remembered by your target audience.

g. Test and Refine: Test your USP with real customers, gather feedback, and refine it based on their responses.

Types of USP

USPs come in various forms, each emphasizing different aspects of your product or service:

a. Price USP: Offering the lowest price in the market, emphasizing affordability and value.

b. Quality USP: Focusing on superior quality, durability, or performance compared to competitors.

c. Convenience USP: Highlighting the ease of use, accessibility, or customer convenience.

d. Innovation USP: Emphasizing cutting-edge technology, unique features, or groundbreaking solutions.

e. Service USP: Showcasing exceptional customer service, personalized support, or extended warranties.

f. Emotional USP: Evoking strong emotions or a sense of belonging, often seen in lifestyle brands.

g. Niche USP: Serving a specific, underserved, or niche market segment.

h. Value USP: Providing a product or service with a compelling balance of quality, features, and price.

Examples of Successful USPs

Here are some real-world examples of successful USPs:

a. FedEx: "When it absolutely, positively has to be there overnight." FedEx built its reputation on guaranteed overnight delivery.

b. Apple: "Think different." Apple's USP revolves around innovative design and user-friendly technology.

c. Volvo: "For life." Volvo's USP centers on safety and durability, appealing to customers looking for reliable family vehicles.

d. M&M's: "Melts in your mouth, not in your hands." M&M's USP highlights their product's resistance to melting, a key feature in the candy market.

e. TOMS: "One for One." TOMS' USP is built on a charitable mission; for every pair of shoes sold, they donate a pair to a child in need.

f. Amazon: "Earth's most customer-centric company." Amazon's USP is its relentless focus on customer satisfaction and convenience.

Implementing Your USP

Once you've defined your USP, it's essential to integrate it into your branding, marketing, and business strategies:

a. Consistent Messaging: Ensure that your USP is consistently communicated in your advertising, website, and other marketing materials.

b. Train Your Team: Educate your team about your USP, empowering them to effectively communicate and embody it.

c. Customer-Centric Approach: Keep your customers at the center of your business, always striving to meet their needs in alignment with your USP.

d. Adapt and Evolve: As your business grows and the market changes, be prepared to adapt and refine your USP to remain relevant.

Measuring the Success of Your USP

The effectiveness of your USP can be gauged through key performance indicators (KPIs):

a. Sales Growth: Monitor changes in sales, especially after implementing or refining your USP.

b. Customer Retention: Assess whether your USP improves customer loyalty and retention rates.

c. Market Share: Observe any growth in your market share, indicating an increasing number of customers choosing your brand.

d. Customer Feedback: Collect and analyze customer feedback to determine if your USP resonates with your target audience.

e. Brand Awareness: Track the increase in brand awareness and recognition as a result of your USP-based marketing efforts.

Conclusion

A strong Unique Selling Proposition is a critical element in differentiating your brand and driving success. By following a structured process to define your USP and integrating it effectively into your business strategies, you can create a compelling message that resonates with your target audience and sets you apart from the competition. Remember that your USP should be flexible and adaptable to evolve with your business and customer needs, ensuring continued success in a dynamic market.

Setting Personal Development Goals: A Path to Self-Improvement and Fulfillment

Introduction

Personal development is a lifelong journey of self-improvement, self-awareness, and growth. To effectively embark on this path, setting personal development goals is essential. These goals act as roadmaps for enhancing your skills, qualities, and knowledge while fostering a sense of purpose and fulfillment. In this comprehensive guide, we will explore the importance of setting personal development goals, provide a step-by-step process for creating them, and offer practical tips for achieving your objectives.

Why Set Personal Development Goals?

Setting personal development goals serves several essential purposes:

   a. Self-Improvement: Goals give you a clear focus on areas of your life that you want to enhance, whether it's your career, relationships, or personal qualities.

   b. Motivation: Goals provide a sense of purpose and motivation, encouraging you to work toward self-improvement.

   c. Self-Awareness: Defining goals requires self-reflection, fostering greater self-awareness and understanding.

   d. Measurable Progress: Goals offer quantifiable metrics for tracking your personal growth and achievements.

e. Fulfillment: Achieving personal development goals can lead to increased self-esteem, happiness, and a sense of accomplishment.

The SMART Goal Setting Framework

When setting personal development goals, it's beneficial to use the SMART framework, which stands for Specific, Measurable, Achievable, Relevant, and Time-bound:

   a. Specific: Goals should be clear and well-defined. Specify exactly what you want to achieve, avoiding vague objectives.

   b. Measurable: Set specific criteria for measuring your progress and determining when you've reached your goal. This might involve numbers, percentages, or other metrics.

   c. Achievable: Ensure that your goals are realistic and attainable. While ambition is essential, setting unattainable goals can lead to frustration and disappointment.

   d. Relevant: Goals should align with your personal values and aspirations. They should make sense within the context of your life.

   e. Time-bound: Establish a clear timeframe for achieving your personal development goals. This adds a sense of urgency and commitment.

The Steps to Setting Personal Development Goals

Follow these steps to set effective personal development goals:

   a. Self-Reflection: Begin by taking time to reflect on your strengths, weaknesses, values, and aspirations. Consider what areas of your life need improvement.

b. Prioritize Areas for Development: Identify the most crucial aspects you want to work on. Prioritization helps you focus your efforts effectively.

c. Set Specific Goals: Define clear and specific personal development goals based on your reflections and priorities. Ensure that your goals adhere to the SMART framework.

d. Break Down Goals: Divide larger goals into smaller, manageable objectives. This makes the path to achieving your goals less daunting and more achievable.

e. Create an Action Plan: Develop a detailed plan that outlines the steps and actions needed to reach your objectives. Specify resources, timelines, and responsibilities.

f. Stay Accountable: Share your goals with a trusted friend, mentor, or coach who can help hold you accountable.

g. Regularly Review and Adjust: Periodically assess your progress, review your goals, and make necessary adjustments based on your experiences and insights.

Common Areas for Personal Development Goals

Personal development goals can encompass various areas of your life:

a. Career: Enhance your professional skills, climb the career ladder, or explore new opportunities.

b. Education: Pursue lifelong learning, gain new knowledge, and develop expertise in a particular field.

c. Health and Wellness: Focus on improving physical health, emotional well-being, or adopting healthier habits.

d. Relationships: Strengthen personal relationships, improve communication, or develop deeper connections with others.

e. Emotional Intelligence: Work on self-awareness, self-regulation, empathy, and social skills.

f. Leadership: Develop leadership skills, effective communication, and the ability to inspire and motivate others.

g. Time Management: Learn to manage your time more efficiently and achieve a better work-life balance.

Tips for Achieving Personal Development Goals

To succeed in your personal development journey, consider these tips:

a. Consistency: Consistently work on your goals, even when progress seems slow. Consistency is key to personal growth.

b. Track Your Progress: Keep a journal or use goal-tracking apps to monitor your progress and stay motivated.

c. Seek Feedback: Request feedback from mentors, friends, or family members to gain insights and suggestions for improvement.

d. Celebrate Achievements: Acknowledge and celebrate your accomplishments, no matter how small. Positive reinforcement can boost motivation.

e. Adaptability: Be open to adjusting your goals and strategies when necessary. Life is full of unexpected changes, and adaptability is a valuable skill.

f. Learn from Setbacks: Understand that setbacks are a natural part of the journey. Use these experiences as opportunities for learning and growth.

Conclusion

Setting personal development goals is a fundamental step toward self-improvement, self-awareness, and overall personal growth. By defining clear, SMART goals and consistently working toward them, you can achieve personal fulfillment, build new skills, and become a better version of yourself. Remember that personal development is a lifelong journey, and the process of setting and achieving goals will help you continuously evolve and lead a more purposeful life.

Developing a Growth Mindset: Unlocking Your Potential for Success

Introduction

A growth mindset is a powerful concept that can transform the way you approach challenges, learning, and personal development. It is the belief that your abilities and intelligence can be developed through dedication and hard work. Developing a growth mindset can significantly impact your life, both personally and professionally. In this comprehensive guide, we will explore the importance of a growth mindset, the steps to develop one, and how it can lead to success and personal growth.

Understanding the Growth Mindset

A growth mindset, as coined by psychologist Carol Dweck, is the belief that abilities and intelligence can be developed through effort, learning, and perseverance. In contrast, a fixed mindset is the belief that abilities are innate and cannot be changed. Individuals with a growth mindset embrace challenges, learn from failures, and see effort as a path to mastery.

The Importance of a Growth Mindset

A growth mindset offers numerous benefits and plays a crucial role in personal development and success:

   a. Resilience: Individuals with a growth mindset are more resilient in the face of setbacks and failures.

b. Learning and Development: Embracing a growth mindset fosters a love for learning and personal development.

c. Adaptability: It enhances adaptability, as individuals are more willing to change and learn from new experiences.

d. Motivation: A growth mindset fuels intrinsic motivation, as the focus shifts from external validation to personal growth and improvement.

e. Achievement: Those with a growth mindset tend to achieve higher levels of success and satisfaction in various aspects of life.

Steps to Develop a Growth Mindset

Developing a growth mindset involves a shift in your perspective and thinking patterns:

a. Self-Awareness: Start by recognizing your existing mindset. Are you more inclined towards a fixed mindset or a growth mindset in certain areas of your life?

b. Embrace Challenges: Embrace challenges and view them as opportunities to learn and grow. Avoid seeking only tasks you're already good at.

c. Accept Mistakes and Failure: Acknowledge that mistakes and failure are part of the learning process. Learn from them rather than avoiding or fearing them.

d. Value Effort and Persistence: Shift your focus from innate talent to effort and persistence as the keys to success.

e. Cultivate a Love for Learning: Develop a love for learning by exploring new interests, acquiring new skills, and taking on intellectual challenges.

f. Seek Constructive Feedback: Welcome constructive criticism and feedback as valuable insights for growth and improvement.

   g. Set Meaningful Goals: Establish clear and meaningful goals that require effort and learning to achieve.

   h. Surround Yourself with Growth-Minded Individuals: Connect with people who also have a growth mindset, as they can encourage and support your journey.

The Impact of a Growth Mindset

A growth mindset can have a profound influence on various aspects of your life:

   a. Academic Success: Students with a growth mindset tend to achieve higher grades and perform better in school.

   b. Career Advancement: In the workplace, individuals with a growth mindset are more likely to be promoted and excel in their careers.

   c. Improved Relationships: A growth mindset can lead to better relationships, as individuals are more willing to learn from conflicts and adapt.

   d. Health and Well-being: It can contribute to better physical and mental health, as individuals are more likely to make efforts toward self-improvement.

   e. Resilience: A growth mindset fosters resilience in the face of adversity and setbacks.

Cultivating a Growth Mindset in Different Areas of Life

You can cultivate a growth mindset in various areas:

a. Career: Embrace challenges at work, seek opportunities for professional development, and view feedback as a chance for growth.

b. Education: Approach learning with curiosity, tackle complex subjects, and consider difficulties as part of the learning process.

c. Relationships: Improve relationships by being open to communication, learning from conflicts, and adapting to the needs of your loved ones.

d. Personal Development: Focus on personal growth and development, setting and achieving meaningful goals, and viewing life as a journey of self-improvement.

Overcoming Challenges in Developing a Growth Mindset

Developing a growth mindset is not always easy and may come with its share of challenges:

a. Fixed Mindset Habits: You may have existing fixed mindset habits that need to be unlearned.

b. Fear of Failure: Overcoming the fear of failure and rejection can be difficult.

c. Impatience: Developing a growth mindset requires patience, as it's a long-term journey with gradual progress.

    d. Perfectionism: Perfectionism can hinder a growth mindset, as it focuses on avoiding mistakes rather than learning from them.

    e. Negative Self-Talk: Negative self-talk and self-limiting beliefs can be obstacles in cultivating a growth mindset.

Case Studies: Real-Life Examples of a Growth Mindset

Numerous successful individuals attribute their achievements to a growth mindset:

   a. Michael Jordan: The legendary basketball player is known for his work ethic and belief that practice and effort are the keys to success.

   b. Elon Musk: The tech entrepreneur and innovator embraces challenges and setbacks as opportunities for growth and improvement.

   c. Oprah Winfrey: The media mogul and philanthropist emphasizes the importance of learning and growth in her life and career.

   d. Albert Einstein: The renowned physicist advocated for continuous learning and adaptation, believing that "Once you stop learning, you start dying."

Conclusion

A growth mindset is a powerful mindset that can transform your life by fostering resilience, adaptability, motivation, and personal development. By recognizing and embracing challenges, valuing effort and persistence, and seeking feedback and learning opportunities, you can develop a growth mindset in various areas of your life. Remember that personal growth is a journey, and a growth mindset will be your constant companion on the path to success and self-improvement.

Leveraging Your "Why" in Marketing: Building Authentic Connections with Your Audience

Introduction

In the dynamic and competitive world of marketing, authenticity and meaningful connections with your audience are more important than ever. One powerful tool for achieving this is leveraging your "why." Your "why" represents your core purpose, values, and motivations as a business or brand. In this comprehensive guide, we will explore the significance of your "why" in marketing, the steps to leverage it effectively, and real-life examples of businesses that have successfully integrated their "why" into their marketing strategies.

Understanding Your "Why" in Marketing

Your "why" is the driving force behind your business or brand. It answers the fundamental question of why you do what you do. It goes beyond merely selling products or services; it encompasses your passion, values, and the positive impact you aim to create in the world. When harnessed in marketing, your "why" helps establish a deep and emotional connection with your audience.

The Importance of Leveraging Your "Why"

Leveraging your "why" in marketing can provide various benefits:

   a. Authenticity: It distinguishes your brand as genuine and purpose-driven, enhancing your credibility and trustworthiness.

b. Emotional Connection: A strong "why" resonates emotionally with your audience, fostering a more profound connection.

c. Loyalty: Customers who share your values and purpose are more likely to become loyal advocates of your brand.

d. Competitive Advantage: A compelling "why" can set you apart from competitors by providing a unique selling point.

e. Inspiration: Your "why" can inspire not only your audience but also your team and stakeholders, rallying them around a common purpose.

Steps to Leverage Your "Why" in Marketing

To effectively leverage your "why" in marketing, follow these steps:

a. Define Your "Why": Start by clearly defining your core purpose, values, and the impact you want to create in the world. This is the foundation of your marketing strategy.

b. Understand Your Audience: Thoroughly research and understand your target audience, including their values, needs, and preferences.

c. Craft a Compelling Story: Develop a narrative that encapsulates your "why" and its significance. This story should resonate with your audience and create an emotional connection.

d. Integrate Your "Why" Into Branding: Your "why" should be seamlessly integrated into your brand's identity, including your logo, tagline, and visual elements.

e. Communicate Authentically: Ensure that your marketing materials, messages, and content authentically reflect your "why."

f. Show Impact: Share real-world examples of how your brand is living out its "why" and making a positive difference.

g. Create Engaging Content: Develop content that aligns with your "why" and speaks to your audience's values and aspirations.

h. Collaborate with Like-Minded Partners: Partner with organizations and individuals who share your "why" to amplify your message.

i. Gather and Share Customer Stories: Showcase customer stories and testimonials that highlight how your brands "why" has positively impacted their lives.

Real-Life Examples of Brands Leveraging Their "Why"

Several brands have successfully integrated their "why" into their marketing strategies:

a. TOMS: TOMS' "why" is built on a mission to provide a pair of shoes to a child in need for every pair sold. This mission is central to their marketing, and they have successfully leveraged it to build a loyal customer base who share their values.

b. Patagonia: Patagonia's "why" is a commitment to environmental sustainability. Their marketing campaigns emphasize their dedication to preserving the planet, resonating with environmentally conscious consumers.

c. Nike: Nike's "why" revolves around empowering athletes and encouraging them to push their limits. Their marketing is built on inspiring stories of athletes who have overcome obstacles to achieve their goals.

d. Dove: Dove's "why" is to promote self-esteem and body positivity. Their marketing campaigns challenge beauty stereotypes and emphasize self-acceptance.

e. Warby Parker: Warby Parker's "why" is to provide affordable, stylish eyeglasses while also giving back. For every pair of glasses sold, they donate to those in need. Their marketing highlights their mission to make a positive impact.

Measuring the Impact of Leveraging Your "Why"

To assess the effectiveness of leveraging your "why" in marketing, consider the following key performance indicators:

a. Customer Engagement: Monitor customer engagement and interaction with your content and messaging related to your "why."

b. Brand Loyalty: Measure the increase in brand loyalty and the number of repeat customers who share your values.

c. Social Media Reach: Track your brand's social media reach and the impact of posts related to your "why."

d. Customer Feedback: Collect and analyze customer feedback and testimonials that reference your "why."

e. Sales and Revenue: Assess the impact on sales and revenue as a result of your "why"-driven marketing efforts.

Conclusion

Leveraging your "why" in marketing is a powerful strategy that can transform your brand and build lasting, authentic connections with your audience. Your "why" is the essence of your brand's purpose and values, and when communicated effectively, it can resonate deeply with your target audience. By defining your "why," crafting a compelling story, and integrating it into your branding and messaging, you can create a marketing strategy that goes beyond products or services, inspiring and engaging your audience on a meaningful level.

Creating a Brand Story that Resonates: The Art of Authentic Branding

Introduction

In a world saturated with brands and products, storytelling has become a powerful tool for businesses to connect with their audiences on a personal and emotional level. A compelling brand story is more than just marketing; it's a way to communicate your brand's values, personality, and purpose. In this comprehensive guide, we will explore the importance of creating a brand story that resonates, the steps to craft an authentic narrative, and real-world examples of businesses that have successfully leveraged their brand stories.

The Power of a Resonating Brand Story

A brand story is more than a series of words and visuals; it is the soul of your brand. It serves several important functions:

   a. Differentiation: It sets your brand apart from competitors and creates a unique identity in the market.

   b. Emotional Connection: A compelling story appeals to your audience's emotions and fosters a deeper connection.

   c. Trust and Credibility: A transparent and authentic story builds trust and credibility with your audience.

   d. Brand Loyalty: A resonating brand story can create loyal customers who feel a sense of alignment with your values.

   e. Attraction: It attracts like-minded individuals and communities who share your brand's purpose.

Steps to Create a Resonating Brand Story

Crafting a brand story that resonates with your audience involves several crucial steps:

a. Know Your Audience: Start by understanding your target audience, their values, interests, and pain points.

b. Define Your Brand's Core Values: Identify the fundamental values that drive your brand. These values should be authentic and non-negotiable.

c. Develop a Compelling Narrative: Create a story that encapsulates your brand's journey, values, and purpose. This narrative should be engaging and emotionally charged.

d. Incorporate Human Elements: Humanize your brand by incorporating relatable elements such as personal experiences, challenges, and triumphs.

e. Keep it Authentic: Authenticity is crucial. Be honest and transparent in your storytelling, as customers can detect insincerity.

f. Visual Storytelling: Use visuals such as images, videos, and graphics to complement and enhance your brand story.

g. Consistency: Ensure that your brand story is consistently reflected across all touchpoints, from your website to social media and marketing materials.

h. Evoke Emotion: Effective storytelling evokes emotions. Your brand story should make your audience feel something, whether it's joy, empathy, or inspiration.

i. Test and Refine: Share your brand story with a trusted circle and gather feedback. Use this feedback to refine and improve your narrative.

Real-Life Examples of Resonating Brand Stories

Several brands have successfully leveraged their brand stories to connect with their audiences:

   a. Nike: Nike's brand story centers around the idea that everyone can be an athlete, emphasizing empowerment and inspiration.

   b. Coca-Cola: Coca-Cola's brand story is built on the themes of happiness, sharing, and togetherness. Their marketing campaigns promote unity and joy.

   c. Patagonia: Patagonia's brand story revolves around environmental sustainability, activism, and a commitment to reducing its ecological footprint.

   d. Apple: Apple's brand story focuses on innovation, creativity, and the idea that they exist to empower individuals through technology.

   e. Dove: Dove's brand story is all about promoting self-esteem and body positivity, challenging stereotypes of beauty.

Measuring the Impact of Your Brand Story

To evaluate the effectiveness of your brand story, consider these key performance indicators:

   a. Brand Awareness: Measure the increase in brand awareness resulting from your story-driven marketing efforts.

   b. Customer Engagement: Track customer engagement with your brand's narrative on social media, website, and other platforms.

   c. Conversion Rates: Analyze the impact of your brand story on conversion rates and sales.

d. Customer Feedback: Gather and evaluate customer feedback to understand how your brand story resonates with your audience.

e. Social Impact: Measure the social impact of your brand's purpose and values, such as the adoption of eco-friendly practices or support for a charitable cause.

Conclusion

Creating a brand story that resonates is a powerful way to connect with your audience on a deeper level and differentiate your brand in a crowded marketplace. Your brand story should be authentic, emotionally engaging, and aligned with your brand's core values. When effectively executed and consistently communicated, a resonating brand story can build trust, loyalty, and long-lasting connections with your customers, making it an invaluable asset in today's business landscape.

Building a Strong Online Presence: Strategies for Success

Introduction

In the digital age, a strong online presence is a fundamental component of success for individuals, businesses, and organizations. It encompasses your visibility, credibility, and engagement on the internet. Building a strong online presence not only boosts your brand's recognition but also opens up opportunities for growth and impact. In this comprehensive guide, we will explore the importance of a strong online presence, the strategies to build one, and the tools to help you along the way.

Understanding the Importance of an Online Presence

A strong online presence is crucial for various reasons:

   a. Brand Visibility: An online presence ensures that your brand is discoverable by a broader audience.

   b. Credibility and Trust: A well-maintained online presence establishes trust and credibility with your audience.

   c. Customer Engagement: Engaging with your audience online allows for meaningful interactions and feedback.

   d. Competitive Advantage: An effective online presence sets you apart from competitors.

   e. Business Growth: It can lead to increased sales, revenue, and growth opportunities.

Strategies to Build a Strong Online Presence

To create a strong online presence, follow these strategies:

a. Define Your Objectives: Start by setting clear objectives for your online presence. Determine what you want to achieve, whether it's brand awareness, customer engagement, lead generation, or something else.

b. Create a Professional Website: Your website is your online headquarters. Ensure it is professional, user-friendly, and mobile-responsive. Optimize it for search engines (SEO) to enhance discoverability.

c. Develop High-Quality Content: Content is king online. Create and share valuable, relevant, and engaging content on your website and social media platforms.

d. Engage on Social Media: Establish a presence on social media platforms relevant to your audience. Regularly share content, engage with followers, and maintain a consistent brand voice.

e. Optimize for SEO: Understand the basics of search engine optimization (SEO) to improve your website's search engine rankings and visibility.

f. Build an Email List: Collect and maintain an email list to communicate with your audience directly and share valuable content.

g. Online Advertising: Consider paid advertising options like Google Ads, Facebook Ads, or sponsored content to reach a broader audience.

h. Encourage Online Reviews: Request and promote positive reviews on platforms like Google, Yelp, and Trustpilot to build trust and credibility.

i. Guest Blogging: Contribute guest posts to reputable websites in your industry to expand your reach and build backlinks to your site.

j. Monitor and Respond: Keep a close eye on your online presence. Respond to comments, feedback, and inquiries promptly.

k. Analyze Data: Use analytics tools to track website traffic, social media engagement, and other key metrics. Adjust your strategies based on this data.

Tools to Help Build Your Online Presence

There are various tools and platforms that can aid in building a strong online presence:

a. Content Management Systems (CMS): Platforms like WordPress, Joomla, and Wix help create and manage websites.

b. Social Media Management Tools: Tools like Hootsuite and Buffer simplify the management and scheduling of social media posts.

c. Email Marketing Platforms: Platforms like Mailchimp, Constant Contact, and SendinBlue facilitate email marketing campaigns.

d. SEO Tools: SEO tools such as Moz, SEMrush, and Ahrefs help with keyword research, backlink analysis, and site optimization.

e. Analytics Tools: Google Analytics and social media analytics provide valuable insights into website and audience performance.

f. Online Advertising Platforms: Google Ads, Facebook Ads, and LinkedIn Ads allow you to create and manage paid advertising campaigns.

g. Reputation Management Tools: Tools like Trustpilot and ReviewTrackers help monitor and improve online reviews and reputation.

Common Pitfalls to Avoid

While building an online presence, be mindful of common pitfalls:

a. Neglecting Mobile Optimization: Ensure your website is mobile-responsive, as a growing number of users access the internet via mobile devices.

b. Inconsistent Branding: Maintain a consistent brand voice and visual identity across all online channels.

c. Ignoring Security: Prioritize website security to protect your online presence from potential threats.

d. Neglecting Offline Engagement: An online presence should complement, not replace, offline engagement with your audience.

e. Overlooking Local SEO: If your business has a physical location, optimize for local SEO to attract nearby customers.

Measuring the Success of Your Online Presence

To evaluate the success of your online presence, consider the following key performance indicators (KPIs):

a. Website Traffic: Monitor the number of visitors, page views, and time spent on your website.

b. Social Media Engagement: Track likes, shares, comments, and follower growth on social media.

c. Email Campaign Metrics: Analyze email open rates, click-through rates, and conversion rates.

d. Conversion Rates: Measure the percentage of website visitors who take a desired action, such as making a purchase or signing up for a newsletter.

e. Online Reviews: Assess the quantity and quality of online reviews and their impact on your brand's reputation.

f. Brand Mentions: Monitor online mentions of your brand across various platforms.

Conclusion

A strong online presence is a valuable asset in the digital era, enabling businesses and individuals to reach and engage with their target audiences effectively. By following the strategies outlined in this guide, maintaining a professional website, creating high-quality content, and leveraging digital tools, you can build an authentic online presence that sets you apart from the competition and fosters trust and credibility with your audience. Regularly monitor and adjust your online presence to stay relevant and responsive to the evolving digital landscape.

The Power of Storytelling in Business Communication

Introduction

Storytelling is a timeless and universal way of sharing information and creating connections. In the world of business communication, storytelling is a powerful tool that can transform data, facts, and strategies into compelling narratives that resonate with audiences. This educational article explores the art of storytelling in business communication, its significance, strategies for effective storytelling, and real-world examples of how successful businesses leverage storytelling to achieve their goals.

The Significance of Storytelling in Business Communication

Storytelling in business communication is not just about relaying facts and figures; it's about engaging, inspiring, and persuading your audience. Here's why storytelling is vital in the business context:

   a. Connection: Stories foster a deep emotional connection, making your audience more receptive to your message.

   b. Memorability: People remember stories far more effectively than data or statistics.

   c. Clarity: Complex information can be simplified and made clearer through the use of narrative.

   d. Persuasion: Stories can be persuasive, influencing your audience to take desired actions.

e. Brand Building: Storytelling helps build and communicate your brand's identity, values, and mission.

Strategies for Effective Storytelling in Business Communication

To effectively integrate storytelling into business communication, follow these strategies:

a. Know Your Audience: Understanding your audience's needs, values, and preferences is essential to crafting stories that resonate.

b. Identify Your Core Message: Define the main point or message you want to convey through your story. Make it clear and concise.

c. Create a Narrative Arc: Stories typically follow a structure with a beginning, middle, and end. Introduce a problem or challenge, present a solution, and conclude with a resolution.

d. Personalize Your Story: Make your story relatable by incorporating personal experiences, anecdotes, or real-life examples.

e. Use Vivid Language: Paint a vivid picture with descriptive and emotional language that captivates your audience.

f. Keep It Simple: Avoid jargon and complex terminology. Simplicity is often more effective.

g. Emphasize Emotion: Emotional content resonates strongly with audiences, so be sure to incorporate feelings and experiences.

h. Add Conflict and Resolution: Most great stories have a conflict that needs to be resolved. Identify the problem and show how your product, service, or solution resolves it.

i. Showcase Characters: Characters bring stories to life. Introduce relatable characters that your audience can connect with.

j. Use Analogies and Metaphors: Analogies and metaphors can simplify complex concepts and make them more accessible.

k. Create a Hook: Begin your story with an engaging and attention-grabbing opening to draw your audience in.

l. Encourage Interaction: Encourage your audience to engage with your story by asking questions or inviting them to share their own experiences.

m. Practice and Refine: Refine your storytelling skills through practice and feedback. The more you tell stories, the better you'll become.

Real-World Examples of Storytelling in Business

Several successful businesses and organizations have harnessed the power of storytelling in their communication strategies:

a. Coca-Cola: Coca-Cola's marketing campaigns often tell heartwarming stories of joy, togetherness, and the importance of sharing.

b. Apple: Apple's product launches are masterclasses in storytelling, using narratives to explain how their innovations will change customers' lives.

c. Patagonia: Patagonia shares stories of environmental activism and their commitment to sustainability, aligning their brand with their core values.

d. Dove: Dove's "Real Beauty" campaign tells stories of self-acceptance, encouraging people to embrace their natural beauty.

Measuring the Impact of Storytelling

Measuring the impact of storytelling can be challenging, but there are ways to gauge its effectiveness:

   a. Audience Engagement: Monitor the level of engagement with your content, including likes, shares, comments, and time spent on your website.

   b. Conversion Rates: Track how storytelling impacts conversion rates, whether it's driving sales, sign-ups, or other desired actions.

   c. Brand Awareness: Measure changes in brand awareness and recognition as a result of your storytelling efforts.

   d. Customer Feedback: Analyze customer feedback, reviews, and testimonials to understand the impact of your stories on their perceptions.

   e. Data Analytics: Utilize website analytics to assess the performance of storytelling elements on your website.

   f. Sales Metrics: Evaluate the correlation between storytelling and sales metrics, such as revenue growth and customer acquisition.

Conclusion

Storytelling in business communication is a potent tool for engaging, persuading, and connecting with your audience. When done effectively, storytelling can help you stand out in a crowded marketplace, communicate your brand's values and mission, and drive your audience to take desired actions. By employing the strategies outlined in this article and drawing inspiration from successful businesses, you can harness the power of storytelling to make a lasting impact in the world of business communication.

Incorporating Your "Why" into Your Brand: Creating Authentic Connections

Introduction

Incorporating your "why" into your brand is a powerful approach that goes beyond traditional marketing. Your "why" represents your core purpose, values, and the driving force behind your business. When you authentically integrate your "why" into your brand, you create a more meaningful and lasting connection with your audience. In this comprehensive guide, we'll explore the importance of infusing your "why" into your brand, the steps to do it effectively, and real-world examples of businesses that have successfully integrated their "why."

The Significance of Your "Why" in Your Brand

Your "why" is the foundation of your brand's identity. Here's why incorporating it is crucial:

  a. Authenticity: It distinguishes your brand as genuine and purpose-driven, enhancing your credibility and trustworthiness.

  b. Emotional Connection: Your "why" resonates emotionally with your audience, fostering a deeper connection.

  c. Loyalty: Customers who share your values and purpose are more likely to become loyal advocates of your brand.

  d. Competitive Advantage: A compelling "why" sets you apart from competitors by providing a unique selling point.

  e. Inspiration: Your "why" can inspire not only your audience but also your team and stakeholders, rallying them around a common purpose.

Steps to Incorporate Your "Why" into Your Brand

To effectively integrate your "why" into your brand, follow these steps:

a. Define Your "Why": Start by clearly defining your core purpose, values, and the impact you want to create in the world. This is the foundation of your brand identity.

b. Understand Your Audience: Thoroughly research and understand your target audience, including their values, needs, and preferences.

c. Craft Your Brand Story: Develop a compelling narrative that encapsulates your "why" and its significance. This story should resonate with your audience and create an emotional connection.

d. Integrate Your "Why" into Branding: Your "why" should be seamlessly integrated into your brand's identity, including your logo, tagline, and visual elements.

e. Communicate Authentically: Ensure that your brand's messaging and content authentically reflect your "why."

f. Show Impact: Share real-world examples of how your brand is living out its "why" and making a positive difference.

g. Create Engaging Content: Develop content that aligns with your "why" and speaks to your audience's values and aspirations.

h. Collaborate with Like-Minded Partners: Partner with organizations and individuals who share your "why" to amplify your message.

i. Gather and Share Customer Stories: Showcase customer stories and testimonials that highlight how your brand's "why" has positively impacted their lives.

Real-Life Examples of Brands Incorporating Their "Why"

Several brands have successfully integrated their "why" into their brand identity:

a. TOMS: TOMS' "why" is built on a mission to provide a pair of shoes to a child in need for every pair sold. This mission is central to their brand, and they have successfully incorporated it into their identity and marketing.

b. Patagonia: Patagonia's "why" revolves around environmental sustainability. Their brand identity is synonymous with their commitment to preserving the planet, resonating with environmentally conscious consumers.

c. Nike: Nike's "why" revolves around empowering athletes and encouraging them to push their limits. Their brand identity reflects this through inspirational storytelling and marketing.

d. Dove: Dove's "why" is to promote self-esteem and body positivity. Their brand identity challenges beauty stereotypes and emphasizes self-acceptance.

e. Warby Parker: Warby Parker's "why" is to provide affordable, stylish eyeglasses while also giving back. Their brand identity highlights their mission to make a positive impact.

Measuring the Impact of Incorporating Your "Why"

To assess the effectiveness of incorporating your "why" into your brand, consider these key performance indicators:

a. Brand Loyalty: Measure the increase in brand loyalty and the number of repeat customers who share your values.

b. Customer Engagement: Track customer engagement with your content and messaging related to your "why."

c. Social Media Reach: Analyze your brand's social media reach and the impact of posts related to your "why."

d. Customer Feedback: Collect and analyze customer feedback and testimonials that reference your "why."

e. Sales and Revenue: Assess the impact on sales and revenue as a result of your "why"-driven brand identity and marketing efforts.

Conclusion

Incorporating your "why" into your brand is a transformative approach that can deepen the connection with your audience, build brand loyalty, and set you apart from competitors. Your "why" is not just a marketing gimmick; it's the soul of your brand, representing your core values and the positive impact you aim to create. By clearly defining your "why," crafting a compelling narrative, and integrating it into your branding and messaging, you can create a brand identity that resonates with your audience and fosters trust, loyalty, and lasting connections.

Section 2:

Progression to Finding Your Ideal Customer

Monitoring and Adjusting Your Business Alignment for Success

Introduction

Business alignment refers to the harmonious integration of your company's strategy, goals, and processes to ensure that all aspects of your organization are working cohesively towards a common objective. However, business alignment is not a one-time endeavor; it's an ongoing process that requires regular monitoring and adjustments to stay in line with changing circumstances, market trends, and internal dynamics. In this comprehensive article, we will explore the importance of monitoring and adjusting your business alignment, the key areas to focus on, and effective strategies to keep your organization on the path to success.

The Significance of Monitoring Business Alignment

Monitoring business alignment is crucial for several reasons:

   a. Adaptability: Markets and industries evolve, and your business alignment must adapt to remain relevant and competitive.

   b. Efficiency: Continuous alignment ensures that your organization's resources are utilized optimally.

   c. Accountability: Monitoring allows you to hold teams and individuals accountable for their roles in achieving alignment.

   d. Customer Satisfaction: By staying aligned with customer needs, you can provide better products and services.

e. Strategic Agility: Regular monitoring and adjustments enable your business to respond effectively to changes in the external environment.

Key Areas to Monitor for Business Alignment

To effectively monitor and adjust your business alignment, focus on these key areas:

a. Business Objectives: Continuously evaluate whether your objectives are in sync with your organization's mission and current market conditions.

b. Strategy: Regularly review and update your strategic plan to adapt to market shifts and emerging opportunities.

c. Communication: Monitor how well your internal and external communications align with your business goals and values.

d. Team Alignment: Ensure that your teams understand and are aligned with the organization's objectives and each other.

e. Performance Metrics: Continuously assess key performance indicators (KPIs) to gauge your progress and identify areas needing improvement.

f. Customer Feedback: Regularly collect and analyze customer feedback to ensure your products and services align with customer needs and expectations.

g. Market Trends: Stay informed about industry trends, technological advancements, and changes in customer behavior that may require adjustments.

h. Employee Satisfaction: Monitor employee satisfaction and engagement to ensure alignment with your company's values and goals.

Strategies for Monitoring and Adjusting Business Alignment

To effectively monitor and adjust your business alignment, consider these strategies:

a. Regular Reviews: Conduct regular reviews of your business objectives, strategy, and performance metrics to identify misalignments.

b. Collaborative Approach: Involve cross-functional teams and department heads in the alignment process to gain diverse perspectives.

c. Technology and Analytics: Utilize technology and data analytics tools to collect and analyze relevant data for alignment assessment.

d. Benchmarking: Compare your performance and alignment with industry benchmarks and best practices.

e. Employee Feedback: Encourage open communication with employees to gather their insights and suggestions for alignment improvements.

f. Continuous Learning: Stay updated on industry trends and innovations through training and professional development to make informed decisions.

g. Scenario Planning: Develop contingency plans to quickly respond to unexpected market changes, ensuring alignment is maintained.

h. Customer-Centric Approach: Place the customer at the center of your alignment efforts, as customer satisfaction is a strong indicator of business alignment.

i. Flexibility and Adaptability: Be willing to adjust your strategic course when necessary, rather than rigidly adhering to outdated plans.

Real-World Examples of Monitoring and Adjusting Business Alignment

Several companies have successfully demonstrated the importance of monitoring and adjusting business alignment:

a. Amazon: Amazon constantly adjusts its business alignment to meet evolving customer needs, expanding into new markets and innovating with products and services like Amazon Web Services and Kindle.

b. Netflix: Netflix started as a DVD rental service but transitioned into a streaming platform, demonstrating its ability to adapt and align with changing technology and customer preferences.

c. Apple: Apple's ability to align its product line with user preferences and technological advancements has made it a leader in the tech industry.

d. IBM: IBM has undergone multiple transformations to align with shifts in technology and services, transitioning from a hardware-focused company to a leading provider of cloud and AI solutions.

e. Zappos: Zappos continually aligns its corporate culture with its mission of delivering exceptional customer service, fostering employee engagement, and customer loyalty.

Measuring the Impact of Monitoring and Adjusting Business Alignment

To measure the impact of your alignment efforts, consider the following key performance indicators (KPIs):

a. Business Performance: Track overall revenue, profitability, and market share to assess the impact of alignment adjustments.

b. Customer Satisfaction: Measure customer satisfaction and retention rates to gauge the success of alignment efforts in meeting customer needs.

c. Employee Engagement: Monitor employee engagement and retention as indicators of organizational alignment.

d. Market Position: Assess your company's market position and competitive advantage to determine the effectiveness of alignment adjustments.

e. Efficiency Metrics: Analyze operational efficiency metrics such as cost savings, reduced errors, and faster time-to-market resulting from alignment.

Conclusion

Incorporating a robust system for monitoring and adjusting your business alignment is essential for your organization's ongoing success. The business landscape is dynamic and ever-changing, and alignment is a continuous process that requires adaptability, collaboration, and a commitment to staying in tune with market conditions and customer needs. By regularly reviewing key areas, employing strategic adjustments, and measuring the impact of alignment efforts, your organization can maintain a competitive edge and continue to thrive in an evolving business environment.

Understanding the Concept of an Ideal Customer

Introduction

In the world of business and marketing, the concept of an "ideal customer" is a fundamental principle that serves as the cornerstone for effective sales and marketing strategies. Understanding who your ideal customer is allows businesses to tailor their products, services, and marketing efforts to better meet the needs and desires of their target audience. In this comprehensive article, we will explore the concept of an ideal customer, why it's important, how to define one, and the benefits of catering to your ideal customer.

What is an Ideal Customer?

An ideal customer, sometimes referred to as a "buyer persona" or "target customer," is a fictional representation of your perfect customer. It's a detailed profile that encompasses their demographics, behaviors, preferences, and pain points. Creating an ideal customer persona helps businesses gain a deeper understanding of their target audience and effectively tailor their strategies to attract and retain these valuable customers.

Why is Defining Your Ideal Customer Important?

Defining your ideal customer is crucial for several reasons:

   a. Targeted Marketing: Understanding your ideal customer allows you to create marketing campaigns that specifically address their needs and desires.

b. Efficient Resource Allocation: It helps you allocate your marketing budget and resources more effectively, ensuring you reach the right audience.

c. Enhanced Customer Relationships: Tailoring your products and services to your ideal customer fosters stronger customer relationships.

d. Increased Sales: Catering to your ideal customer's preferences can lead to higher conversion rates and increased sales.

e. Better Product Development: Knowing your ideal customer enables you to develop products that address their pain points and preferences.

f. Competitive Advantage: It sets you apart from competitors who may not be as focused on serving their ideal customers.

How to Define Your Ideal Customer

Defining your ideal customer requires a systematic approach:

a. Market Research: Conduct thorough market research to gather data on your existing customer base, competition, and industry trends.

b. Customer Segmentation: Segment your audience based on demographics, psychographics, and behavioral characteristics.

c. Create Buyer Personas: Develop detailed profiles of your ideal customers, including their age, gender, income, values, goals, challenges, and preferences.

d. Validate with Data: Use real data and feedback from your existing customers to refine your ideal customer personas.

e. Continuously Update: Ideal customer profiles may evolve over time, so regularly update and refine them as your business grows.

Benefits of Catering to Your Ideal Customer

Catering to your ideal customer offers numerous advantages:

a. Improved Marketing ROI: Targeted marketing campaigns directed at your ideal customer are more likely to yield a higher return on investment (ROI).

b. Increased Customer Satisfaction: Products and services tailored to your ideal customer's preferences result in higher customer satisfaction.

c. Brand Loyalty: Customers who feel understood and valued are more likely to become loyal advocates of your brand.

d. Reduced Marketing Costs: Focusing on your ideal customer saves marketing costs by avoiding efforts directed at less relevant audiences.

e. Word-of-Mouth Marketing: Satisfied ideal customers are more likely to recommend your products or services to others.

f. Faster Decision-Making: Knowing your ideal customer helps streamline product development and marketing decision-making.

Real-World Examples of Defining Ideal Customers

Several businesses have effectively defined their ideal customers and reaped the benefits:

a. Apple: Apple's ideal customer persona focuses on individuals who value innovation, design, and seamless integration of technology into their daily lives.

b. Starbucks: Starbucks caters to the ideal customer who appreciates quality coffee, a comfortable environment, and a sense of community.

c. Tesla: Tesla's ideal customer is typically someone who values sustainability, cutting-edge technology, and high-performance electric vehicles.

d. Patagonia: Patagonia serves the ideal customer who is passionate about outdoor activities and environmental sustainability.

e. Amazon: Amazon caters to a wide range of ideal customers, from busy parents seeking convenience to tech enthusiasts looking for a vast selection of products.

Conclusion

Understanding the concept of an ideal customer is a pivotal step in creating a successful business. By defining and catering to your ideal customer, you can tailor your products, services, and marketing efforts to resonate with your target audience, resulting in higher customer satisfaction, brand loyalty, and increased sales. Regularly review and update your ideal customer personas to stay aligned with market changes and evolving customer needs, ensuring your business remains adaptable and competitive in the long term.

Defining Demographic and Psychographic Characteristics

Introduction

In the fields of marketing, advertising, and business strategy, understanding your target audience is paramount. Two key aspects of understanding your audience are demographic and psychographic characteristics. These characteristics provide valuable insights into who your customers are, what they value, and how they make purchasing decisions. In this comprehensive article, we will explore the definitions of demographic and psychographic characteristics, their significance, methods to define them, and practical applications in business and marketing.

Demographic Characteristics

Demographic characteristics are quantifiable, objective traits that define a population. They provide a basic understanding of who your audience is in terms of tangible attributes. Common demographic characteristics include:

  a. Age: The age range of your audience, such as "18-24" or "25-34."

  b. Gender: Whether your audience is predominantly male, female, or diverse.

  c. Location: Geographical location or region, including city, state, or country.

  d. Income: The income level of your audience, whether it's "low income," "middle income," or "high income."

e. Education: The highest level of education your audience has attained, such as "high school," "college," or "postgraduate."

f. Occupation: The type of work or industry your audience is employed in.

g. Marital Status: Whether your audience is single, married, divorced, or in a domestic partnership.

h. Family Size: The number of people in the household, such as "single," "small family," or "large family."

Psychographic Characteristics

Psychographic characteristics delve into the psychological and behavioral aspects of your audience. They provide insights into their values, beliefs, interests, and lifestyles. Common psychographic characteristics include:

a. Values and Beliefs: The principles and convictions that guide your audience's decision-making and behavior.

b. Interests and Hobbies: The activities, hobbies, and pastimes that your audience is passionate about.

c. Lifestyle: The way your audience lives, including factors like diet, exercise, and spending habits.

d. Personality Traits: The personality characteristics that shape your audience's behavior, such as introverted, extroverted, or adventurous.

e. Attitudes: The general attitudes and opinions your audience holds towards certain topics or issues.

f. Social Class: The social and economic status of your audience, which can influence their lifestyle and consumption habits.

g. Opinions and Values: The values and beliefs your audience holds regarding specific topics, such as sustainability or social responsibility.

h. Behavioral Habits: The purchasing habits and preferences of your audience, including brand loyalty and online shopping behaviors.

The Significance of Demographic and Psychographic Characteristics

Understanding demographic and psychographic characteristics is essential for several reasons:

a. Targeted Marketing: These characteristics enable businesses to create tailored marketing campaigns that resonate with their audience.

b. Personalization: Knowing your audience's demographics and psychographics allows for personalized product and service recommendations.

c. Market Segmentation: Demographic and psychographic characteristics are key to segmenting your audience and targeting specific market niches.

d. Product Development: Businesses can design products and services that cater to the needs, preferences, and values of their target audience.

e. Customer Engagement: Effective understanding of these characteristics leads to more engaging and relevant communication with customers.

Methods to Define Demographic and Psychographic Characteristics

To define demographic and psychographic characteristics, businesses can employ various methods:

a. Surveys and Questionnaires: Collect data by directly asking your audience about their demographic and psychographic attributes.

b. Market Research: Leverage market research to gather data on customer behavior, values, and preferences.

c. Social Media Insights: Analyze data from social media platforms to understand the interests and behaviors of your audience.

d. Data Analytics: Use data analytics tools to gain insights from website visits, clicks, and interactions.

e. Customer Feedback: Pay attention to customer feedback and reviews to understand their opinions and preferences.

f. Focus Groups: Conduct focus group discussions to gather deeper insights into the psychographic aspects of your audience.

Practical Applications in Business and Marketing

Understanding demographic and psychographic characteristics has numerous practical applications in business and marketing:

a. Targeted Advertising: Use this knowledge to create advertising campaigns that resonate with specific demographics and psychographics.

b. Product Development: Develop products that align with the values, interests, and preferences of your target audience.

c. Content Creation: Create content that caters to the psychographic characteristics of your audience, ensuring it's relevant and engaging.

d. Market Segmentation: Divide your audience into segments based on their demographics and psychographics, tailoring your strategies accordingly.

e. Personalization: Offer personalized recommendations and experiences based on the attributes and behaviors of your audience.

Conclusion

Demographic and psychographic characteristics are essential tools for understanding your target audience. By defining these characteristics, businesses can create more effective marketing strategies, personalized product offerings, and engaging customer experiences. The combination of demographic and psychographic insights provides a holistic view of your audience, enabling you to meet their needs and build lasting relationships. This deeper understanding is key to a successful and customer-centric approach in the business and marketing world.

Conducting Market Research to Identify Your Target Audience

Introduction

Identifying and understanding your target audience is a pivotal step in any successful business or marketing strategy. Market research plays a crucial role in this process, providing valuable insights into the preferences, behaviors, and needs of your potential customers. In this comprehensive article, we will delve into the importance of conducting market research to identify your target audience, the key steps involved, and the tools and techniques available to gather the necessary data for a well-informed decision-making process.

The Significance of Identifying Your Target Audience

Defining your target audience is fundamental for several reasons:

   a. Targeted Marketing: It enables you to create highly targeted and effective marketing campaigns that reach the right people.

   b. Efficient Resource Allocation: You can allocate your resources (time, budget, and personnel) more effectively by focusing on the most receptive audience.

   c. Better Product Development: Understanding your audience's needs and preferences helps in designing products and services that cater to them.

   d. Enhanced Customer Relationships: A better understanding of your audience fosters stronger and more meaningful customer relationships.

e. Competitive Advantage: Businesses that know their target audience well are better positioned to compete in the market.

Key Steps in Conducting Market Research

To identify your target audience through market research, follow these key steps:

a. Define Your Objectives: Clearly outline your research objectives, specifying what you want to learn and achieve.

b. Gather Secondary Data: Start by collecting existing data and information from sources such as industry reports, government statistics, and competitor analysis.

c. Primary Research: Conduct primary research by gathering data directly from your target audience. This can be done through surveys, interviews, focus groups, or observations.

d. Analyze Competitor Audiences: Study the audiences of your competitors to identify common traits, preferences, and potential gaps in the market.

e. Create Buyer Personas: Develop detailed buyer personas that encapsulate the characteristics and attributes of your ideal customers.

f. Segment Your Market: Divide your audience into segments based on demographic, geographic, psychographic, and behavioral criteria.

g. Analyze Data: Analyze the data you've collected to identify trends, preferences, and unique characteristics within each segment.

h. Prioritize Segments: Prioritize segments based on their alignment with your business goals and resources.

Tools and Techniques for Market Research

Several tools and techniques can aid in conducting market research:

a. Surveys and Questionnaires: Online or offline surveys and questionnaires are a versatile way to gather data directly from your target audience.

b. Focus Groups: Conduct focus group discussions to gain qualitative insights into audience preferences and opinions.

c. Online Analytics: Utilize web analytics tools to track user behavior on your website and gather insights into online customer behavior.

d. Social Media Insights: Social media platforms offer data on user demographics, interests, and behaviors that can be valuable in defining your audience.

e. Market Research Reports: Explore industry-specific market research reports to access valuable data and trends.

f. Customer Feedback: Pay close attention to customer feedback and reviews to understand their likes, dislikes, and expectations.

g. Competitor Analysis: Study your competitors' customer base to identify overlaps and differences in your potential audience.

h. Demographic Data Sources: Gather demographic data from government sources, census data, or industry-specific databases.

The Role of Buyer Personas

Buyer personas are fictional representations of your ideal customers, based on data and research. Creating buyer personas helps humanize your target audience and provides a clear and relatable understanding of who you are trying to reach. Each persona should include:

a. Demographics: Age, gender, income, education, and location.

b. Psychographics: Interests, values, lifestyles, and behavior.

c. Pain Points: The problems or challenges they face that your product or service can address.

d. Goals: What they hope to achieve through their interactions with your business.

e. Communication Preferences: The channels and methods they prefer for communication.

f. Buying Behavior: Their purchasing habits and decision-making process.

Benefits of Target Audience Identification

The process of conducting market research to identify your target audience offers numerous benefits:

a. Effective Communication: Tailor your messaging and content to resonate with your audience's preferences and needs.

b. Improved ROI: Targeted marketing efforts are more likely to yield a higher return on investment (ROI).

c. Enhanced Product Development: Design products and services that meet the specific needs of your target audience.

d. Customer Loyalty: Customers who feel understood and valued are more likely to become loyal advocates of your brand.

e. Efficient Resource Allocation: Avoid wasting resources on reaching audiences that aren't relevant to your business.

Conclusion

Conducting market research to identify your target audience is a foundational step in building a successful business. By understanding the preferences, behaviors, and needs of your potential customers, you can create more effective marketing campaigns, develop products and services that cater to their requirements, and build lasting and meaningful relationships. This knowledge also positions your business to adapt to changing market conditions and evolving customer demands, ensuring long-term success in a dynamic business landscape.

Creating Customer Personas: A Guide to Understanding Your Audience

Introduction

Understanding your target audience is essential for crafting successful marketing strategies and building lasting customer relationships. Customer personas, also known as buyer personas or marketing personas, are semi-fictional representations of your ideal customers. They provide businesses with a detailed profile of their target audience, helping them tailor their products, services, and marketing efforts to meet their customers' needs and preferences. In this comprehensive article, we will explore the importance of creating customer personas, the steps involved in their creation, and real-world examples to illustrate their significance.

The Significance of Creating Customer Personas

Creating customer personas is vital for several reasons:

   a. Targeted Marketing: Personas help businesses create highly targeted marketing campaigns that resonate with specific customer segments.

   b. Personalization: By understanding your audience's needs and behaviors, you can offer personalized product recommendations and experiences.

   c. Efficient Resource Allocation: You can allocate your marketing budget and resources more effectively by focusing on the most receptive audience.

d. Better Product Development: A deep understanding of your audience's needs and preferences helps in designing products and services that cater to them.

e. Enhanced Customer Relationships: Understanding your audience fosters stronger and more meaningful customer relationships.

f. Competitive Advantage: Businesses that know their customer personas well are better positioned to compete in the market.

Steps to Create Customer Personas

To create effective customer personas, follow these key steps:

a. Market Research: Conduct market research to gather data on your existing customer base, competition, and industry trends.

b. Customer Segmentation: Segment your audience based on demographic, geographic, psychographic, and behavioral characteristics.

c. Create Detailed Profiles: Develop detailed profiles for each customer persona, including their age, gender, income, values, goals, challenges, and preferences.

d. Validate with Data: Use real data and feedback from your existing customers to refine your customer personas.

e. Prioritize Personas: Prioritize customer personas based on their alignment with your business goals and resources.

Elements of a Customer Persona

A well-crafted customer persona should include the following elements:

a. Demographics: Age, gender, income, education, and location.

   b. Psychographics: Interests, values, lifestyles, and behavior.

   c. Pain Points: The problems or challenges they face that your product or service can address.

   d. Goals: What they hope to achieve through their interactions with your business.

   e. Communication Preferences: The channels and methods they prefer for communication.

   f. Buying Behavior: Their purchasing habits and decision-making process.

Real-World Examples of Customer Personas

Several businesses have effectively created customer personas to improve their marketing and product development strategies:

   a. HubSpot: HubSpot uses customer personas to tailor content and marketing efforts for various segments, such as "Marketing Mary" and "Sales Sam."

   b. Airbnb: Airbnb has created customer personas like "The Experience Seeker" and "The Young Professional" to guide its product and marketing decisions.

   c. Cisco: Cisco uses detailed customer personas to understand the specific challenges and needs of its diverse customer base.

   d. Buffer: Buffer, a social media management platform, created personas like "Social Media Manager Sarah" and "Small Business Owner Sam" to tailor its product features.

e. Adidas: Adidas developed customer personas like "The Athlete" and "The Street Styler" to customize marketing campaigns for different target audiences.

Benefits of Customer Personas

The creation of customer personas offers numerous benefits:

a. Targeted Marketing: Tailored marketing campaigns are more likely to resonate with specific customer segments.

b. Personalization: Personalized product recommendations and experiences lead to increased customer satisfaction.

c. Enhanced Product Development: Products and services that align with customer needs result in higher product adoption and satisfaction.

d. Customer Loyalty: Customers who feel understood and valued are more likely to become loyal advocates of your brand.

e. Efficient Resource Allocation: Focused marketing efforts save resources by avoiding unproductive outreach.

Conclusion

Creating customer personas is a fundamental step in building a successful business. By defining detailed profiles of your ideal customers, you can tailor your products, services, and marketing efforts to resonate with their needs and preferences. This deep understanding positions your business to create more effective marketing campaigns, develop products that cater to your target audience, and build lasting and meaningful relationships with your customers. Regularly review and update your customer personas to stay aligned with market changes and evolving customer needs, ensuring your business remains adaptable and competitive in a dynamic business landscape.

Analyzing Your Existing Customer Base: A Guide to Informed Business Growth

Introduction

Analyzing your existing customer base is a critical step for any business looking to grow and thrive. Understanding your current customers' behaviors, preferences, and demographics provides valuable insights that can guide your marketing, product development, and customer retention strategies. In this comprehensive article, we will explore the importance of analyzing your existing customer base, the key steps and methods involved, and practical applications for informed business growth.

The Significance of Analyzing Your Existing Customer Base

Analyzing your existing customer base is crucial for several reasons:

   a. Customer Retention: Understanding your current customers' needs and preferences enables you to retain and build long-term relationships with them.

   b. Targeted Marketing: Data-driven insights help you create more targeted and effective marketing campaigns, which can lead to higher conversion rates.

   c. Product Development: Analysis can reveal opportunities for enhancing your existing products or developing new ones tailored to customer demands.

d. Resource Allocation: You can allocate your marketing budget more effectively by focusing on the customers most likely to make repeat purchases.

e. Competitive Advantage: Businesses that know their customers well can stay ahead of the competition by delivering superior products and services.

Key Steps in Analyzing Your Existing Customer Base

To effectively analyze your existing customer base, follow these key steps:

a. Data Collection: Gather data on your customers, including purchase history, behavior on your website or app, demographics, and feedback.

b. Customer Segmentation: Segment your customer base into distinct groups based on factors like demographics, purchasing behavior, and psychographics.

c. Develop Customer Profiles: Create detailed profiles for each customer segment, highlighting key attributes, behaviors, and preferences.

d. Analyze Data: Utilize data analytics tools to extract meaningful insights from the information you've gathered.

e. Identify Trends: Look for patterns, trends, and commonalities among different customer segments to gain deeper insights.

f. Segment Prioritization: Prioritize customer segments based on their value to your business and their potential for growth.

Methods and Tools for Analyzing Your Customer Base

Several methods and tools can aid in the analysis of your existing customer base:

a. Data Analytics: Utilize data analytics tools to mine and analyze customer data, looking for trends and patterns.

b. CRM Systems: Customer Relationship Management (CRM) systems provide a central repository for customer data and insights.

c. Surveys and Feedback: Collect customer feedback through surveys, reviews, and customer service interactions to gain insights into customer satisfaction and preferences.

d. Customer Segmentation: Segment your customer base using demographic, geographic, psychographic, and behavioral criteria.

e. Sales Data: Analyze sales data to understand purchasing patterns and customer preferences.

f. Website and App Analytics: Use web analytics tools to track customer behavior on your website or app.

Practical Applications for Informed Business Growth

Analyzing your existing customer base offers several practical applications for business growth:

a. Customer Retention Strategies: Use insights to develop personalized strategies that retain and build long-term relationships with your existing customers.

b. Targeted Marketing Campaigns: Create marketing campaigns that are tailored to specific customer segments, increasing the chances of success.

c. Product Development: Identify opportunities for product improvements or new product offerings that align with customer needs and preferences.

d. Cross-Selling and Upselling: Use insights to recommend complementary products or upsell to existing customers.

e. Pricing Strategies: Adjust pricing strategies based on customer behavior and willingness to pay.

f. Resource Allocation: Efficiently allocate marketing budgets by focusing on the most profitable customer segments.

Real-World Examples of Customer Base Analysis

Numerous businesses have successfully analyzed their customer bases to drive growth:

a. Amazon: Amazon analyzes customer data to make product recommendations, optimize its website, and tailor marketing campaigns.

b. Spotify: Spotify uses customer listening habits to curate personalized playlists and recommend new music based on user preferences.

c. Netflix: Netflix analyzes customer viewing habits to suggest content and create original series tailored to their audience.

d. Starbucks: Starbucks uses purchase data to personalize its loyalty program and offer promotions to customers based on their preferences.

e. Zappos: Zappos analyzes customer feedback and purchase data to enhance its customer service and improve product offerings.

Conclusion

Analyzing your existing customer base is a fundamental step in understanding your customers, retaining their loyalty, and guiding informed business growth. By collecting and analyzing data, segmenting customers, and developing detailed profiles, you can uncover insights that inform your marketing strategies, product development, and customer retention efforts. Staying adaptable and responsive to customer behavior and preferences is essential in a dynamic business landscape, and a thorough analysis of your existing customer base is an invaluable tool for staying ahead of the competition and delivering a superior customer experience.

Segmenting Your Audience for Tailored Marketing: A Comprehensive Guide

Introduction

In the world of marketing, a one-size-fits-all approach rarely yields the best results. To create effective marketing campaigns, it's crucial to segment your audience based on their unique characteristics, behaviors, and preferences. This process, known as audience segmentation, allows businesses to target specific groups with tailored marketing messages. In this comprehensive article, we will explore the importance of audience segmentation, the key steps involved, various segmentation criteria, and practical applications in marketing for businesses of all sizes.

The Significance of Audience Segmentation

Audience segmentation is pivotal for several reasons:

   a. Targeted Marketing: Segmentation helps you create marketing campaigns that resonate with specific customer segments.

   b. Personalization: Tailored messaging and content lead to increased customer engagement and satisfaction.

   c. Improved ROI: Targeted marketing efforts tend to yield a higher return on investment (ROI) as they reach a more receptive audience.

   d. Enhanced Product Development: Insights from segmentation can guide product and service development to align with customer needs.

e. Customer Retention: Better understanding of customer segments allows you to develop strategies for retaining and nurturing existing customers.

Key Steps in Audience Segmentation

To effectively segment your audience, follow these key steps:

a. Data Collection: Gather data on your customers, including demographic information, purchase history, online behavior, and psychographics.

b. Define Segmentation Criteria: Identify the criteria or characteristics that will form the basis of your segmentation, such as age, location, or purchasing habits.

c. Create Customer Profiles: Develop detailed profiles for each customer segment, highlighting key attributes, behaviors, and preferences.

d. Analyze Data: Use data analytics tools to extract meaningful insights from the information you've gathered.

e. Segment Prioritization: Prioritize customer segments based on their alignment with your business goals and resources.

Segmentation Criteria

Audience segmentation can be based on various criteria. Here are some common segmentation categories:

a. Demographics: Characteristics like age, gender, income, education, and location.

b. Geographic: Location-based segmentation, such as region, city, or climate.

c. Psychographics: Audience values, beliefs, interests, lifestyle, and behaviors.

d. Behavioral: Segmentation based on customer actions, such as purchase history, website activity, or engagement with marketing content.

e. Firmographic: Business-to-business (B2B) segmentation criteria, including company size, industry, and revenue.

f. Occasion-Based: Segmentation according to specific events, seasons, or holidays.

g. Benefits Sought: Segmenting by the primary benefit or solution customers are seeking.

h. Usage: Frequency of product or service usage.

i. Customer Lifecycle: Where customers are in their journey with your business, such as new, repeat, or lapsed customers.

Practical Applications in Marketing

Segmenting your audience has a multitude of practical applications in marketing:

a. Tailored Messaging: Create marketing messages and content that resonate with specific customer segments.

b. Customized Offers: Develop personalized offers and promotions based on the needs and preferences of each segment.

c. Channel Selection: Choose the most effective marketing channels for reaching each segment.

   d. Product Recommendations: Use data from segment analysis to suggest products or services that align with each segment's preferences.

   e. Email Marketing: Segment your email list to send relevant content and offers to different customer groups.

   f. Ad Campaigns: Craft targeted ad campaigns on platforms like social media and search engines to reach specific segments.

   g. Content Creation: Develop content that addresses the interests and pain points of your various customer segments.

Real-World Examples of Audience Segmentation

Numerous businesses use audience segmentation to enhance their marketing strategies:

   a. Amazon: Amazon uses sophisticated segmentation to recommend products based on customers' previous purchases and browsing behavior.

   b. Netflix: Netflix segments its audience to recommend shows and movies tailored to users' viewing history and preferences.

   c. Spotify: Spotify creates personalized playlists and recommends music based on users' listening habits and preferences.

   d. Sephora: Sephora segments its customers to provide personalized product recommendations and offers through its Beauty Insider program.

e. Starbucks: Starbucks tailors its promotions and rewards programs to different customer segments, such as loyal customers and occasional visitors.

Conclusion

Audience segmentation is a fundamental strategy in modern marketing, enabling businesses to deliver more relevant and effective campaigns. By collecting and analyzing data, defining segmentation criteria, and creating customer profiles, businesses can gain a deeper understanding of their customers and build more meaningful relationships with them. This knowledge also positions businesses to make data-driven decisions, ensuring they create marketing campaigns, products, and services that cater to the unique preferences and needs of their diverse customer segments. Audience segmentation is a valuable tool for staying competitive and responsive to changing market dynamics in the ever-evolving world of marketing.

Identifying Your Audience's Pain Points: A Comprehensive Guide

Introduction

In the world of marketing and business, understanding your audience's pain points is a crucial step towards creating effective solutions and building lasting customer relationships. A pain point refers to a problem, challenge, or need that your target audience faces. By identifying these pain points, you can tailor your products, services, and marketing strategies to provide value and address the specific issues your audience encounters. In this comprehensive article, we will explore the importance of identifying your audience's pain points, the methods for doing so, and the practical applications for businesses seeking to meet their customers' needs.

The Significance of Identifying Your Audience's Pain Points

Identifying your audience's pain points is pivotal for several reasons:

   a. Customer-Centric Approach: It allows you to develop products and services that directly address the challenges and needs of your target audience.

   b. Targeted Marketing: Understanding your audience's pain points enables you to create marketing campaigns that resonate and provide solutions.

   c. Enhanced Customer Relationships: Tailoring your offerings to alleviate pain points fosters stronger and more meaningful customer relationships.

d. Competitive Advantage: Businesses that effectively address pain points are more likely to outshine competitors in the market.

   e. Innovation: Pain point identification can lead to innovative solutions and new product or service ideas.

Key Steps in Identifying Pain Points

To effectively identify your audience's pain points, follow these key steps:

   a. Research: Conduct thorough market research to gather insights into your target audience, their behaviors, and their challenges.

   b. Survey and Questionnaires: Use surveys and questionnaires to gather direct feedback from your audience about their pain points.

   c. Customer Feedback: Pay close attention to customer reviews, support tickets, and feedback to identify recurring issues or challenges.

   d. Competitor Analysis: Analyze the pain points your competitors are addressing and look for gaps or unmet needs.

   e. Data Analysis: Utilize data analytics tools to identify patterns in customer behavior and pain point identification.

Methods for Identifying Pain Points

Several methods can be employed to identify your audience's pain points:

   a. Customer Surveys: Create surveys with open-ended questions and ask your audience about their biggest challenges and frustrations.

b. Social Media Monitoring: Monitor social media channels and discussions to identify common complaints or problems related to your industry.

c. Customer Support Interactions: Review customer support interactions to understand the most frequently reported issues.

d. Focus Groups: Conduct focus group discussions to gain deeper insights into pain points and customer challenges.

e. Online Reviews and Feedback: Analyze online reviews and feedback on platforms like Yelp, Google Reviews, and Amazon to uncover recurring pain points.

Practical Applications for Addressing Pain Points

Once you've identified your audience's pain points, there are various practical applications:

a. Product and Service Improvement: Use insights to enhance existing products or services to better meet customer needs.

b. New Product Development: Identify opportunities to create new products or services that address specific pain points.

c. Content Creation: Develop content that educates and provides solutions to common pain points.

d. Tailored Marketing: Create marketing campaigns that directly address the pain points of your target audience.

e. Customer Support: Train customer support teams to effectively address and resolve the identified pain points.

Real-World Examples of Addressing Pain Points

Numerous businesses have effectively addressed their audience's pain points:

a. Apple: Apple addressed the pain point of music piracy with the introduction of the iTunes Store, making it convenient for customers to purchase and download music legally.

b. Uber: Uber addressed the pain point of transportation by providing a convenient and reliable ride-sharing service.

c. Slack: Slack addressed communication and collaboration pain points by offering a centralized platform for teams to communicate and share information.

d. Amazon: Amazon addressed the pain point of online shopping convenience by providing a user-friendly platform with a wide selection and fast delivery.

e. Zillow: Zillow addressed the pain point of finding real estate listings by providing a user-friendly platform for homebuyers and renters.

Conclusion

Identifying your audience's pain points is a foundational step in building a customer-centric business. By conducting research, surveys, and analyzing customer feedback, you can gain insights into the challenges and needs of your target audience. These insights enable you to create products, services, and marketing campaigns that directly address pain points, providing value and building stronger customer relationships. Continuously listening to your audience and adapting to their evolving needs is essential for long-term success and competitiveness in the ever-changing business landscape. Addressing pain points is not just a strategy; it's a commitment to providing solutions and improving the lives of your customers.

Conducting Surveys and Interviews for Insights: A Comprehensive Guide

Introduction

Surveys and interviews are powerful tools for gathering insights and valuable information from individuals. Whether you're a researcher, a business owner, or a marketer, these methods can help you better understand your target audience, customers, or participants. In this comprehensive article, we will explore the significance of conducting surveys and interviews, the key steps involved, best practices, and practical applications to obtain valuable insights for various purposes.

The Significance of Conducting Surveys and Interviews

Conducting surveys and interviews is crucial for several reasons:

   a. Informed Decision-Making: Gathering insights from surveys and interviews provides valuable data for making well-informed decisions.

   b. Customer-Centric Approach: Understanding the perspectives and needs of your audience or participants allows you to tailor your products, services, or strategies to better meet their requirements.

   c. Market Research: Surveys and interviews are key components of market research, helping businesses gain insights into customer behavior and preferences.

   d. Academic Research: Researchers use surveys and interviews to collect data for studies, theses, and academic projects.

e. Continuous Improvement: Regularly conducting surveys and interviews allows organizations to continuously improve and adapt to changing circumstances.

Key Steps in Conducting Surveys and Interviews

To effectively conduct surveys and interviews for insights, follow these key steps:

a. Define Objectives: Clearly outline your research objectives, specifying what you want to learn and achieve.

b. Design Questions: Create questions that align with your objectives and are clear, concise, and unbiased.

c. Select Participants: Choose a representative sample of participants or respondents from your target population.

d. Choose the Method: Decide whether to conduct surveys, interviews, or a combination of both.

e. Prepare Materials: Develop survey forms, questionnaires, or interview guides.

f. Conduct the Surveys/Interviews: Administer the surveys or interviews following your prepared materials.

g. Collect and Record Data: Systematically collect and record the data obtained from surveys and interviews.

h. Analyze Data: Use data analysis techniques and tools to draw insights from the collected information.

i. Report Findings: Summarize your findings and communicate the insights to relevant stakeholders or your audience.

Best Practices for Effective Surveys and Interviews

To maximize the effectiveness of your surveys and interviews, consider these best practices:

a. Keep Questions Clear and Unbiased: Ensure that questions are easy to understand and free from any biases that might influence responses.

b. Use Open-Ended and Closed-Ended Questions: Incorporate both types of questions to gather qualitative and quantitative data.

c. Test Your Surveys/Interviews: Pilot-test your surveys or interview guides to identify and address any issues before conducting the main research.

d. Respect Participant Privacy: Assure respondents that their information will be kept confidential and that their privacy will be respected.

e. Offer Incentives: Consider offering incentives to participants to encourage their participation.

f. Analyze Data Thoroughly: Apply appropriate data analysis methods to extract meaningful insights.

g. Communicate Findings: Share your findings with relevant stakeholders or your audience in a clear and comprehensible manner.

Practical Applications for Gaining Insights

Surveys and interviews can be applied in various contexts to gain insights, including:

a. Market Research: Use surveys and interviews to understand customer behavior, preferences, and market trends.

b. Product Development: Gather insights to design and improve products and services according to customer needs.

c. Customer Feedback: Collect feedback from customers to gauge their satisfaction and identify areas for improvement.

d. Academic Research: Conduct surveys and interviews for academic studies and research projects.

e. Human Resources: Use interviews and surveys to assess employee satisfaction, collect feedback, and improve the workplace.

f. Nonprofit Organizations: Gather insights to understand the needs and preferences of beneficiaries and donors.

Real-World Examples of Surveys and Interviews

Numerous organizations and businesses have successfully conducted surveys and interviews to gain insights:

a. Apple: Apple conducts user surveys and interviews to collect feedback for product development and design.

b. Netflix: Netflix interviews viewers to gain insights into their preferences and improve content recommendations.

c. McDonald's: McDonald's uses customer surveys to improve menu offerings and service quality.

d. Government Agencies: Government agencies conduct surveys to collect data for policy development, public health, and social services.

e. Universities: Universities use surveys and interviews for academic research, course evaluations, and student feedback.

Conclusion

Conducting surveys and interviews is a valuable and versatile method for gaining insights in various fields, from business and marketing to academic research and policy development. By following the key steps and best practices outlined in this guide, you can effectively collect and analyze data to make informed decisions, improve products and services, and better meet the needs and preferences of your target audience. Surveys and interviews empower organizations to adopt a customer-centric approach, respond to changing circumstances, and continuously enhance their offerings to remain competitive and responsive to evolving needs.

Using Social Listening to Understand Customer Needs: A Comprehensive Guide

Introduction

In the age of digital communication and social media, understanding customer needs and preferences has become more accessible than ever through the practice of social listening. This powerful tool allows businesses to monitor online conversations, track mentions of their brand, and gather insights from social media and online discussions. In this comprehensive article, we will explore the importance of using social listening to understand customer needs, the key steps involved, best practices, and practical applications for businesses seeking to enhance their customer-centric approach.

The Significance of Using Social Listening

Using social listening to understand customer needs is pivotal for several reasons:

  a. Real-Time Insights: Social listening provides real-time access to customer sentiments and opinions.

  b. Customer-Centric Approach: It allows businesses to align their products and services with the expressed needs and preferences of their target audience.

  c. Competitive Advantage: Staying informed about customer needs enables businesses to outshine competitors in responding to changing market dynamics.

d. Improved Products and Services: The data gathered through social listening can guide product development and service improvement.

e. Crisis Management: Early detection of issues and concerns allows businesses to address problems promptly and maintain their reputation.

Key Steps in Using Social Listening

To effectively use social listening to understand customer needs, follow these key steps:

a. Define Objectives: Clearly outline your research objectives and what you aim to achieve through social listening.

b. Select Tools: Choose social listening tools and platforms that suit your needs and budget.

c. Monitor Social Media Channels: Set up alerts and monitoring systems for relevant social media channels and websites.

d. Gather and Analyze Data: Collect data from online conversations and analyze it for insights into customer needs.

e. Categorize Insights: Group insights into categories such as product feedback, feature requests, and customer sentiments.

f. Report Findings: Summarize and communicate the findings to relevant stakeholders in a clear and actionable manner.

Best Practices for Effective Social Listening

To maximize the effectiveness of your social listening efforts, consider these best practices:

a. Choose the Right Tools: Select social listening tools that match your business objectives and needs.

b. Set Up Alerts: Configure alerts for specific keywords, mentions, or hashtags relevant to your brand and industry.

c. Act in Real Time: Address customer needs and concerns promptly, demonstrating your commitment to customer satisfaction.

d. Maintain Data Privacy: Ensure that the data you collect adheres to data protection and privacy regulations.

e. Continuously Update and Adapt: Stay flexible and adaptable in your approach, as customer needs and preferences can change.

f. Engage with Customers: Interact with customers online to show that you value their opinions and needs.

Practical Applications for Understanding Customer Needs

Using social listening to understand customer needs can be applied in various contexts, including:

a. Product Development: Gather insights to inform the creation of new products or the improvement of existing ones.

b. Customer Support: Address customer issues and concerns in real time, providing better service and support.

c. Content Creation: Develop content that resonates with customer interests and needs.

d. Marketing Campaigns: Tailor marketing campaigns to address the expressed needs and preferences of your audience.

e. Reputation Management: Use social listening to monitor your online reputation and address negative feedback or crises.

Real-World Examples of Successful Social Listening

Numerous businesses have harnessed the power of social listening to understand customer needs:

a. Coca-Cola: Coca-Cola used social listening to monitor customer conversations and discovered a demand for more sustainable packaging, leading to their "World Without Waste" initiative.

b. JetBlue: JetBlue employs social listening to address customer issues and respond to queries promptly through their @JetBlueCheeps Twitter handle.

c. Pampers: Pampers used social listening to identify parents' concerns about diaper leaks, leading to product improvements and a positive customer response.

d. Lego: Lego uses social listening to gather feedback on their products and to identify trends in children's preferences.

e. Spotify: Spotify leverages social listening to create personalized playlists and recommend music based on user interests and needs.

Conclusion

Using social listening to understand customer needs is a critical practice in the digital age. It enables businesses to stay informed about customer opinions, concerns, and preferences in real time, leading to a customer-centric approach. Social listening is a dynamic and adaptable tool that empowers businesses to meet customer needs and remain competitive in a customer-driven landscape.

Exploring Customer Journey Mapping: A Comprehensive Guide

Introduction

Understanding your customers' experiences and interactions with your brand is vital for creating a seamless and customer-centric approach to business. Customer journey mapping is a powerful tool that allows businesses to visualize and analyze every step of the customer's experience, from initial contact to post-purchase interactions. In this comprehensive article, we will explore the importance of customer journey mapping, the key steps involved, best practices, and practical applications to help businesses enhance their customer experience.

The Significance of Customer Journey Mapping

Customer journey mapping is crucial for several reasons:

   a. Customer-Centric Approach: It enables businesses to see their brand through the eyes of the customer and tailor their offerings accordingly.

   b. Improved Customer Experience: By identifying pain points and opportunities, businesses can make necessary improvements to enhance the customer experience.

   c. Identifying Touchpoints: It helps businesses identify all the touchpoints where customers interact with their brand, enabling more effective communication and engagement.

   d. Enhanced Retention: Understanding the customer journey allows businesses to address customer needs and concerns promptly, improving customer satisfaction and retention.

   e. Data-Driven Decision-Making: The insights gained from customer journey mapping guide data-driven decision-making and resource allocation.

Key Steps in Customer Journey Mapping

To effectively map the customer journey, follow these key steps:

a. Define Objectives: Clearly outline what you aim to achieve with your customer journey map and the specific goals you want to accomplish.

b. Identify Customer Personas: Create detailed customer personas to represent the different segments of your audience.

c. Map the Journey: Chart the stages and touchpoints of the customer journey, starting from the initial awareness of your brand to post-purchase interactions.

d. Gather Data: Collect data through surveys, interviews, customer feedback, and analytics to gain insights into customer experiences.

e. Analyze and Document: Analyze the data to identify customer pain points, satisfaction points, and areas for improvement.

f. Visualize the Map: Create a visual representation of the customer journey map, including each touchpoint and the customer's emotional state at each stage.

g. Share and Iterate: Communicate the map with relevant stakeholders, gather feedback, and continuously iterate and improve the map.

Best Practices for Effective Customer Journey Mapping

To maximize the effectiveness of your customer journey mapping, consider these best practices:

a. Start with Customer Personas: Develop detailed customer personas to better understand your target audience.

b. Involve Cross-Functional Teams: Collaborate with teams from different departments, such as marketing, sales, and customer support, to gather a holistic view of the customer journey.

c. Capture Emotions: Consider the emotional state of the customer at each stage of the journey, as emotions play a significant role in decision-making.

d. Focus on Pain Points: Pay special attention to identifying pain points and areas where the customer experience can be improved.

e. Continuously Update: The customer journey is not static, so regularly update your map to reflect changes in customer behavior and market dynamics.

f. Communicate Findings: Share the customer journey map with relevant stakeholders and ensure that it is understood and acted upon throughout the organization.

Practical Applications of Customer Journey Mapping

Customer journey mapping can be applied in various contexts, including:

a. Marketing: Create targeted marketing campaigns that align with the customer journey, increasing the chances of customer engagement.

b. Product Development: Identify opportunities for creating new products or enhancing existing ones to better meet customer needs.

c. Customer Support: Tailor customer support strategies to address customer concerns and questions at each stage of their journey.

d. Sales: Understand the customer journey to optimize the sales process and improve conversion rates.

e. Website and User Experience: Design websites and user experiences that align with the customer journey, making it more intuitive and engaging.

Real-World Examples of Successful Customer Journey Mapping

Numerous businesses have harnessed the power of customer journey mapping to enhance the customer experience:

a. Disney: Disney has mastered the art of customer journey mapping by creating a magical and memorable experience at every touchpoint, from the moment guests arrive at the park to the end of their visit.

b. Apple: Apple carefully maps the customer journey, ensuring that every interaction with its products, whether in-store or online, is intuitive and enjoyable.

c. Zappos: Zappos excels in customer service by tailoring the customer journey to provide a seamless shopping experience, including hassle-free returns and exceptional customer support.

d. Airbnb: Airbnb maps the customer journey for both hosts and guests, creating a platform that caters to their unique needs and expectations.

e. Starbucks: Starbucks provides a consistent and enjoyable customer journey, from mobile ordering to in-store service, to enhance the overall experience.

Conclusion

Customer journey mapping is a valuable practice that empowers businesses to view their brand from the customer's perspective and create a seamless and customer-centric experience. By following the key steps, best practices, and practical applications outlined in this guide, organizations can gather valuable insights to enhance their customer experience, improve product development, optimize marketing efforts, and foster customer loyalty. Understanding the customer journey is a dynamic and adaptive process that empowers businesses to remain competitive and responsive to changing market dynamics and evolving customer needs.

Analyzing Customer Feedback for Improvement: A Comprehensive Guide

Introduction

Customer feedback is a valuable resource for businesses seeking to improve their products, services, and overall customer experience. Analyzing this feedback enables organizations to gain valuable insights, identify areas for enhancement, and address customer concerns promptly. In this comprehensive article, we will explore the importance of analyzing customer feedback for improvement, the key steps involved, best practices, and practical applications to help businesses continuously enhance their offerings and better serve their customers.

The Significance of Analyzing Customer Feedback

Analyzing customer feedback is pivotal for several reasons:

   a. Customer-Centric Approach: It demonstrates a commitment to customer satisfaction and the willingness to listen to customer voices.

   b. Quality Improvement: Customer feedback can reveal areas in need of enhancement, leading to improved products and services.

   c. Issue Resolution: Identifying and addressing customer concerns promptly can help prevent dissatisfaction and potential churn.

   d. Competitive Advantage: Businesses that actively use customer feedback to improve their offerings often outshine competitors.

   e. Data-Driven Decision-Making: Insights from customer feedback serve as a valuable data source for informed decision-making.

Key Steps in Analyzing Customer Feedback

To effectively analyze customer feedback for improvement, follow these key steps:

a. Collect Feedback: Gather customer feedback through various channels such as surveys, reviews, social media, and direct customer interactions.

b. Categorize and Organize: Sort the feedback into categories, such as positive comments, constructive criticism, or recurring issues.

c. Prioritize Feedback: Identify the most critical and common feedback for immediate attention.

d. Analyze the Data: Use data analysis tools and techniques to draw insights from the feedback data.

e. Report and Communicate: Summarize the findings and communicate them to relevant stakeholders and teams within the organization.

f. Develop an Action Plan: Create a detailed plan to address the issues identified in the feedback analysis.

g. Implement Improvements: Execute the action plan, making the necessary changes and enhancements.

h. Monitor Progress: Continuously monitor the impact of the improvements and gather ongoing feedback.

Best Practices for Effective Customer Feedback Analysis

To maximize the effectiveness of your customer feedback analysis efforts, consider these best practices:

a. Act Swiftly: Address urgent and severe issues promptly to demonstrate responsiveness to customer concerns.

   b. Combine Quantitative and Qualitative Analysis: Blend quantitative data (ratings, scores) with qualitative insights (comments, suggestions) for a comprehensive view.

   c. Ensure Data Privacy: Adhere to data protection regulations and maintain customer data privacy when handling feedback.

   d. Engage Cross-Functional Teams: Collaborate with teams from various departments to implement improvements effectively.

   e. Close the Feedback Loop: Provide feedback to customers on the changes made as a result of their input to foster trust and loyalty.

   f. Continuously Monitor: Customer feedback analysis is an ongoing process; regularly gather and analyze feedback to stay responsive to changing customer needs.

Practical Applications for Improvement

Analyzing customer feedback can be applied in various contexts, including:

   a. Product Development: Use feedback to enhance existing products or design new ones that align with customer needs and expectations.

   b. Service Improvement: Identify areas of improvement in customer service and support, leading to more satisfied customers.

   c. Marketing Strategies: Adjust marketing campaigns based on customer feedback to make them more effective.

d. Website and User Experience: Improve website design and user experience according to customer comments and suggestions.

e. Reputation Management: Respond to negative reviews and comments to maintain a positive online reputation.

Real-World Examples of Successful Customer Feedback Analysis

Numerous businesses have harnessed the power of customer feedback analysis to enhance their offerings:

a. Amazon: Amazon actively analyzes customer feedback to improve its product recommendations and customer service.

b. Airbnb: Airbnb uses customer feedback to make improvements in the user experience, security, and customer service.

c. Starbucks: Starbucks gathers and analyzes customer feedback to create new products, enhance the in-store experience, and tailor its loyalty program.

d. Delta Airlines: Delta Airlines uses customer feedback to improve its services, addressing issues such as delays and baggage handling.

Conclusion

By following the key steps, best practices, and practical applications outlined in this guide, organizations can utilize customer feedback to continuously improve their products, services, and overall customer experience. Being responsive to customer concerns and suggestions empowers businesses to remain competitive, build customer loyalty, and adapt to the evolving needs and preferences of their audience. Customer feedback analysis is not just a process; it's a commitment to delivering value and satisfaction to your customers.

Creating Empathy Maps to Understand Your Audience: A Comprehensive Guide

Introduction

Understanding your target audience on a deep, emotional level is key to creating products, services, and marketing campaigns that resonate with them. Empathy maps are a powerful tool that allows businesses to gain insights into the thoughts, feelings, needs, and aspirations of their audience. In this comprehensive article, we will explore the importance of creating empathy maps to understand your audience, the key steps involved, best practices, and practical applications to help businesses build stronger connections and offer more customer-centric solutions.

The Significance of Creating Empathy Maps

Empathy maps play a crucial role in audience understanding for several reasons:

   a. Customer-Centric Approach: They enable businesses to view the world through the eyes of their audience, fostering a customer-centric approach.

   b. Enhanced Communication: Understanding your audience's thoughts and feelings allows for more effective and targeted messaging.

   c. Product and Service Improvement: Insights from empathy maps guide the development of products and services that meet customer needs and aspirations.

   e. Problem Solving: Identifying customer pain points and challenges is vital for effective problem-solving.

Key Steps in Creating Empathy Maps

To effectively create empathy maps for your audience, follow these key steps:

a. Define Your Audience: Clearly identify the target audience you want to understand.

b. Gather Information: Collect data and insights about your audience through surveys, interviews, social media, and market research.

c. Identify Personas: Create detailed customer personas that represent different segments within your audience.

d. Create the Empathy Map: Develop an empathy map that visually represents the thoughts, feelings, needs, aspirations, and pain points of your customer personas.

e. Analyze and Iterate: Continuously gather feedback and data to refine and improve your empathy maps over time.

Best Practices for Effective Empathy Maps

To maximize the effectiveness of your empathy maps, consider these best practices:

a. Start with Research: Gather data from primary and secondary sources to inform your empathy maps.

b. Collaborate: Involve cross-functional teams from marketing, product development, customer support, and other relevant departments to gain a holistic view.

c. Use Visuals: Create visual representations of empathy maps, making it easier for stakeholders to grasp and relate to the audience's feelings and needs.

d. Empathize and Validate: Put yourself in the shoes of your audience and validate your empathy maps through customer feedback.

e. Regularly Update: Keep your empathy maps up to date as your audience's needs, preferences, and pain points evolve.

Practical Applications for Understanding Your Audience

Creating empathy maps can be applied in various contexts, including:

a. Product Development: Use empathy maps to guide product design and feature development that aligns with audience needs.

b. Marketing Campaigns: Develop marketing strategies and content that resonate with your audience's emotions and aspirations.

c. Customer Support: Train customer support teams to better understand and address customer concerns.

d. Brand Messaging: Craft messaging and branding that speaks directly to your audience's values and needs.

e. User Experience Design: Create user experiences that align with your audience's preferences and pain points.

Real-World Examples of Successful Empathy Mapping

Numerous businesses have utilized empathy maps to better understand their audience and create more effective strategies:

a. Airbnb: Airbnb uses empathy maps to understand both hosts and guests, enabling them to develop features and experiences that cater to their needs and aspirations.

b. Design Thinking Firms: Many design thinking companies use empathy maps to inform the design process, ensuring that products and services address user needs.

c. Nonprofit Organizations: Nonprofits use empathy maps to better understand the communities they serve and develop initiatives that align with their values and challenges.

d. Consumer Goods Companies: Companies like Procter & Gamble and Unilever use empathy maps to design products and marketing campaigns that resonate with consumers.

e. Technology Startups: Technology startups create empathy maps to gain insights into user pain points and design user-friendly applications and platforms.

Conclusion

Creating empathy maps is a valuable practice for businesses that aim to connect with their audience on a deeper, emotional level. By following the key steps, best practices, and practical applications outlined in this guide, organizations can utilize empathy maps to build stronger relationships, develop products and services that meet customer needs and aspirations, and craft marketing campaigns that resonate with their audience's emotions. The continuous use of empathy maps empowers businesses to stay competitive, respond to changing customer dynamics, and foster lasting customer loyalty. In a customer-driven world, understanding and empathizing with your audience is not just a strategy; it's a commitment to delivering value and creating meaningful connections, and foster lasting customer loyalty. In a customer-driven world, understanding and empathizing with your audience is not just a strategy; it's a commitment to delivering value and creating meaningful connections.

Identifying Common Challenges Your Audience Faces: A Comprehensive Guide

Introduction

Understanding the challenges your target audience faces is a critical step in building a customer-centric approach to business. Whether you're a marketer, product developer, or service provider, recognizing and addressing your audience's pain points and obstacles is key to meeting their needs effectively. In this comprehensive article, we will explore the significance of identifying common challenges your audience faces, the key steps involved, best practices, and practical applications for businesses seeking to improve their offerings and customer relationships.

The Significance of Identifying Common Challenges

Identifying the common challenges your audience faces is pivotal for several reasons:

   a. Customer-Centric Approach: It enables businesses to focus on customer needs and concerns, fostering a customer-centric culture.

   b. Problem Solving: Understanding pain points and challenges empowers businesses to develop solutions that alleviate customer frustrations.

   c. Tailored Marketing: Using insights into common challenges allows for more targeted marketing campaigns that resonate with your audience.

d. Competitive Advantage: Businesses that effectively address customer challenges tend to outperform competitors.

e. Product and Service Improvement: Insights into audience challenges guide product development and service enhancements.

Key Steps in Identifying Common Challenges

To effectively identify common challenges your audience faces, follow these key steps:

a. Define Your Audience: Clearly outline who your target audience is, including demographics, preferences, and behaviors.

b. Gather Data: Collect data through surveys, interviews, focus groups, social media monitoring, and market research.

c. Analyze the Data: Examine the collected data to identify recurring pain points and challenges your audience encounters.

d. Categorize Challenges: Group identified challenges into categories, making it easier to prioritize and address them.

e. Validate Insights: Validate your findings by seeking feedback and input from your audience to ensure accuracy.

f. Prioritize Challenges: Prioritize the most critical and common challenges to address first.

Best Practices for Identifying Common Challenges

To maximize the effectiveness of your efforts in identifying common challenges, consider these best practices:

a. Gather Diverse Data: Use a variety of data sources, including surveys, interviews, and social media monitoring, to gain a comprehensive view.

   b. Leverage Technology: Utilize data analysis tools and software to streamline the process and identify patterns.

   c. Engage Cross-Functional Teams: Collaborate with teams from various departments, such as marketing, product development, and customer support, to gain a holistic view.

   d. Continuously Listen: Keep an ear to the ground and continuously gather and analyze data to stay responsive to evolving challenges.

   e. Empathize with Your Audience: Put yourself in your audience's shoes to better understand their frustrations and concerns.

Practical Applications for Addressing Common Challenges

Identifying common challenges your audience faces can be applied in various contexts, including:

   a. Product Development: Use insights into challenges to guide product and feature enhancements.

   b. Marketing Campaigns: Create marketing campaigns that directly address and offer solutions to common challenges.

   c. Customer Support: Train customer support teams to be well-equipped to handle and resolve common challenges.

   d. Content Creation: Develop content that educates and provides solutions to your audience's typical pain points.

   e. Strategic Planning: Utilize insights into common challenges to inform long-term business strategies and goals.

Real-World Examples of Identifying Common Challenges

Numerous businesses have successfully identified common challenges their audience faces:

a. Apple: Apple identified the challenge of file sharing among users and developed AirDrop as a solution.

b. Amazon: Amazon recognized the challenge of time-consuming shopping and introduced one-click shopping for convenience.

c. Slack: Slack addressed the challenge of workplace communication and collaboration by creating a centralized platform.

d. Zillow: Zillow identified the challenge of finding real estate listings and provided an easy-to-use platform for homebuyers and renters.

e. Uber: Uber recognized the challenge of transportation accessibility and created an efficient ride-sharing solution.

Conclusion

Identifying the common challenges your audience faces is a foundational step in providing customer-centric solutions and building lasting customer relationships. By following the key steps, best practices, and practical applications outlined in this guide, organizations can gain valuable insights into the challenges and pain points of their audience, allowing them to create products, services, and marketing campaigns that directly address these concerns. Addressing common challenges is not just a strategy; it's a commitment to providing solutions and improving the lives of your customers. In a customer-driven world, understanding and addressing your audience's challenges is the key to success and lasting customer loyalty.

Understanding the Emotional Aspect of Pain Points: A Comprehensive Guide

Introduction

Pain points, in the context of business and customer experience, refer to the specific problems, frustrations, or challenges that individuals face. They are critical for businesses to identify and address because they offer insights into what's preventing customers from achieving their goals or experiencing satisfaction. However, it's equally important to recognize that pain points often have emotional components. Understanding the emotional aspect of pain points is key to creating effective solutions and building stronger customer relationships. In this comprehensive article, we will explore the significance of understanding the emotional aspect of pain points, how to identify them, and best practices for addressing them.

The Significance of Understanding Emotional Pain Points

Recognizing and addressing emotional pain points is pivotal for several reasons:

a. Improved Customer Experience: By addressing emotional pain points, businesses can enhance the overall customer experience, making it more positive and satisfying.

b. Customer Retention: Understanding and resolving emotional pain points can foster loyalty and prevent customer churn.

c. Customer-Centric Approach: Recognizing the emotional aspects of pain points reflects a commitment to a customer-centric culture within the organization.

   d. Product and Service Enhancement: Insights into the emotional dimension of pain points guide the development of products and services that cater to customer needs and emotions.

   e. Empathy Building: It helps businesses build empathy and stronger connections with their customers.

Identifying Emotional Pain Points

To effectively identify emotional pain points, follow these steps:

   a. Conduct Customer Research: Gather data through surveys, interviews, and feedback forms to understand customer experiences and emotions.

   b. Look for Patterns: Analyze the data to identify recurring emotional pain points and feelings associated with specific challenges or frustrations.

   c. Consider Non-Verbal Clues: Sometimes, emotional pain points are conveyed through non-verbal cues such as tone of voice or body language.

   d. Empathize with Customers: Put yourself in the shoes of your customers to understand their emotions and frustrations.

   e. Seek Feedback: Actively seek feedback from your customers about their experiences and emotions.

Best Practices for Addressing Emotional Pain Points

To effectively address emotional pain points, consider these best practices:

a. Listen Actively: Pay close attention to customer feedback, both verbal and non-verbal, to understand their emotional responses.

b. Empathize: Show empathy by acknowledging and validating your customers' emotions and frustrations.

c. Provide Solutions: Develop and implement solutions that not only resolve practical issues but also consider the emotional aspects of the pain points.

d. Communicate Transparently: Keep customers informed about the actions you're taking to address their emotional pain points.

e. Train Your Teams: Educate and train your customer support and frontline teams to handle emotional pain points with empathy and care.

f. Gather Feedback Continuously: Make it a habit to collect ongoing feedback to ensure that emotional pain points are being effectively addressed.

Examples of Emotional Pain Points

Emotional pain points can manifest in various forms, such as:

a. Frustration: When customers find your website or product challenging to use, they may feel frustrated.

b. Annoyance: Inefficient processes or lack of information can lead to annoyance.

c. Anxiety: Uncertainty about a product's reliability or safety can cause anxiety.

d. Anger: Inadequate customer support or poor service can trigger anger in customers.

e. Confusion: When customers can't understand your instructions or communication, they may become confused.

f. Disappointment: Unmet expectations can result in disappointment.

Addressing Emotional Pain Points in Different Contexts

Understanding and addressing emotional pain points can be applied in various contexts:

a. Customer Support: Train your support teams to handle emotional pain points with empathy and provide solutions that address both practical and emotional concerns.

b. User Experience Design: Design user experiences that consider the emotional aspects of pain points, making interactions smoother and more pleasant.

c. Product Development: Use insights into emotional pain points to guide product improvements and feature development.

d. Marketing Campaigns: Create campaigns that resonate emotionally with your audience, showing that you understand and care about their concerns.

e. Crisis Management: In times of crises or negative incidents, address customer emotions by showing empathy, transparency, and commitment to resolution.

Conclusion

Understanding the emotional aspect of pain points is a vital step toward delivering a superior customer experience and building stronger customer relationships. By recognizing and addressing emotional pain points, businesses demonstrate their commitment to customer satisfaction, empathy, and customer-centric values. It is not just about resolving practical issues; it's about acknowledging and responding to the emotions and frustrations of your customers. In a customer-driven world, understanding and addressing the emotional aspects of pain points are the keys to success, customer loyalty, and lasting relationships.

Prioritizing Pain Points for Addressing: A Comprehensive Guide

Introduction

In the world of business and customer experience, "pain points" refer to specific issues or challenges that customers encounter while interacting with a product, service, or organization. Identifying and addressing these pain points is a crucial part of improving customer satisfaction and building strong, lasting relationships. However, not all pain points are created equal; some have a more significant impact on customers' experiences than others. Prioritizing pain points for addressing is essential to allocate resources effectively and deliver the most value to your customers. In this comprehensive article, we will explore the significance of prioritizing pain points, the key steps involved, best practices, and practical applications for businesses seeking to enhance their customer-centric approach.

The Significance of Prioritizing Pain Points

Prioritizing pain points is essential for several reasons:

a. Customer-Centric Approach: It demonstrates a commitment to putting the customer's needs first, fostering a customer-centric culture.

b. Efficient Resource Allocation: Prioritization allows businesses to allocate their resources, time, and efforts effectively, focusing on what matters most to customers.

c. Enhanced Customer Satisfaction: Addressing the most significant pain points results in improved customer satisfaction and loyalty.

d. Competitive Advantage: Businesses that actively identify and prioritize pain points often outperform competitors.

e. Problem Resolution: By focusing on the most pressing issues, businesses can tackle challenges more efficiently and effectively.

Key Steps in Prioritizing Pain Points

To effectively prioritize pain points for addressing, follow these key steps:

a. Gather Data: Collect data through surveys, interviews, customer feedback, and market research to identify pain points.

b. Analyze the Data: Examine the collected data to understand the frequency, severity, and impact of each pain point on customer experiences.

c. Categorize Pain Points: Group the identified pain points into categories, such as technical issues, communication problems, or service delays.

d. Weight the Severity: Assign a severity score to each pain point based on its impact on customers and the business.

e. Prioritize Based on Data: Use the data-driven analysis to prioritize pain points from the most to least severe.

f. Seek Stakeholder Input: Consult with relevant teams and stakeholders to ensure alignment and a holistic perspective.

Best Practices for Prioritizing Pain Points

To maximize the effectiveness of your efforts in prioritizing pain points, consider these best practices:

   a. Align with Business Goals: Ensure that the prioritization aligns with your business objectives and values.

   b. Involve Cross-Functional Teams: Collaboration between different departments and teams provides a more comprehensive view of pain points.

   c. Use Data Analysis Tools: Leverage data analysis tools and techniques to process and interpret customer feedback effectively.

   d. Communicate Transparently: Keep stakeholders informed about the prioritization process and the reasons behind the chosen order.

   e. Regularly Reevaluate: Periodically reassess the prioritization to adapt to changing customer needs and emerging pain points.

Practical Applications for Prioritization

Prioritizing pain points can be applied in various contexts, including:

   a. Product Development: Guide product and feature development to tackle the most critical pain points that impact customer satisfaction.

   b. Customer Support: Focus support efforts on addressing the most severe pain points, ensuring quick issue resolution.

   c. Service Enhancement: Improve customer service processes and policies to address the most critical customer pain points.

   d. Marketing Strategies: Tailor marketing campaigns to speak directly to the pain points that resonate with your audience.

e. User Experience Design: Design user experiences that prioritize addressing the most severe pain points to create a more pleasant interaction.

Real-World Examples of Prioritizing Pain Points

Many successful businesses prioritize pain points to enhance customer experiences:

a. Apple: Apple is known for its focus on addressing pain points related to product reliability and user-friendliness, which has led to customer loyalty.

b. Amazon: Amazon prioritizes pain points like delivery time uncertainty to improve customer trust.

c. Southwest Airlines: The airline consistently ranks high in customer satisfaction by prioritizing quick issue resolution and support for travelers.

d. Starbucks: Starbucks emphasizes a customer-centric approach by addressing pain points like long wait times in their cafes.

e. Airbnb: Airbnb addresses pain points related to trust and safety to create a more comfortable environment for its users.

Conclusion

Prioritizing pain points for addressing is a fundamental aspect of delivering superior customer experiences and building stronger customer relationships. By focusing on the most significant challenges first, businesses can significantly improve customer satisfaction and loyalty. Effective prioritization is not just about solving problems; it's about understanding and responding to the needs and preferences of your customers.

Using Data Analysis to Pinpoint Critical Issues: A Comprehensive Guide

Introduction

In today's data-driven world, businesses have access to an abundance of information. Harnessing the power of data is essential for understanding and improving various aspects of operations. Data analysis plays a crucial role in identifying and pinpointing critical issues that affect an organization's performance and customer satisfaction. In this comprehensive article, we will explore the significance of using data analysis to pinpoint critical issues, the key steps involved, best practices, and practical applications for businesses aiming to make data-driven decisions and enhance their performance.

The Significance of Using Data Analysis

Using data analysis to pinpoint critical issues is pivotal for several reasons:

   a. Informed Decision-Making: Data analysis provides a factual basis for making informed decisions, reducing the reliance on intuition.

   b. Early Detection: Data analysis allows organizations to detect critical issues early, before they escalate into major problems.

   c. Improved Efficiency: By identifying issues, organizations can allocate resources more efficiently to tackle the most critical concerns.

   d. Enhanced Customer Satisfaction: Pinpointing critical issues that impact customer experiences helps in addressing them promptly.

   e. Competitive Advantage: Businesses that effectively use data analysis to address critical issues outperform competitors.

Key Steps in Using Data Analysis

To effectively use data analysis to pinpoint critical issues, follow these key steps:

a. Data Collection: Gather relevant data from various sources, including customer feedback, sales records, customer service interactions, and operational reports.

b. Data Cleaning: Ensure that the collected data is accurate, complete, and free from errors or inconsistencies.

c. Data Transformation: Convert raw data into a format suitable for analysis, which may involve aggregating, summarizing, or restructuring the data.

d. Data Analysis: Utilize data analysis techniques and tools to identify patterns, trends, anomalies, and correlations within the data.

e. Issue Prioritization: Rank the identified issues based on their impact, severity, and urgency to focus on critical problems.

f. Root Cause Analysis: Investigate the underlying causes of critical issues to address the source of the problem, not just its symptoms.

g. Action Planning: Develop a detailed plan to address and resolve the critical issues based on the data analysis findings.

h. Implementation: Execute the action plan to address the critical issues, making the necessary changes and improvements.

i. Monitoring and Evaluation: Continuously monitor the progress and impact of the solutions to ensure they effectively address the critical issues.

Best Practices for Data Analysis

To maximize the effectiveness of using data analysis to pinpoint critical issues, consider these best practices:

a. Define Clear Objectives: Clearly define the goals and objectives of your data analysis to ensure alignment with organizational priorities.

b. Cross-Functional Collaboration: Involve teams from various departments to gain a comprehensive view and insights into critical issues.

c. Use Advanced Tools: Utilize data analysis software and tools to streamline the process and uncover complex patterns.

d. Regularly Collect Data: Ensure the continuous gathering of relevant data to stay responsive to changing circumstances.

e. Communicate Findings: Share the results and insights of data analysis with relevant stakeholders and teams.

Practical Applications for Data Analysis

Data analysis can be applied in various contexts, including:

a. Customer Experience Improvement: Analyze customer feedback and interactions to pinpoint critical issues affecting customer satisfaction.

b. Product Quality Enhancement: Use data analysis to identify defects or issues in product quality, leading to improvements.

c. Operations Optimization: Analyze operational data to identify bottlenecks or inefficiencies that hinder productivity.

d. Sales and Marketing Strategies: Use data analysis to identify trends and customer behaviors that impact sales and marketing strategies.

e. Risk Management: Analyze data to detect potential risks and vulnerabilities in business operations.

Real-World Examples of Using Data Analysis

Numerous businesses have successfully used data analysis to pinpoint critical issues and improve their operations:

a. Netflix: Netflix uses data analysis to personalize recommendations and enhance user engagement.

b. Amazon: Amazon employs data analysis to optimize its supply chain and predict customer preferences.

c. Walmart: Walmart utilizes data analysis to optimize inventory management and reduce waste.

d. Uber: Uber uses data analysis to forecast rider demand and manage driver supply efficiently.

e. Starbucks: Starbucks analyzes customer purchase data to tailor promotions and store layouts.

Conclusion

Using data analysis to pinpoint critical issues is a crucial step in improving operations, customer satisfaction, and overall performance. By following the key steps, best practices, and practical applications outlined in this guide, organizations can harness the power of data to make informed decisions, efficiently allocate resources, and address the most critical issues promptly. Data analysis is not just a process; it's a commitment to data-driven decision-making and continuous improvement. In a data-driven world, understanding and addressing critical issues is the key to success and ongoing growth.

Assessing the Impact of Pain Points on Decision-Making: A Comprehensive Guide

Introduction

In the realm of business and customer experience, pain points refer to specific issues or challenges that individuals face during interactions with products, services, or organizations. These pain points can significantly influence decision-making processes, both for customers and businesses. Assessing the impact of pain points on decision-making is a crucial step in understanding customer behavior and improving the decision-making processes within your organization. In this comprehensive article, we will explore the significance of assessing the impact of pain points, the key steps involved, best practices, and practical applications for businesses aiming to enhance their customer-centric approach and decision-making processes.

The Significance of Assessing the Impact of Pain Points

Assessing the impact of pain points is pivotal for several reasons:

   a. Informed Decision-Making: Understanding how pain points influence decision-making allows businesses to make more informed choices and improve processes.

   b. Customer-Centric Approach: It demonstrates a commitment to understanding and addressing customer needs, fostering a customer-centric culture.

c. Enhanced Customer Satisfaction: By addressing pain points effectively, businesses can significantly improve customer satisfaction and loyalty.

d. Competitive Advantage: Businesses that actively assess the impact of pain points often outperform competitors.

e. Efficient Resource Allocation: Knowing the significance of pain points helps in allocating resources more efficiently to tackle critical issues.

Key Steps in Assessing the Impact of Pain Points

To effectively assess the impact of pain points on decision-making, follow these key steps:

a. Identify Pain Points: Begin by identifying the pain points that customers encounter during their interactions with your products or services.

b. Gather Data: Collect data through surveys, interviews, customer feedback, and market research to understand the prevalence and severity of these pain points.

c. Analyze the Data: Utilize data analysis techniques and tools to identify patterns, trends, and correlations between pain points and decision-making behavior.

d. Categorize Pain Points: Group the identified pain points into categories, such as usability issues, service delays, communication problems, and pricing concerns.

e. Assess Decision-Making Impact: Evaluate how these pain points influence customer decision-making, such as purchase choices, brand loyalty, and repeat business.

f. Prioritize Pain Points: Rank the pain points based on their influence on decision-making to focus on the most impactful issues.

g. Seek Stakeholder Input: Consult with relevant teams and stakeholders to ensure alignment and a holistic perspective.

Best Practices for Assessing the Impact of Pain Points

To maximize the effectiveness of your efforts in assessing the impact of pain points, consider these best practices:

a. Use Data Analysis Tools: Leverage data analysis software and tools to streamline the process and uncover complex relationships between pain points and decision-making behavior.

b. Define Clear Objectives: Clearly define the goals and objectives of your assessment to ensure alignment with organizational priorities.

c. Cross-Functional Collaboration: Involve teams from various departments to gain a comprehensive view and insights into the impact of pain points.

d. Communicate Findings: Share the results and insights of your assessment with relevant stakeholders and teams to encourage data-driven decision-making.

e. Regularly Reevaluate: Periodically reassess the impact of pain points to adapt to changing customer needs and emerging pain points.

Practical Applications for Assessment

Assessing the impact of pain points can be applied in various contexts, including:

a. Product Development: Identify how pain points influence product choices and make informed decisions about product features and improvements.

b. Marketing Strategies: Understand the impact of pain points on brand perception and tailor marketing campaigns to address these issues.

c. Customer Service: Assess how pain points affect customer service interactions and optimize support processes accordingly.

d. User Experience Design: Use insights into the impact of pain points to design user experiences that address critical issues and enhance usability.

e. Pricing Strategies: Determine how pricing-related pain points influence purchasing decisions and adjust pricing strategies accordingly.

Real-World Examples of Impact Assessment

Numerous businesses have successfully assessed the impact of pain points on decision-making:

a. Apple: Apple assesses how user experience pain points influence brand loyalty and decision-making regarding product upgrades and new purchases.

b. Amazon: Amazon evaluates the impact of pain points related to shipping and delivery on customer satisfaction and purchase decisions.

c. Netflix: Netflix studies how content discovery pain points affect user engagement and content consumption choices.

d. Uber: Uber assesses the impact of pain points such as wait times and surge pricing on user decisions to use the platform.

e. Starbucks: Starbucks analyzes the influence of pain points like wait times and order accuracy on customer choices and loyalty.

Conclusion

Assessing the impact of pain points on decision-making is a fundamental aspect of understanding customer behavior and making more informed choices in your organization. By following the key steps, best practices, and practical applications outlined in this guide, businesses can better align their operations, marketing strategies, and product development efforts with customer needs and preferences. Assessing the impact of pain points is not just a process; it's a commitment to data-driven decision-making, customer satisfaction, and lasting customer relationships. In a customer-centric world, understanding and addressing the impact of pain points on decision-making is the key to success and ongoing growth.

Creating a Pain Point Scorecard: A Comprehensive Guide

Introduction

A pain point scorecard is a valuable tool for businesses seeking to systematically assess and prioritize the challenges and frustrations their customers encounter. By quantifying and categorizing pain points, organizations can make informed decisions about which issues to address first, ultimately improving customer satisfaction and loyalty. In this comprehensive article, we will explore the significance of creating a pain point scorecard, the key steps involved, best practices, and practical applications for businesses aiming to enhance their customer-centric approach and decision-making processes.

The Significance of Creating a Pain Point Scorecard

Creating a pain point scorecard is pivotal for several reasons:

   a. Informed Decision-Making: A pain point scorecard provides a data-driven basis for making decisions about which issues to address, reducing reliance on intuition.

   b. Prioritization: It enables organizations to prioritize pain points based on their severity, frequency, and impact on customer satisfaction.

   c. Customer-Centric Approach: A scorecard reflects a commitment to understanding and addressing customer needs and fostering a customer-centric culture.

   d. Efficient Resource Allocation: The scorecard helps in allocating resources efficiently by focusing efforts on the most critical issues.

e. Competitive Advantage: Businesses that actively create and use pain point scorecards often outperform competitors by addressing customer frustrations systematically.

Key Steps in Creating a Pain Point Scorecard

To effectively create a pain point scorecard, follow these key steps:

a. Identify Pain Points: Begin by identifying the pain points that customers encounter during their interactions with your products or services.

b. Define Scoring Criteria: Establish clear criteria for scoring pain points, considering factors like frequency, severity, and impact on customer satisfaction.

c. Gather Data: Collect data through surveys, interviews, customer feedback, and market research to understand the prevalence and impact of these pain points.

d. Score Pain Points: Use the established criteria to assign scores to each pain point, quantifying their severity and influence on customer experiences.

e. Categorize Pain Points: Group the identified pain points into categories or themes, such as usability issues, service delays, communication problems, or pricing concerns.

f. Calculate Total Scores: Calculate the total scores for each category by summing the scores of individual pain points within that category.

g. Prioritize Categories: Rank the categories based on their total scores to identify which themes represent the most significant customer challenges.

h. Seek Stakeholder Input: Consult with relevant teams and stakeholders to ensure alignment and a holistic perspective.

Best Practices for Creating a Pain Point Scorecard

To maximize the effectiveness of your pain point scorecard, consider these best practices:

   a. Use a Consistent Scoring System: Ensure that the scoring criteria are applied consistently to all pain points for accurate comparisons.

   b. Define Clear Objectives: Clearly define the goals and objectives of your scorecard to ensure alignment with organizational priorities.

   c. Cross-Functional Collaboration: Involve teams from various departments to gain a comprehensive view and insights into pain points.

   d. Communicate Findings: Share the results and insights of your scorecard with relevant stakeholders and teams to encourage data-driven decision-making.

   e. Regularly Update: Periodically update the pain point scorecard to adapt to changing customer needs and emerging pain points.

Practical Applications for a Pain Point Scorecard

A pain point scorecard can be applied in various contexts, including:

   a. Product Development: Use the scorecard to identify the most critical pain points that impact customer satisfaction and guide product improvements.

   b. Customer Support: Prioritize customer support efforts by addressing the most severe pain points, ensuring quick issue resolution.

c. Marketing Strategies: Tailor marketing campaigns to speak directly to the pain points that resonate with your audience.

   d. User Experience Design: Design user experiences that prioritize addressing the most significant pain points to create a more pleasant interaction.

   e. Operations Optimization: Analyze operational pain points to identify bottlenecks or inefficiencies that hinder productivity.

Real-World Examples of Pain Point Scorecards

Many successful businesses use pain point scorecards to enhance customer experiences:

   a. Airbnb: Airbnb uses a pain point scorecard to categorize and prioritize customer challenges and improve the overall guest experience.

   b. Southwest Airlines: The airline utilizes a scorecard to assess and prioritize customer feedback and pain points in its ongoing commitment to passenger satisfaction.

   c. Zappos: Zappos employs a pain point scorecard to systematically address issues related to customer service, ensuring a seamless shopping experience.

   d. Uber: Uber uses a scorecard to rank and address driver and rider pain points, enhancing its ride-sharing platform.

   e. Microsoft: Microsoft incorporates a pain point scorecard to gather and prioritize customer feedback for its software and service improvements.

Conclusion

Creating a pain point scorecard is a fundamental step in understanding and addressing customer challenges systematically. By following the key steps, best practices, and practical applications outlined in this guide, businesses can better align their operations, marketing strategies, and product development efforts with customer needs and preferences. A pain point scorecard is not just a tool; it's a commitment to data-driven decision-making, customer satisfaction, and lasting customer relationships. In a customer-centric world, understanding and addressing pain points through a scorecard is the key to success and ongoing growth.

Crafting Messaging that Resonates with Pain Points: A Comprehensive Guide

Introduction

In the world of marketing and communication, understanding and addressing customer pain points is essential for creating messaging that resonates and connects with your target audience. Pain points represent the challenges, frustrations, and problems that individuals experience in their lives. Crafting messaging that effectively speaks to these pain points can be a powerful way to capture attention, build trust, and drive desired actions. In this comprehensive article, we will explore the significance of crafting messaging that resonates with pain points, the key steps involved, best practices, and practical applications for businesses seeking to enhance their customer-centric communication strategies.

The Significance of Crafting Messaging that Resonates with Pain Points

Crafting messaging that resonates with pain points is crucial for several reasons:

  a. Audience Engagement: Tailoring your messaging to pain points captures the attention of your audience, making your communication more relatable and engaging.

  b. Empathy and Connection: Addressing pain points demonstrates empathy and understanding, fostering a stronger emotional connection with your audience.

c. Problem Solving: Messaging that resonates with pain points can showcase how your product or service offers solutions to the challenges your audience faces.

d. Brand Trust: Businesses that demonstrate an understanding of their audience's pain points are more likely to gain the trust of potential customers.

e. Call to Action: Effective pain point messaging can lead to clear and compelling calls to action that prompt the desired response from your audience.

Key Steps in Crafting Messaging that Resonates with Pain Points

To effectively craft messaging that resonates with pain points, follow these key steps:

a. Identify Pain Points: Start by identifying the pain points that your target audience encounters in their daily lives or when interacting with your products or services.

b. Customer Personas: Develop detailed customer personas to understand your audience's demographics, psychographics, behaviors, and motivations.

c. Pain Point Prioritization: Prioritize the identified pain points based on their severity and relevance to your audience.

d. Empathetic Language: Use empathetic language that acknowledges and understands the challenges your audience faces.

e. Pain Point Connection: Create a clear connection between your product or service and the resolution of the identified pain points.

f. Benefits-Oriented: Highlight the benefits of your offering as they relate to the specific pain points, emphasizing how they provide relief or solutions.

   g. Storytelling: Craft compelling stories that illustrate how your product or service has successfully addressed pain points for others.

   h. Clear Call to Action: Include a clear and action-oriented call to action (CTA) that guides your audience toward taking the next steps.

   i. Test and Refine: Continuously test and refine your messaging to ensure it resonates effectively with your audience's pain points.

Best Practices for Crafting Messaging

To maximize the effectiveness of crafting messaging that resonates with pain points, consider these best practices:

   a. Deep Customer Understanding: Invest time in understanding your audience's pain points, needs, and preferences through research and data analysis.

   b. Emotional Appeal: Tap into the emotional aspect of pain points to create messaging that connects on a personal level.

   c. Problem-Solution Alignment: Ensure that your messaging aligns your audience's pain points with your product or service as the solution.

   d. Testimonials and Social Proof: Incorporate testimonials and social proof to show that others have successfully overcome similar pain points with your offering.

   e. Clarity and Simplicity: Craft messaging that is clear, concise, and easy for your audience to understand.

Practical Applications for Crafting Messaging

Crafting messaging that resonates with pain points can be applied in various contexts, including:

a. Marketing Campaigns: Tailor your marketing campaigns to address the specific pain points of your target audience.

b. Product Descriptions: Create product descriptions that highlight how your offering resolves customer pain points.

c. Content Marketing: Develop content that addresses pain points, positioning your brand as a helpful resource.

d. Customer Service: Train your customer service representatives to communicate with empathy and address customer pain points effectively.

e. Sales Presentations: Craft sales presentations that directly connect your product or service to the resolution of pain points.

Real-World Examples of Pain Point Messaging

Many successful businesses have effectively used pain point messaging in their marketing and communication:

a. Nike: Nike's "Just Do It" campaign speaks to the pain points of procrastination and inaction by motivating individuals to take action and pursue their goals.

b. Apple: Apple's messaging often centers on the pain point of complexity in technology, emphasizing simplicity and user-friendliness.

c. Coca-Cola: Coca-Cola addresses the pain point of thirst and refreshment with its messaging, portraying its products as the perfect solutions.

d. Airbnb: Airbnb's messaging resonates with the pain point of expensive and impersonal hotel stays by offering unique and affordable accommodations.

e. Dove: Dove's "Real Beauty" campaign effectively resonates with the pain point of unrealistic beauty standards and encourages self-acceptance.

Conclusion

Crafting messaging that resonates with pain points is a fundamental aspect of customer-centric communication and effective marketing. By following the key steps, best practices, and practical applications outlined in this guide, businesses can better understand and address customer challenges, foster emotional connections, and guide their audience toward taking desired actions. Crafting messaging that speaks to pain points is not just a strategy; it's a commitment to empathy, problem-solving, and building lasting relationships with your audience. In a customer-centric world, understanding and addressing pain points is the key to successful and impactful communication.

Developing Solutions to Address Customer Pain Points: A Comprehensive Guide

Introduction

In the world of business, customer satisfaction is paramount. Addressing customer pain points is not only an opportunity but also an obligation for businesses to provide value, build trust, and retain loyal customers. Developing effective solutions to address these pain points is essential for ensuring that customers have positive experiences and remain engaged with your brand. In this comprehensive article, we will explore the significance of developing solutions for customer pain points, the key steps involved, best practices, and practical applications for businesses seeking to enhance their customer-centric approach and improve their products and services.

The Significance of Addressing Customer Pain Points

Addressing customer pain points is pivotal for several reasons:

   a. Customer Satisfaction: Resolving pain points leads to improved customer satisfaction, which is essential for retaining customers and building loyalty.

   b. Competitive Advantage: Businesses that actively address customer pain points often outperform competitors by offering superior products or services.

c. Customer-Centric Approach: It demonstrates a commitment to understanding and meeting customer needs, fostering a customer-centric culture.

d. Product and Service Improvement: By identifying and addressing pain points, businesses can continuously improve their offerings.

e. Long-Term Relationships: Addressing pain points not only retains existing customers but also helps to create lasting, mutually beneficial relationships.

Key Steps in Developing Solutions for Customer Pain Points

To effectively develop solutions for customer pain points, follow these key steps:

a. Identify Pain Points: Begin by identifying and thoroughly understanding the specific pain points that customers encounter during their interactions with your products or services.

b. Gather Customer Feedback: Actively seek feedback from customers through surveys, interviews, reviews, and direct communication channels.

c. Prioritize Pain Points: Rank the identified pain points based on their impact on customer satisfaction, frequency of occurrence, and alignment with your business goals.

d. Cross-Functional Collaboration: Involve teams from various departments to collaborate on finding solutions, as different perspectives can lead to more effective problem-solving.

e. Ideate Solutions: Brainstorm potential solutions to address each prioritized pain point, considering a range of ideas and strategies.

f. Test and Validate: Prototype, test, and validate the solutions to ensure they effectively resolve the identified pain points.

   g. Develop a Rollout Plan: Create a plan for implementing the solutions, which may involve changes to processes, products, services, or customer communication.

   h. Monitor and Evaluate: Continuously monitor the results and impact of the implemented solutions to make adjustments as needed.

Best Practices for Developing Solutions

To maximize the effectiveness of developing solutions for customer pain points, consider these best practices:

   a. Data-Driven Decision-Making: Base your solutions on data and evidence from customer feedback and market research.

   b. Customer Involvement: Involve customers in the solution development process, considering their input and feedback.

   c. Continuous Improvement: Recognize that addressing pain points is an ongoing process, and consistently seek to improve and evolve your solutions.

   d. Empathy and Understanding: Approach the development of solutions with a deep understanding of the emotional and practical aspects of customer pain points.

   e. Clear Communication: Clearly communicate the changes and solutions to customers, ensuring they understand how their pain points are being addressed.

Practical Applications for Developing Solutions

Developing solutions for customer pain points can be applied in various contexts, including:

a. Product Development: Enhance existing products or create new ones to directly address customer pain points.

b. Customer Support: Improve customer support processes and training to effectively address and resolve customer pain points.

c. Service Enhancement: Enhance the quality of services, addressing customer pain points in service delivery and customer interactions.

d. Marketing Strategies: Craft marketing messages that highlight how your products or services effectively resolve customer pain points.

e. User Experience Design: Redesign user experiences to prioritize addressing the most significant customer pain points, making interactions more pleasant.

Real-World Examples of Pain Point Solutions

Numerous businesses have successfully developed solutions to address customer pain points:

a. Apple: Apple consistently updates its products to address pain points related to user-friendliness and product reliability.

b. Amazon: Amazon addresses pain points related to delivery times and reliability through its Prime service.

c. Zappos: Zappos has built its reputation on superior customer service, addressing pain points in the online shopping experience.

d. Airbnb: Airbnb addresses pain points related to trust and safety by implementing rigorous identity verification and host/guest review systems.

e. Starbucks: Starbucks has improved its customer service and ordering processes to address pain points like long wait times and order accuracy.

Conclusion

Developing solutions to address customer pain points is a fundamental aspect of improving customer satisfaction, building trust, and creating lasting customer relationships. By following the key steps, best practices, and practical applications outlined in this guide, businesses can better understand customer challenges and foster a culture of customer-centricity and continuous improvement. Addressing customer pain points is not just a strategy; it's a commitment to empathy, problem-solving, and providing exceptional value to your customers. In a customer-centric world, understanding and addressing pain points is the key to success and long-term growth.

Personalizing Your Approach for Each Customer: A Comprehensive Guide

Introduction

In today's highly competitive business landscape, one-size-fits-all approaches are no longer effective. To stand out and create meaningful connections with customers, personalization is key. Personalizing your approach for each customer involves tailoring your communication, products, and services to meet individual needs and preferences. In this comprehensive article, we will explore the significance of personalization, the key steps involved, best practices, and practical applications for businesses aiming to enhance their customer-centric approach and build stronger, more lasting relationships with their customers.

The Significance of Personalizing Your Approach

Personalizing your approach for each customer is pivotal for several reasons:

a. Customer Satisfaction: Personalization leads to higher customer satisfaction by demonstrating that you understand and value each customer's unique needs.

b. Customer Loyalty: Personalized experiences often result in increased customer loyalty, as customers are more likely to stick with businesses that cater to their preferences.

c. Competitive Advantage: Businesses that offer personalized services and communication have a competitive edge over those with generic, mass-market approaches.

d. Enhanced Engagement: Personalization drives better customer engagement, increasing the chances of repeat business and referrals.

e. Data Utilization: Personalization relies on data, enabling businesses to make data-driven decisions that improve the customer experience.

Key Steps in Personalizing Your Approach

To effectively personalize your approach for each customer, follow these key steps:

a. Data Collection: Gather customer data through various sources, including surveys, website analytics, purchase history, and customer feedback.

b. Customer Segmentation: Divide your customer base into segments based on common characteristics, behaviors, and preferences.

c. Analyze Data: Use data analysis tools to identify patterns and trends within customer segments.

d. Customize Communication: Craft personalized messages, content, and offers tailored to each customer segment.

e. Product and Service Personalization: Modify your products or services to cater to the specific needs and preferences of each customer segment.

f. Personalization Platforms: Utilize customer relationship management (CRM) systems and personalization software to streamline the process.

g. Feedback Loop: Continuously collect feedback and data to refine and adapt your personalization strategies.

Best Practices for Personalization

To maximize the effectiveness of personalizing your approach, consider these best practices:

   a. Respect Privacy: Ensure that you handle customer data with care and in compliance with data protection regulations.

   b. Start Simple: Begin with basic personalization, such as addressing customers by their names and sending relevant product recommendations.

   c. Test and Iterate: Regularly test different personalization strategies and adapt them based on performance and customer feedback.

   d. Train Your Team: Educate your team on the importance of personalization and how to effectively implement it in their roles.

   e. Be Transparent: Inform customers about how their data is being used to personalize their experiences and obtain their consent.

Practical Applications for Personalization

Personalization can be applied in various contexts, including:

   a. Email Marketing: Craft personalized email campaigns that address customer interests and behaviors.

   b. E-commerce: Offer product recommendations and personalized shopping experiences based on customer browsing and purchase history.

   c. Content Marketing: Tailor content to individual preferences, increasing engagement and relevance.

   d. Customer Support: Use customer data to personalize support interactions and provide more efficient solutions.

e. Loyalty Programs: Create personalized loyalty programs that offer rewards based on customer behaviors and preferences.

Real-World Examples of Personalization

Many successful businesses employ personalization to enhance customer experiences:

a. Amazon: Amazon's product recommendation engine suggests items based on a customer's browsing and purchase history.

b. Netflix: Netflix personalizes content recommendations based on viewing history and user preferences.

c. Spotify: Spotify curates personalized playlists and recommendations based on user listening habits.

d. Starbucks: Starbucks' mobile app offers personalized offers, rewards, and recommendations to individual customers.

e. Airbnb: Airbnb personalizes property recommendations and travel guides based on user search history and preferences.

Conclusion

Personalizing your approach for each customer is a fundamental aspect of creating memorable customer experiences, building trust, and fostering customer loyalty. By following the key steps, best practices, and practical applications outlined in this guide, businesses can create more meaningful connections with their customers and improve their overall satisfaction. Personalization is not just a strategy; it's a commitment to understanding and catering to the unique needs of each customer. In a customer-centric world, personalizing your approach is the key to success and ongoing growth.

Mapping Pain Point Solutions to Your Product/Service: A Comprehensive Guide

Introduction

In today's customer-centric business landscape, understanding and addressing the pain points of your target audience is crucial. Once you've identified these pain points, it's equally important to map solutions to your products or services. This process not only improves your offerings but also demonstrates a commitment to providing value and enhancing customer satisfaction. In this comprehensive article, we will explore the significance of mapping pain point solutions, the key steps involved, best practices, and practical applications for businesses seeking to align their products and services with customer needs more effectively.

The Significance of Mapping Pain Point Solutions

Mapping pain point solutions to your product or service is essential for several reasons:

   a. Customer Satisfaction: Addressing pain points leads to higher customer satisfaction by offering practical solutions to their challenges.

   b. Improved Customer Retention: Satisfied customers are more likely to remain loyal, reducing churn and increasing customer lifetime value.

   c. Competitive Advantage: Businesses that proactively address pain points stand out in the market, gaining a competitive edge.

d. Enhanced Brand Reputation: Addressing pain points builds trust and a positive brand reputation as customers perceive you as a solution-oriented company.

   e. Customer-Centric Focus: Aligning your offerings with pain point solutions fosters a customer-centric culture within your organization.

Key Steps in Mapping Pain Point Solutions

To effectively map pain point solutions to your product or service, follow these key steps:

   a. Identify Pain Points: Begin by identifying and thoroughly understanding the specific pain points that your target audience encounters during their interactions with your industry or related products and services.

   b. Cross-Functional Collaboration: Involve teams from various departments to gain a comprehensive view of how your product or service can address identified pain points.

   c. Ideate Solutions: Brainstorm potential solutions and adaptations to your product or service that would effectively resolve the identified pain points.

   d. Test and Validate: Prototype, test, and validate the solutions to ensure they successfully resolve the identified pain points without creating new challenges.

   e. Product/Service Adjustments: Modify your product or service based on the validated solutions, ensuring they effectively address customer pain points.

   f. Communication and Training: Train your teams to communicate the product or service changes effectively, both internally and externally.

g. Continuous Improvement: Continuously monitor the results and impact of the implemented solutions and make adjustments as needed.

Best Practices for Mapping Pain Point Solutions

To maximize the effectiveness of mapping pain point solutions, consider these best practices:

a. Data-Driven Decisions: Base your solutions on data and feedback from customers, ensuring you address their most pressing pain points.

b. Prioritize Impactful Solutions: Focus on solutions that have the most significant impact on customer satisfaction and loyalty.

c. Customer Involvement: Involve customers in the solution development process, consider their input, and gather feedback to ensure your solutions align with their expectations.

d. Scalability: Ensure that the solutions can be scaled effectively to meet the needs of your entire customer base.

e. Stay Agile: Be open to adaptation and quick adjustments as customer pain points evolve or new ones arise.

Practical Applications for Mapping Pain Point Solutions

Mapping pain point solutions can be applied in various contexts, including:

a. Product Development: Enhance existing products or create new ones that directly address customer pain points.

b. Service Enhancement: Improve the quality of your services to address customer pain points in service delivery and interactions.

c. User Experience Design: Redesign user experiences to prioritize addressing the most significant customer pain points, making interactions more pleasant.

d. Process Optimization: Analyze operational pain points to identify bottlenecks or inefficiencies and optimize processes to address them.

e. Marketing Strategies: Develop marketing messages and campaigns that highlight how your products or services effectively resolve customer pain points.

Real-World Examples of Pain Point Solutions

Many successful businesses have effectively mapped pain point solutions to their products and services:

a. Uber: Uber addressed the pain point of unreliable taxis by providing a user-friendly app that allows customers to book rides quickly and conveniently.

b. Airbnb: Airbnb addressed the pain point of expensive and impersonal hotel stays by offering unique, affordable accommodations and experiences.

c. Apple: Apple's user-friendly devices addressed the pain point of complicated technology, providing products that are intuitive and easy to use.

d. Amazon: Amazon improved the convenience of shopping, addressing the pain point of busy schedules, with features like one-click purchasing and fast delivery.

e. Zappos: Zappos resolved the pain point of impersonal online shopping with exceptional customer service, free shipping, and hassle-free returns.

Conclusion

Mapping pain point solutions to your product or service is a fundamental aspect of improving customer satisfaction, building trust, and creating lasting customer relationships. By following the key steps, best practices, and practical applications outlined in this guide, businesses can effectively address customer challenges and foster a culture of customer-centricity and continuous improvement. Addressing customer pain points is not just a strategy; it's a commitment to empathy, problem-solving, and providing exceptional value to your customers. In a customer-centric world, mapping pain point solutions is the key to success and ongoing growth.

Building Trust Through Addressing Pain Points

Introduction

Trust is the foundation of any healthy relationship, whether it's in personal life or business. In the business world, building trust with your customers or clients is vital for long-term success. One effective way to establish trust is by addressing pain points. Pain points are the specific challenges, problems, or concerns that your target audience faces. By identifying and addressing these pain points, you can demonstrate empathy, competence, and a commitment to meeting your customers' needs. In this article, we'll explore the importance of addressing pain points in building trust and provide a comprehensive guide on how to do it effectively.

Understanding Pain Points

1. Identifying Pain Points:

To address pain points effectively, you first need to identify them. This involves understanding your target audience, conducting research, and actively listening to your customers. Pain points can vary greatly between industries, demographics, and even individual customers. Common pain points might include pricing concerns, slow customer support, product defects, or a lack of necessary features. Conduct surveys, focus groups, and market research to uncover these pain points.

2. Prioritizing Pain Points:

Not all pain points are created equal. Some may be minor inconveniences, while others could be deal-breakers. Prioritize the pain points based on their severity and the number of customers they affect. This helps you allocate your resources and efforts more effectively.

Addressing Pain Points

1. Communication:

Once you've identified and prioritized pain points, open a channel of communication with your customers. Let them know you're actively seeking to improve their experience. Transparency is essential in building trust. Share your plans for addressing their concerns and keep them updated on progress.

2. Empathy:

Show genuine empathy toward your customers' pain points. Understand their frustrations and concerns and let them know you're committed to finding solutions. This humanizes your brand and shows that you care about their well-being.

3. Quality Solutions:

Effective problem-solving is the key to addressing pain points. Invest in developing high-quality solutions that directly alleviate the identified issues. Whether it's improved customer service, better product features, or a more competitive pricing model, make sure your solutions are practical and customer-focused.

4. Consistency:

Consistency is critical for trust-building. Ensure that the solutions you provide are consistently implemented and maintained. This means following through on your promises and continuously monitoring and adjusting your approach as necessary.

Case Study: Amazon's Approach to Addressing Pain Points

Amazon, a global e-commerce giant, is a prime example of a company that excels in addressing customer pain points. They have identified and addressed several common pain points, such as:

a. Shipping Delays: Amazon introduced Amazon Prime for faster shipping, addressing the pain point of delayed deliveries.

b. Product Quality Concerns: Amazon created AmazonBasics, its own line of reliable, low-cost products to address quality concerns.

c. Returns and Refunds: Amazon has a hassle-free return policy that eases customer concerns about returns and refunds.

By consistently addressing these pain points, Amazon has built a reputation for trustworthiness, customer-centricity, and reliability.

Maintaining Trust

Building trust is an ongoing process. Once you've effectively addressed pain points and established trust with your customers, it's essential to maintain it. Here are some key principles to keep in mind:

1. Continual Improvement: Never stop seeking ways to enhance your products, services, and customer experiences. New pain points may arise, and old ones might resurface.

2. Feedback Loop: Maintain an open feedback loop with your customers. Encourage them to share their experiences, concerns, and suggestions.

3. Adaptability: Be ready to adapt to changes in your industry, market, and customer preferences. Stagnation can erode trust.

4. Deliver on Promises: Consistently deliver on your promises and commitments. This reinforces the trust you've built.

Conclusion

Building trust through addressing pain points is a dynamic and ongoing process. By identifying, prioritizing, and effectively resolving your customers' concerns, you demonstrate a genuine commitment to their well-being. This, in turn, fosters trust and loyalty, which are invaluable in the world of business. Remember that trust takes time to develop, but it can be easily lost if not carefully maintained. By consistently addressing pain points and making customer satisfaction a top priority, you can create a strong foundation of trust that will benefit your business for years to come.

Measuring the Effectiveness of Your Solutions

Introduction

In both business and personal life, we constantly encounter problems and seek solutions. Whether you're running a company, managing a project, or simply trying to improve your daily routines, measuring the effectiveness of the solutions you implement is crucial. Effectiveness evaluation provides valuable insights into whether your chosen approach is achieving the desired outcomes or whether adjustments are needed. In this comprehensive guide, we will explore various methods and strategies to measure the effectiveness of your solutions.

Define Clear Objectives and Metrics

Before implementing any solution, it's essential to define clear objectives and the key performance indicators (KPIs) that will help measure the solution's success. Your objectives should be specific, measurable, achievable, relevant, and time-bound (SMART). When you have well-defined goals, you can create a roadmap for success.

Pre-Implementation Baseline Data

Gathering baseline data before implementing a solution is essential. This data serves as a reference point for measuring the solution's effectiveness. For instance, if you're introducing a new marketing strategy, collect data on key metrics like website traffic, conversion rates, and revenue before making any changes.

Key Performance Indicators (KPIs)

KPIs are measurable values that reflect the performance of your solution. Depending on your objectives, KPIs can encompass a wide range of metrics, including financial indicators (e.g., revenue, ROI), customer satisfaction (e.g., NPS scores), efficiency (e.g., project completion time), and more. Each KPI should directly align with your objectives.

Surveys and Feedback

Collecting feedback from relevant stakeholders, including employees, customers, or project team members, can provide valuable qualitative data. Surveys, interviews, and focus groups can help you understand their perspectives and experiences regarding the solution. This data can complement quantitative metrics and provide insights into the solution's overall impact.

Comparative Analysis

Comparing the performance of your solution to a previous state or to industry benchmarks can be highly informative. For example, if you're improving your website's loading speed, compare the new speed to the old one or to industry standards to assess the solution's impact.

Cost-Benefit Analysis

Calculate the costs associated with implementing your solution and compare them to the benefits it provides. This cost-benefit analysis (CBA) helps you determine if the solution is financially viable and if the benefits outweigh the expenses.

A/B Testing

In scenarios where you have multiple potential solutions or variations, A/B testing can help you identify which one is more effective. This method involves running two or more versions concurrently and comparing their performance. A/B testing is commonly used in marketing, web design, and product development.

Post-Implementation Data

Continuously collect data and monitor the solution's performance after implementation. Real-time data allows you to identify trends and make necessary adjustments as early as possible. Regularly updated data is crucial for long-term success.

Feedback Loops

Create mechanisms for ongoing feedback and improvement. Encourage stakeholders to share their experiences and suggestions and be ready to adapt based on their input. This iterative approach helps maintain and enhance the solution's effectiveness over time.

Reporting and Visualization

Utilize data visualization tools and reports to present your findings in a clear and understandable manner. Visualizing data through charts, graphs, and dashboards can help stakeholders quickly grasp the solution's impact.

Conclusion

Measuring the effectiveness of your solutions is a critical aspect of decision-making and problem-solving in various domains. By defining clear objectives, utilizing KPIs, collecting data, and employing analysis techniques, you can gain a deeper understanding of whether your solutions are achieving the desired outcomes. Remember that the evaluation process should be ongoing, with a willingness to adjust and adapt as needed. An effective solution isn't static; it's a dynamic response to changing circumstances and the pursuit of continuous improvement.

The Power of Testimonials and Success Stories

Introduction

Testimonials and success stories are potent tools for businesses, organizations, and individuals seeking to build trust, establish credibility, and showcase their achievements. Whether you are running a business, a nonprofit, or promoting a personal brand, gathering and sharing testimonials and success stories can significantly impact your reputation and influence others. In this comprehensive guide, we will explore the importance of testimonials and success stories, how to gather them effectively, and how to leverage them to achieve your goals.

The Significance of Testimonials and Success Stories

1. Establishing Credibility

Testimonials and success stories offer third-party validation of your capabilities. They serve as evidence that you have satisfied customers or helped individuals achieve their goals, establishing credibility and trust.

2. Building Trust

Trust is a cornerstone of any successful relationship, and it's equally crucial in business or personal branding. Testimonials and success stories build trust by showcasing real experiences and outcomes, assuaging doubts and uncertainties.

3. Social Proof

Human behavior is often influenced by the actions and opinions of others. Testimonials and success stories provide social proof, demonstrating that others have benefited from your products, services, or expertise, making it more likely that new customers or followers will do the same.

Gathering Testimonials

1. Request Permission

Before using someone's testimonial, ensure you have their explicit consent. Reach out to customers, clients, or individuals whose experiences align with your goals and ask for permission to use their words.

2. Timing MattersCapture testimonials at the right time. Ideally, ask for feedback immediately after a positive experience or achievement. The details will be fresher in their minds, leading to more authentic and compelling testimonials.

3. Make it Easy

Simplify the process for your customers or clients to provide testimonials. Offer a variety of channels, such as online forms, email, or social media, and guide them through the process with clear instructions.

4. Offer Incentives

Incentives, such as discounts, freebies, or recognition, can motivate individuals to share their experiences. However, ensure that incentives do not compromise the authenticity of the testimonials.

5. Personalize the Request

Tailor your request for testimonials to the individual's specific experience. Ask them to share the details that are most relevant to your goals, making their responses more compelling.

Creating Compelling Success Stories

1. Choose Relevant Subjects

Select success stories that align with your goals and resonate with your target audience. Look for cases that demonstrate the benefits of your products, services, or expertise in a clear and relatable way.

2. Structure the Story

Craft a narrative that outlines the problem, the solution (your product or service), and the results. A compelling structure engages the reader or viewer and keeps them invested in the story.

3. Use Real Data

Include quantifiable data to support your success stories. This might include statistics, metrics, or before-and-after comparisons. Hard numbers provide additional credibility.

4. Include Visuals

Visual elements, such as photos or videos, add authenticity and relatability to your success stories. They help humanize the individuals or customers behind the story.

Leveraging Testimonials and Success Stories

1. Share on Multiple Platforms

Distribute your testimonials and success stories on various platforms, including your website, social media, marketing materials, and email campaigns. Wider exposure increases the chances of reaching your target audience.

2. Integrate into Sales and Marketing

Use testimonials in your sales and marketing efforts. Incorporate them into your sales pitches, website copy, and advertising materials to enhance your credibility and influence purchasing decisions.

3. Case Study Content

Create in-depth case studies that delve into the details of success stories. These can be used as valuable content for blogs, ebooks, or whitepapers, attracting potential customers and providing insights into your offerings.

Conclusion

Testimonials and success stories are invaluable assets for establishing credibility, building trust, and providing social proof. When gathered effectively and leveraged strategically, they can significantly enhance your reputation and influence your target audience. By focusing on the authenticity and relatability of these stories, you can create a powerful narrative that resonates with those you aim to reach. Remember, the impact of these stories is not just in the words themselves but in the real experiences and outcomes they represent.

Section 3: Effective Communication Without Being Salesy

The Psychology of Sales and Persuasion

Introduction

Sales and persuasion are at the heart of many aspects of our lives, from convincing someone to buy a product to influencing colleagues in the workplace. Understanding the psychology behind these processes is essential for success. This comprehensive guide delves into the psychology of sales and persuasion, exploring key principles, strategies, and techniques that can help individuals and businesses become more effective at persuading others to take desired actions.

The Psychology of Persuasion

1. Reciprocity

Reciprocity is a fundamental principle of persuasion. It posits that when you do something for someone, they feel a social obligation to return the favor. In sales, offering value, whether it's in the form of information, a sample, or a small gift, can create a sense of reciprocity, making potential customers more inclined to make a purchase.

2. Scarcity

The scarcity principle is based on the idea that people value things more when they are perceived as rare or in short supply. Limited-time offers, exclusive deals, or highlighting product scarcity can boost sales by tapping into the fear of missing out (FOMO) in customers.

3. Authority

Credibility plays a significant role in persuasion. People are more likely to follow the advice or buy from someone they perceive as an authority figure. Establish your expertise in your field and utilize authority figures in your marketing to boost trust and influence.

4. Consistency

Consistency is the principle that individuals tend to act in ways that align with their past behavior and commitments. By getting someone to commit to a small action or belief related to your product or service, you can influence them to make more significant commitments, such as a purchase.

5. Liking

People are more likely to be persuaded by those they know, like, and trust. Building rapport, finding common ground, and demonstrating genuine interest in others are all strategies for increasing likability and, subsequently, persuasion.

The Psychology of Sales

1. Understand Customer Needs

Effective salespeople focus on understanding their customers' needs, pain points, and desires. This psychological insight enables them to tailor their approach and product offerings to precisely match what the customer is looking for.

2. Use Social Proof

The concept of social proof is based on the idea that people look to others for guidance when making decisions. Utilize testimonials, reviews, and case studies to demonstrate that others have had positive experiences with your product or service.

3. Overcome Objections

Objections are natural in the sales process. Effective salespeople are adept at addressing objections with empathy, understanding, and facts.

By acknowledging and overcoming objections, they build trust and move closer to a sale.

4. Create a Sense of Urgency

The psychology of sales often involves creating a sense of urgency. Limited-time offers, deadlines, or highlighting the consequences of inaction can motivate customers to make a decision quickly.

5. Emotional Storytelling

Emotions play a significant role in decision-making. Telling compelling stories that resonate with customers on an emotional level can make your product or service more relatable and desirable.

Persuasion Techniques

1. Framing

How information is presented can significantly impact how it's perceived. Framing involves presenting information in a way that highlights the positive aspects or the potential loss if someone doesn't take action.

2. Anchoring

Anchoring is a technique where you present a high-value option before offering a lower-priced option. This makes the lower-priced option appear more attractive and can lead to increased sales.

3. The Decoy Effect

The decoy effect involves introducing a third, less attractive option to make the second option look more appealing. It can influence decision-making by directing people toward a specific choice.

4. Psychological Pricing

Price perception can be manipulated through psychological pricing. For example, pricing a product at $9.99 instead of $10 creates the perception of a significantly lower cost.

Conclusion

Understanding the psychology of sales and persuasion is essential for individuals and businesses seeking to influence others effectively. By employing the principles and techniques outlined in this comprehensive guide, you can become a more persuasive and successful communicator. Whether you're in sales, marketing, leadership, or simply looking to enhance your personal persuasive abilities, the knowledge of human psychology and the strategies for utilizing it can significantly improve your outcomes. Remember, ethical persuasion is built on trust, empathy, and a genuine desire to provide value to others.

Building Rapport with Potential Customers

Introduction

Building rapport with potential customers is a fundamental skill in sales and business development. It's the foundation of a positive, trusting relationship that can lead to successful transactions and long-term customer loyalty. In this comprehensive guide, we will explore the importance of building rapport, the psychology behind it, and practical strategies to establish genuine connections with potential customers.

The Importance of Building Rapport

1. Trust and Credibility

Rapport-building is crucial for establishing trust and credibility. When potential customers feel comfortable and connected with you, they are more likely to trust your recommendations and engage with your products or services.

2. Communication

Rapport enhances communication. When you have a strong rapport with someone, they are more open and willing to share their needs, concerns, and expectations. This, in turn, allows you to tailor your offerings to their specific requirements.

3. Customer Retention

A strong rapport can lead to long-term customer relationships. Satisfied and connected customers are more likely to return and become loyal advocates for your brand.

The Psychology of Rapport Building

1. Empathy

Empathy is the ability to understand and share the feelings of another. Demonstrating empathy is key to building rapport because it shows you genuinely care about your potential customers' needs and concerns. Actively listen to their thoughts and feelings and respond with compassion and understanding.

2. Non-Verbal Communication

Non-verbal cues, such as body language, facial expressions, and tone of voice, play a significant role in building rapport. Maintain good eye contact, use open and welcoming body language, and ensure your tone is warm and friendly.

3. Active Listening

Active listening is the art of paying full attention to the speaker, processing their words, and responding thoughtfully. Ask open-ended questions to encourage potential customers to share more about themselves, their needs, and their pain points. Show that you value what they say by summarizing or reflecting on their words.

4. Common Ground

Establishing common ground or shared interests helps foster rapport. Find topics or experiences that you both relate to, such as shared hobbies, experiences, or values. These shared connections can create a bond and make conversations more enjoyable.

Practical Strategies for Building Rapport

1. Do Your Homework

Before interacting with potential customers, research their background, preferences, and needs. This knowledge allows you to start conversations with relevant and engaging topics, showcasing your genuine interest in their concerns.

2. Personalize Your Approach

Tailor your interactions to the individual. Address them by name, remember previous conversations or interactions, and show that you've paid attention to their unique circumstances.

3. Be Authentic

Authenticity is key to building rapport. Be yourself and let your genuine personality shine through. Trying to be someone you're not will come across as insincere.

4. Use Positive Reinforcement

Positivity goes a long way in building rapport. Offer sincere compliments, express appreciation, and maintain an optimistic attitude. Positivity is contagious and can create a pleasant interaction.

5. Find Shared Goals

Discover and highlight shared goals and objectives. When potential customers see that you're aligned in your objectives, they are more likely to trust your guidance and recommendations.

6. Be Patient

Building rapport takes time. Don't rush the process or push for a sale too soon. Allow the connection to develop naturally.

Conclusion

Building rapport with potential customers is not just a sales technique; it's a foundation for lasting, meaningful relationships. When you connect on a personal level, demonstrate empathy, and actively listen, you create an environment in which trust, credibility, and loyalty can flourish. By following the strategies and principles outlined in this comprehensive guide, you can improve your rapport-building skills and create valuable connections that lead to success in business and beyond.

Creating a Genuine Connection with Your Audience

Introduction

In today's information-saturated world, connecting with your audience on a deeper, more personal level has become crucial. Whether you are a content creator, marketer, educator, or public speaker, creating a genuine connection with your audience can make the difference between a fleeting interaction and a loyal, engaged following. This comprehensive guide explores the importance of building authentic connections, the psychological underpinnings, and practical strategies to foster meaningful relationships with your audience.

The Importance of Creating a Genuine Connection

1. Trust and Relatability

Genuine connections breed trust and relatability. When your audience perceives you as authentic and sincere, they are more likely to trust your message, recommendations, and intentions.

2. Engagement

Audiences are more likely to engage with content and participate in discussions when they feel a personal connection. This engagement not only boosts interaction but also helps you better understand your audience's needs, preferences, and feedback.

3. Brand Loyalty

Creating a genuine connection with your audience can result in long-term brand loyalty. Loyal followers are not only repeat customers but also enthusiastic advocates who spread the word about your content, products, or services.

The Psychology of Creating a Connection

1. Authenticity

Authenticity is the bedrock of creating a genuine connection. Audiences value individuals and brands that stay true to their values, beliefs, and principles. Embracing your authentic self fosters a sense of trust and resonance with your audience.

2. Empathy

Empathy is the ability to understand and share the feelings of others. It plays a critical role in creating a connection because it shows that you genuinely care about your audience's needs, challenges, and emotions. Listening actively and empathizing with your audience fosters trust and connection.

3. Storytelling

Humans have a natural affinity for stories. Narratives, when used effectively, can create an emotional connection. Share personal stories, case studies, or anecdotes that allow your audience to see the human side of your brand or persona.

4. Vulnerability

Being vulnerable means sharing your challenges, mistakes, and imperfections. This transparency can be powerful in building a connection because it humanizes you and makes you more relatable. Vulnerability fosters trust and invites others to open up as well.

Practical Strategies for Creating a Genuine Connection

1. Understand Your Audience

To create a genuine connection, you must understand your audience's demographics, preferences, values, and pain points. Use surveys, data analytics, and audience feedback to gain insight into their needs.

2. Personalize Your Communication

Tailor your communication to your audience. Address them by name, acknowledge their interests, and cater your content to their unique preferences.

3. Active Listening

Actively listen to your audience's feedback and concerns. Respond thoughtfully and show that you value their input. Encourage open dialogue and collaboration.

4. Consistency

Consistency in your messaging, tone, and content is essential for creating a connection. It builds trust and reliability, as your audience knows what to expect from you.

Engage in Conversations

Actively engage in conversations with your audience through comments, messages, and social media interactions. Respond to questions and comments promptly and with genuine interest.

6. Seek Feedback

Ask for feedback from your audience and use it to improve your content and services. This not only demonstrates your commitment to their needs but also helps you evolve to meet those needs better.

Conclusion

Creating a genuine connection with your audience is about more than just selling a product or delivering information; it's about building trust, empathy, and lasting relationships. By embracing authenticity, practicing empathy, and using storytelling, you can make your audience feel heard, valued, and understood. Following the practical strategies outlined in this comprehensive guide will help you foster meaningful connections with your audience, ultimately leading to more significant engagement, loyalty, and success in your field. Remember, it's the human touch that turns a casual audience into a dedicated community.

The Art of Active Listening: A Comprehensive Guide

Introduction

Active listening is a powerful skill that plays a critical role in effective communication and building strong relationships. It involves not only hearing words but also fully engaging with the speaker, understanding their message, and responding thoughtfully. In this comprehensive guide, we will explore the art of active listening, its importance, the psychology behind it, and practical techniques to become a better active listener.

Understanding Active Listening

1. Definition of Active Listening

Active listening is a communication technique that involves fully focusing, understanding, and retaining what a speaker is saying. It goes beyond passive hearing, as active listeners show genuine interest, ask questions, and provide feedback to the speaker.

2. The Importance of Active Listening

Active listening is essential in various contexts, including personal relationships, professional settings, and conflict resolution. It fosters better understanding, reduces misunderstandings, and can improve empathy and rapport. Additionally, it enhances problem-solving and decision-making.

The Psychology of Active Listening

1. Empathy

Empathy is at the core of active listening. It's the ability to understand and share the feelings of another person. By actively listening and showing empathy, you acknowledge the speaker's emotions and make them feel heard and valued.

2. Non-Verbal Communication

Non-verbal cues, such as eye contact, facial expressions, and body language, are vital for active listening. These cues convey your engagement and interest in the speaker's message, reinforcing that you are fully present in the conversation.

3. Questioning and Clarification

Asking open-ended questions and seeking clarification is another crucial aspect of active listening. These techniques help you gain a deeper understanding of the speaker's perspective and encourage them to express themselves more fully.

4. Reflective Responses

Reflective responses involve paraphrasing or summarizing the speaker's message to show that you have been actively listening and comprehending their words. This technique confirms the accuracy of your understanding and provides the speaker with feedback.

Practical Techniques for Active Listening

1. Maintain Eye Contact

Eye contact is a non-verbal cue that communicates attentiveness and respect. Maintain appropriate eye contact without making the speaker uncomfortable and be mindful of cultural differences in this regard.

2. Remove Distractions

Eliminate distractions to ensure your full attention is on the speaker. This means silencing your phone, turning off notifications, and finding a quiet, interruption-free environment.

3. Avoid Interrupting

Refrain from interrupting the speaker, even if you have a strong urge to respond or share your perspective. Wait for an appropriate pause to provide your input.

4. Use Verbal Cues

Engage with the speaker through verbal cues such as "I see," "I understand," or "Tell me more." These cues indicate that you are actively listening and encourage the speaker to continue sharing.

5. Paraphrase and Summarize

Occasionally paraphrase or summarize the speaker's words to confirm your understanding and show that you are engaged in the conversation. For example, "So, what I'm hearing is..." or "To clarify, you're saying..."

6. Provide Feedback

Offer constructive feedback or validation to the speaker to let them know you value their input and perspective. This can include statements like "I appreciate your insight" or "Thank you for sharing your thoughts."

Conclusion

Active listening is a skill that can greatly enhance your communication abilities and relationships. By focusing on empathy, non-verbal cues, questioning, and feedback, you can become a more effective active listener. Practice this art in both personal and professional settings to improve your understanding of others, foster stronger connections, and become a more empathetic and compassionate communicator. Active listening is not just about hearing; it's about truly understanding and valuing the voices of those around you.

The Art of Asking Open-Ended Questions to Uncover Needs: A Comprehensive Guide

Introduction

In the realm of effective communication, the ability to uncover needs and gather essential information is a valuable skill. Asking open-ended questions is a powerful technique that facilitates deep and meaningful conversations. In this comprehensive guide, we will explore the art of asking open-ended questions to uncover needs, its significance, the psychology behind it, and practical techniques to master this essential skill.

Understanding Open-Ended Questions

1. Definition of Open-Ended Questions

Open-ended questions are queries that encourage a thoughtful and detailed response, typically more than a simple "yes" or "no." These questions begin with words like "what," "how," "why," "tell me about," and "describe."

2. The Importance of Open-Ended Questions

Open-ended questions are crucial in various settings, including sales, customer service, personal relationships, counseling, and problem-solving. They allow you to gain a deeper understanding of the other person's perspective, needs, and feelings. Open-ended questions also promote active listening and empathy.

The Psychology of Open-Ended Questions

1. Encouraging Thought and Reflection

Open-ended questions prompt individuals to think and reflect on their experiences and feelings. By giving them the space to elaborate, you are more likely to uncover deeper needs and concerns.

2. Demonstrating Interest

When you ask open-ended questions, you convey genuine interest in the other person's thoughts and feelings. This interest fosters trust and encourages the speaker to be more open and honest in their responses.

3. Empowering the Speaker

Open-ended questions empower the speaker to share their perspective and take an active role in the conversation. This engagement can lead to more profound insights and a clearer understanding of their needs.

4. Encouraging Elaboration

Open-ended questions encourage elaboration and provide a platform for individuals to express themselves fully. This comprehensive feedback is essential for identifying needs and addressing concerns effectively.

Practical Techniques for Asking Open-Ended Questions

1. Start with Question Words

Begin your questions with words like "what," "how," "why," "tell me about," "describe," or "walk me through." These words naturally lead to open-ended responses.

2. Use Neutral Language

Ensure your questions are free from judgment or bias. Use neutral language that does not lead the respondent toward a particular answer. For instance, instead of saying, "Don't you think this product is great?" you can ask, "What are your thoughts on this product?"

3. Avoid Double-Barreled Questions

Double-barreled questions combine two or more questions in one, which can lead to confusion and limited responses. For example, avoid asking, "Do you like the design and the functionality of this product?" Instead, ask two separate questions: "What do you think of the design?" and "How about the functionality?"

4. Be Patient and Listen Actively

Allow the respondent time to think and respond. Active listening is essential, as it shows your genuine interest and respect for their thoughts. Avoid interrupting and use non-verbal cues to show your attentiveness.

5. Encourage Further Exploration

When the respondent provides an answer, follow up with additional open-ended questions to delve deeper into the topic. For example, "Can you tell me more about that?" or "What led you to that conclusion?"

Conclusion

Asking open-ended questions is an art that can significantly enhance your communication and problem-solving skills. By using this technique, you can uncover needs, facilitate meaningful conversations, and foster trust and understanding in various personal and professional settings. Practice the strategies outlined in this comprehensive guide to become a more effective communicator and uncover the needs of those you engage with. Remember, open-ended questions are not just tools for information gathering; they are keys to unlocking deeper insights and building stronger connections.

Avoiding Common Sales Pitfalls

Introduction

Sales is a dynamic and rewarding profession, but it can also be filled with challenges and pitfalls that hinder success. Understanding these common mistakes and learning how to avoid them is crucial for sales professionals looking to excel in their careers. In this comprehensive guide, we will explore various sales pitfalls, their consequences, and practical strategies to avoid them.

The Common Sales Pitfalls

1. Lack of Research and Preparation

One of the most common pitfalls is failing to research and prepare adequately before engaging with potential customers. This can result in poor first impressions and ineffective sales pitches.

2. Overemphasis on Product Features

Focusing solely on product features and specifications rather than understanding the customer's needs and providing solutions is a significant pitfall. Customers want to know how your product or service can address their specific problems.

3. Ignoring Objections

Ignoring or mishandling objections from potential customers can derail the sales process. Objections are valuable opportunities to address concerns and build trust.

4. Lack of Active Listening

Not actively listening to the customer can lead to misunderstandings, missed cues, and ineffective communication. Active listening is essential for building rapport and uncovering needs.

5. Rushing the Sale

Attempting to close the deal too quickly without properly understanding the customer's requirements or building trust is a common pitfall. Rushing the sale often leads to lost opportunities.

The Consequences of Sales Pitfalls

1. Lost Sales Opportunities

Failing to address customers' needs and concerns can result in lost sales opportunities. Customers are more likely to buy from someone who understands their specific situation.

2. Damaged Reputation

Frequent sales mistakes can damage your reputation and lead to negative word-of-mouth. Customers who have negative experiences are more likely to share them with others.

3. Missed Upsell and Cross-Sell Opportunities

Neglecting to identify opportunities for upselling or cross-selling can result in missed revenue. Existing customers are often more open to additional purchases when their needs are properly understood.

4. Increased Churn Rate

Customers who feel misunderstood or unsatisfied with their experience are more likely to switch to competitors, resulting in an increased churn rate.

Practical Strategies to Avoid Common Sales Pitfalls

1. Research and Preparation

Invest time in researching your customers, their industries, and their pain points. Be prepared to tailor your approach to meet their specific needs.

2. Consultative Selling

Adopt a consultative selling approach by focusing on understanding customer needs and providing tailored solutions. Ask open-ended questions and actively listen to their responses.

3. Handling Objections

Learn to handle objections effectively by acknowledging them, asking clarifying questions, and providing relevant information or solutions. Objections are opportunities to address concerns and build trust.

4. Active Listening

Cultivate active listening skills by giving your full attention to the customer, maintaining eye contact, and asking clarifying questions. Practice empathy and seek to understand their perspective.

5. Build Relationships

Focus on building long-term relationships rather than solely closing sales. Building trust and rapport takes time but results in loyal customers who return and refer others.

6. Sales Training and Continuous Learning

Invest in sales training and continuous learning to stay updated on best practices, industry trends, and effective sales techniques. Stay adaptable and open to new strategies.

Conclusion

Avoiding common sales pitfalls is essential for sales professionals looking to succeed in a highly competitive field. By understanding these mistakes, their consequences, and employing practical strategies to address them, you can improve your sales skills and build better relationships with customers. Remember, successful sales is not just about selling a product or service; it's about understanding and addressing the unique needs and concerns of your customers. By avoiding pitfalls and focusing on providing value, you can achieve long-term success in the sales profession.

Mastering Consultative Selling Techniques

Introduction

In the ever-evolving world of sales, consultative selling has become a critical approach for building trust, understanding customer needs, and driving successful transactions. This comprehensive guide will delve into the art of consultative selling, its significance, the psychology behind it, and practical strategies to excel in this sales technique.

Understanding Consultative Selling

1. Definition of Consultative Selling

Consultative selling is a customer-centric approach that prioritizes understanding the customer's needs, challenges, and goals. Instead of simply pushing products or services, consultative sellers act as trusted advisors who provide tailored solutions based on the customer's unique situation.

2. The Importance of Consultative Selling

Consultative selling is essential in a modern sales landscape where customers are more informed and expect personalized, value-driven interactions. It builds trust, enhances customer relationships, and leads to more substantial, long-term business success.

The Psychology of Consultative Selling

1. Empathy

Empathy is a cornerstone of consultative selling. Understanding and sharing the customer's feelings and perspective allows you to connect with them on a deeper level, demonstrating that you genuinely care about their needs.

2. Active Listening

Active listening is key to consultative selling. It involves giving your full attention, asking probing questions, and empathizing with the customer. This approach helps you uncover their pain points, desires, and priorities.

3. Problem Solving

Consultative selling is about identifying and solving the customer's problems or fulfilling their needs. Instead of merely selling a product, you're providing a solution that directly addresses their challenges.

4. Relationship Building

Building strong customer relationships is a central goal of consultative selling. It's about becoming a trusted advisor whom the customer can rely on for guidance and support, fostering loyalty and repeat business.

Practical Techniques for Consultative Selling

1. Research Your Customers

Start by thoroughly researching your customers, their industries, and pain points. This enables you to engage with a deeper understanding of their needs.

2. Ask Open-Ended Questions

Open-ended questions encourage customers to express themselves more fully. Questions like "What are your biggest challenges?" or "How would you like to see your business grow?" are examples of effective open-ended questions.

3. Active Listening

Listen actively by giving your full attention and using non-verbal cues like nodding and maintaining eye contact. Summarize or paraphrase what the customer says to confirm your understanding.

4. Empathize and Validate

Show empathy by acknowledging the customer's feelings and validating their concerns. Statements like "I understand how that can be frustrating" or "I appreciate you sharing your perspective" convey empathy.

5. Tailor Solutions

Based on the information gathered, provide customized solutions that address the customer's specific needs. Highlight how your product or service aligns with their goals and resolves their challenges.

6. Overcome Objections

Anticipate objections and be prepared to address them. Use objections as opportunities to further discuss how your solution can benefit the customer.

7. Follow Up and Maintain Relationships

After the sale, continue to build the relationship through follow-ups, offering support, and providing additional value. This can lead to repeat business and referrals.

Conclusion

Mastering consultative selling techniques is an invaluable skill for sales professionals looking to excel in today's customer-centric environment. By understanding the psychology behind consultative selling, practicing active listening, and providing tailored solutions, you can build lasting customer relationships, foster trust, and achieve long-term success in the field. Remember, consultative selling is not just about closing deals; it's about helping customers meet their needs, overcome challenges, and achieve their goals through the products or services you offer.

Demonstrating Empathy in Sales Conversations

Introduction

In the world of sales, empathy is a vital skill that can make the difference between a transaction and a lasting customer relationship. Demonstrating empathy in sales conversations is not only a way to connect with customers on a personal level but also to understand their needs and concerns better. This comprehensive guide explores the importance of empathy, the psychology behind it, and practical strategies for infusing empathy into your sales conversations.

Understanding the Importance of Empathy in Sales

1. What Is Empathy?

Empathy is the ability to understand and share the feelings of another. In sales, it means not only comprehending the customer's perspective but also genuinely caring about their needs, desires, and challenges.

2. The Importance of Empathy in Sales

Empathy is crucial in sales for several reasons:

  - Building Trust: Empathy fosters trust as it shows you are interested in the customer as an individual, not just as a potential sale.

  - Identifying Needs: By understanding the customer's emotions and challenges, you can identify their underlying needs and provide tailored solutions.

- Enhancing Communication: Empathy improves communication by making customers feel heard and valued, leading to more open and constructive conversations.

- Building Customer Loyalty: Demonstrating empathy can lead to long-term customer relationships and loyalty as customers appreciate your understanding and support.

The Psychology of Empathy

1. Cognitive Empathy vs. Emotional Empathy

Empathy comes in two main forms:

- Cognitive Empathy: Understanding the customer's perspective and thoughts.

- Emotional Empathy: Sharing the customer's emotions and feelings.

Both forms are essential in sales conversations, as they help you comprehend the customer's needs and feelings.

2. Mirror Neurons

Mirror neurons are brain cells that fire both when we experience an emotion and when we see someone else experiencing it. They play a crucial role in understanding and responding to the emotions of others. In sales, using mirror neurons to understand and respond to the customer's emotions is a powerful tool.

Practical Strategies for Demonstrating Empathy

1. Active Listening

Active listening is a fundamental technique for demonstrating empathy. It involves giving your full attention, maintaining eye contact, and using non-verbal cues like nodding and mirroring to show that you are engaged and focused on the customer.

2. Asking Open-Ended Questions

Encourage the customer to express themselves more fully by asking open-ended questions. These questions invite deeper responses and allow the customer to share their thoughts and feelings.

3. Reflect and Validate Emotions

When the customer shares their emotions, validate their feelings by acknowledging and empathizing with them. Phrases like "I can see that you're frustrated" or "I understand how that can be challenging" convey empathy.

4. Share Personal Stories

Sharing relevant personal stories or experiences can help the customer feel more connected to you. Stories that demonstrate your understanding of their situation can create a sense of shared experience.

5. Tailor Solutions

Based on the customer's emotions, needs, and concerns, provide solutions that are specifically aligned with their situation. Explain how your product or service can address their challenges and fulfill their desires.

6. Follow-Up and Offer Support

After the sale, continue to demonstrate empathy by following up and offering ongoing support. Showing that you care about the customer's experience and success can strengthen the relationship.

Conclusion

Empathy is a cornerstone of successful sales conversations. By understanding the psychology of empathy and employing practical strategies, you can connect with customers on a deeper level, comprehend their needs, and build lasting relationships. Demonstrating empathy is not just a sales tactic; it's a commitment to understanding and valuing the emotions and experiences of your customers. By infusing empathy into your sales conversations, you can become a trusted advisor and build a loyal customer base that values your genuine care and support.

Handling Objections with Grace and Professionalism

Introduction

In the world of sales, objections are a common and often necessary part of the process. Handling objections with grace and professionalism is crucial for sales professionals looking to maintain a positive customer experience and close deals successfully. This comprehensive guide explores the importance of objection handling, the psychology behind it, and practical strategies to address objections effectively and professionally.

Understanding the Importance of Objection Handling

1. What Are Objections?

Objections are concerns, doubts, or questions that potential customers raise during the sales process. They can be related to price, product features, timing, competition, or other factors.

2. The Importance of Objection Handling

Handling objections effectively is essential for several reasons:

  - Building Trust: Addressing objections professionally shows your commitment to understanding the customer's concerns and building trust.

  - Avoiding Misunderstandings: Failing to address objections can lead to misunderstandings and lost opportunities.

- Identifying Needs: Objections often reveal underlying needs or challenges that can guide you to provide the right solutions.

- Closing Deals: Skilled objection handling can lead to successful deal closures and satisfied customers.

The Psychology of Objection Handling

1. Understanding Customer Perspective

Empathy and understanding are at the core of objection handling. You must put yourself in the customer's shoes to comprehend their concerns and feelings.

2. Addressing Emotional Needs

Customers may have emotional objections, such as fear, frustration, or uncertainty. It's essential to address these emotional needs, not just logical ones.

3. Problem-Solving

Objection handling is a form of problem-solving. You are working collaboratively with the customer to identify and resolve their concerns or challenges.

4. Building Rapport

Professionally addressing objections can help you build rapport. Customers are more likely to trust and continue the conversation with someone who handles objections with respect and expertise.

Practical Strategies for Handling Objections with Grace and Professionalism

1. Listen Actively

Begin by actively listening to the customer's objection. Give them your full attention, avoid interrupting, and use non-verbal cues like nodding to show you are engaged.

2. Pause and Reflect

After the customer presents their objection, take a moment to pause and reflect on what they've said. This shows that you respect their viewpoint and are taking their concern seriously.

3. Clarify and Ask Questions

Ask the customer clarifying questions to gain a deeper understanding of their objection. Questions like "Can you tell me more about that?" or "What specific concerns do you have?" can help uncover the root of the objection.

4. Acknowledge and Empathize

Acknowledge the customer's objection and empathize with their concerns. Use statements like "I understand how that can be a concern" or "I appreciate your honesty."

5. Present Solutions

Offer a well-thought-out solution to address the objection. Highlight how your product or service can alleviate the customer's concerns or challenges. Focus on the value you can provide.

6. Handle Objections as Opportunities

View objections as opportunities to further demonstrate your expertise and understanding. Addressing objections professionally can strengthen the customer's confidence in your ability to meet their needs.

7. Close with a Clear Action

Once you've addressed the objection and provided a solution, guide the conversation toward the next steps. Clearly outline what the customer should expect and encourage them to take action.

8. Follow-Up

After handling objections, follow up with the customer to ensure their satisfaction and address any lingering concerns. This shows your commitment to their success and builds rapport.

Conclusion

Handling objections with grace and professionalism is a critical skill in sales. By understanding the importance of objection handling, the psychology behind it, and practicing the practical strategies outlined in this comprehensive guide, you can address objections effectively and build strong customer relationships. Remember that objection handling is not just about overcoming hurdles; it's about collaborating with customers to find the best solutions and build lasting trust. Professional objection handling can set you apart as a trusted advisor and lead to successful deal closures and satisfied customers.

Crafting Compelling Sales Pitches

Introduction

In the world of sales, a compelling sales pitch is your most powerful tool. A well-crafted pitch not only captures your audience's attention but also persuades them to take action. This comprehensive guide explores the art of crafting compelling sales pitches, its importance, the psychology behind it, and practical strategies to create pitches that win over your audience.

Understanding the Importance of a Compelling Sales Pitch

1. What Is a Sales Pitch?

A sales pitch is a concise, persuasive message designed to attract, engage, and convince potential customers about the value of your product or service.

2. The Importance of a Compelling Sales Pitch

A compelling sales pitch is crucial for several reasons:

  - Capturing Attention: In a crowded marketplace, your pitch must stand out and grab your audience's attention.

  - Building Interest: Your pitch should pique the audience's interest and motivate them to learn more.

  - Converting Interest into Action: The ultimate goal of a pitch is to persuade your audience to take the desired action, whether it's making a purchase or signing up for a service.

The Psychology of Crafting Compelling Sales Pitches

1. Know Your Audience

Understanding your audience is fundamental to crafting a compelling pitch. You must be aware of their needs, desires, pain points, and preferences.

2. Storytelling

Storytelling is a powerful technique in sales. People connect with stories, and a well-told story can help your audience visualize how your product or service can improve their lives.

3. Emotional Appeal

Appealing to emotions can make your pitch more compelling. People often make purchasing decisions based on emotion, so incorporating relatable, positive emotions into your pitch can be persuasive.

4. Building Trust

Trust is essential in sales. Your pitch should convey trustworthiness, professionalism, and authenticity. Use data, statistics, and testimonials to build credibility.

5. Overcoming Objections

Anticipate and address potential objections in your pitch. When you proactively handle objections, it shows your thoroughness and commitment to meeting your audience's concerns.

Practical Strategies for Crafting Compelling Sales Pitches

1. Start with a Hook

Begin your pitch with a compelling hook that grabs your audience's attention. It could be a surprising fact, a relatable story, or a challenging question.

2. Define the Problem

Clearly articulate the problem or challenge your audience is facing. By acknowledging the issue, you show your understanding of their situation.

3. Present Your Solution

After defining the problem, introduce your product or service as the solution. Explain how it can address the challenge and improve the audience's life.

4. Highlight Key Benefits

Focus on the benefits of your product or service. How will it make the audience's life better, easier, or more enjoyable? Be specific and relatable.

5. Use Social Proof

Incorporate social proof by including customer testimonials, case studies, or reviews. Positive experiences from others can build trust and credibility.

6. Offer Value Proposition

Clearly state your value proposition. What sets your product or service apart from the competition? What unique value do you bring to your customers?

7. Call to Action

End your pitch with a clear and compelling call to action. Tell the audience exactly what you want them to do next, whether it's making a purchase, signing up, or requesting more information.

8. Practice and Refine

Crafting a compelling sales pitch takes practice. Review and refine your pitch based on feedback and results. Continuously improve your messaging to better resonate with your audience.

Conclusion

A compelling sales pitch is the foundation of your sales efforts. By understanding the importance of a great pitch, delving into the psychology behind it, and practicing the practical strategies outlined in this comprehensive guide, you can create pitches that engage and persuade your audience effectively. Remember that a compelling pitch is not just about selling; it's about building relationships and offering solutions that genuinely benefit your customers. With the right pitch, you can inspire action, drive results, and build lasting customer loyalty.

Creating Value-Driven Proposals

Introduction

In the world of business and professional interactions, the ability to communicate effectively can make the difference between success and failure. When it comes to presenting proposals, it is crucial to strike a balance between convincing stakeholders and avoiding the perception of being overly salesy. This article delves into the art of creating value-driven proposals, highlighting how you can communicate persuasively while maintaining a genuine and informative approach.

Know Your Audience

Before crafting a proposal, it's essential to understand your audience thoroughly. In-depth research into their needs, challenges, and goals is the foundation of effective communication. Tailor your proposal to address the specific concerns and interests of your audience. Personalization enhances the relevance and appeal of your proposal.

Start with a Strong Value Proposition

The value proposition forms the core of your proposal. It encapsulates the promise of value you intend to deliver. When constructing your value proposition, emphasize what sets your proposal apart from others. How does it solve your audience's problems or enhance their lives? Make it clear, concise, and compelling.

Utilize Storytelling

Engage your audience by using a storytelling approach in your proposal. Narratives are not only memorable but also resonate deeply with people. Share success stories, case studies, or anecdotes that illustrate the practical impact of your proposal. Stories make your proposal more relatable and persuasive, connecting on a personal level.

Emphasize Benefits over Features

While it is important to describe the features of your proposal, it is equally critical to emphasize the benefits. Features outline what your proposal does, while benefits explain how these features will improve your audience's situation. Highlight the specific advantages and positive outcomes that embracing your proposal will bring.

Offer Proof of Concept

To build credibility, provide concrete evidence of your proposal's effectiveness. This can include statistics, testimonials, or data that substantiate your claims. Incorporating social proof, such as endorsements from satisfied clients or industry experts, can further strengthen your proposal's credibility.

Tailor Your Proposal

Generic proposals rarely resonate with diverse audiences. To be effective, customize your proposal to address the specific needs and interests of each audience. Utilize language and examples that they can relate to, demonstrating how your proposal aligns with their unique goals and challenges.

Foster Transparency

Transparency is a cornerstone of value-driven proposals. Avoid concealing vital information or overselling your proposal. Be honest about potential drawbacks or challenges, addressing them proactively. Demonstrating transparency builds trust and establishes your credibility.

Address Objections and Concerns

Anticipate objections and concerns that your audience might raise and address them in your proposal. Acknowledging potential issues and providing solutions or mitigations shows that you have considered their perspective and are committed to a collaborative, problem-solving approach.

Provide a Clear Call to Action (CTA)

End your proposal with a well-defined call to action (CTA). Your CTA should guide your audience on the next steps they need to take. Whether it's scheduling a meeting, signing a contract, or making a purchase, ensure that your CTA is actionable and straightforward, leaving no room for ambiguity.

Follow Up

After presenting your proposal, be sure to follow up with your audience. This demonstrates your dedication and willingness to engage with them. The follow-up provides an opportunity to answer questions, address concerns, and continue nurturing a positive and lasting relationship.

Conclusion

Creating value-driven proposals hinges on effective communication without resorting to aggressive sales tactics. By understanding your audience, building a strong value proposition, weaving engaging stories, emphasizing benefits, and backing your claims with evidence, you can deliver proposals that genuinely resonate with your stakeholders. Remember that transparency, addressing objections, and providing a clear call to action are all key elements in a successful value-driven proposal. These principles will help you communicate your proposals effectively, build trust, and foster positive, long-lasting relationships with your audience.

Developing trust in your relationships

Introduction

Trust is the bedrock of any healthy and enduring relationship. Whether it's in personal, professional, or social settings, the bonds we form with others are rooted in the level of trust we share. Let's explore the crucial principles of developing trust in your relationships and the significance of trust in nurturing strong, lasting connections.

Self-Trust: The Foundation

Trust in external relationships begins with trust in yourself. It's crucial to be honest with yourself, establish boundaries, and consistently adhere to your values and commitments. Self-trust sets the stage for building trust with others.

Open and Honest Communication

Effective communication is the cornerstone of trust. Open and honest conversations enable individuals to understand each other, express their thoughts and feelings, and communicate openly. When both parties engage in transparent communication, it fosters a sense of safety and reliability within the relationship.

Reliability and Consistency

Reliability is a fundamental aspect of trust. Consistently keeping your promises and fulfilling commitments demonstrates that you can be counted on. Whether it's punctuality for a meeting, delivering on agreements, or simply being there for someone in times of need, reliability is the bedrock of trust.

Vulnerability and Empathy

Building trust often requires vulnerability. Sharing your thoughts, emotions, and fears allows others to connect with your authentic self. At the same time, being empathetic and receptive to the vulnerabilities of others fosters a sense of safety and trust in the relationship.

Mutual Respect

Respect is a non-negotiable element of trust. It's crucial to respect each other's boundaries, opinions, and individuality. Respecting the autonomy and agency of those in your relationships establishes trust and sets a solid foundation for mutual understanding.

Consistency in Behavior

Consistency in your actions and behavior is essential for building trust. When you exhibit predictability and stability, it becomes easier for others to rely on you. Inconsistency or erratic behavior can erode trust quickly.

Deliver on Promises

Making commitments and keeping them is a critical aspect of trust-building. When you promise to do something, whether it's a small favor or a significant task, following through on your commitments reinforces your reliability and trustworthiness.

Honesty and Transparency

Honesty is the linchpin of trust. Being forthright and transparent in your interactions helps build trust. Concealing information or being deceptive can damage trust irreparably.

Admit Mistakes and Apologize

No one is infallible. Acknowledging your mistakes and apologizing when you've wronged someone is a sign of integrity and builds trust. Admitting faults shows your willingness to take responsibility for your actions and make amends.

Establish Boundaries

Setting and respecting personal boundaries is essential in building trust. Boundaries ensure that both parties feel safe and secure within the relationship. Understanding and adhering to each other's boundaries is a mark of respect and trustworthiness.

Time and Patience

Trust takes time to develop. It's not an overnight achievement but a gradual process. Be patient and allow your relationships to grow naturally. Rushing the process can have the opposite effect and weaken trust.

Forgiveness

Mistakes and misunderstandings will occur in any relationship. Forgiving and moving forward is crucial in maintaining trust. Holding grudges or harboring resentment can erode trust over time.

Conclusion

Trust is the bedrock of any successful and enduring relationship. By focusing on self-trust, open communication, reliability, vulnerability, mutual respect, and other key principles, you can create and nurture trust in your relationships. Building trust is a continuous effort, but the rewards are substantial—strong, enduring, and fulfilling connections that enrich your personal, professional, and social life. Remember, trust is a two-way street, and by demonstrating trustworthiness, you can inspire trust in others.

Weaving Narratives: Using Storytelling to Illustrate Solutions

Introduction

Storytelling is a powerful and timeless method of communication. It transcends cultural boundaries and connects with our most fundamental human instincts. In the realm of education, business, and problem-solving, storytelling can be a potent tool for illustrating solutions and conveying complex ideas. This educational article explores the art of using storytelling to illustrate solutions, showcasing its effectiveness and providing practical tips on implementation.

The Power of Storytelling in Problem-Solving

1. Engaging Your Audience

One of the most significant advantages of storytelling is its capacity to captivate and engage an audience. When illustrating solutions, a compelling narrative draws listeners or readers into the scenario. This engagement encourages active participation and enhances comprehension.

2. Simplifying Complexity

Solutions to many problems can be intricate and multifaceted. Storytelling simplifies these complexities by breaking down the solution into a narrative form. Stories provide a clear, structured, and memorable way to convey information, making it more accessible to a broad audience.

3. Emotional Connection

Storytelling appeals to emotions, creating a profound connection with the audience. Emotional engagement can help individuals not only understand the solution but also feel its impact. This connection can motivate people to adopt or support the solution.

Practical Tips for Using Storytelling to Illustrate Solutions

1. Begin with a Strong Opening

A good story starts with a captivating opening. Hook your audience with a powerful, attention-grabbing introduction. You might use a relatable problem or challenge to set the stage for the solution.

2. Craft a Relatable Protagonist

In your story, create a protagonist or central character that your audience can relate to. This character should encounter a problem or challenge that mirrors the real-world issue you're addressing.

3. Establish the Problem

Clearly define the problem or challenge faced by your protagonist. Use vivid language and details to make the situation relatable. This sets the stage for the solution to come.

4. Present the Solution

Introduce the solution within the narrative. Make sure it's presented as a natural response to the problem. This can be a real-life solution or a metaphorical one, depending on the context.

5. Show the Benefits

Illustrate the benefits of the solution in your story. This could involve detailing how the protagonist's life or circumstances improve after adopting the solution. Use concrete examples and vivid descriptions.

6. Address Challenges

Acknowledge potential challenges or obstacles that might arise when implementing the solution. Realistic portrayals of hurdles and how they are overcome add depth to your narrative and provide valuable insights.

7. Conclude with a Strong Message

Wrap up your story with a clear and impactful message. Summarize the solution and its benefits, leaving your audience with a memorable takeaway.

8. Encourage Reflection and Action

After telling your story, encourage your audience to reflect on the solution and consider how it might be applied in their own lives or situations. You can also prompt them to take specific actions related to the solution.

Examples of Storytelling in Problem-Solving

1. Case Studies

In business and education, case studies are frequently used to illustrate solutions. These real-world examples outline problems, challenges, and the steps taken to resolve them, offering practical insights for similar situations.

2. Metaphorical Narratives

Sometimes, complex issues are best explained through metaphorical narratives. For instance, a story about a struggling forest ecosystem can symbolize the importance of biodiversity and conservation.

3. Personal Anecdotes

Personal stories can be highly effective in illustrating solutions. Sharing experiences and lessons learned from one's own life can make the solution more relatable and credible.

Conclusion

Storytelling is a dynamic and persuasive method of illustrating solutions to problems and challenges. By engaging your audience, simplifying complexity, and creating emotional connections, storytelling can effectively convey solutions and motivate action. When crafting your narratives, remember to begin with a strong opening, create relatable characters, define the problem, present the solution, highlight the benefits, address challenges, and conclude with a powerful message. Through the art of storytelling, you can make complex ideas and solutions accessible and inspiring.

Mastering Communication: Employing the "Feel, Felt, Found" Method

Introduction

Effective communication is the cornerstone of success in various aspects of life, from business negotiations to interpersonal relationships. The "Feel, Felt, Found" method is a powerful communication technique that helps individuals empathize with others, relate to their experiences, and ultimately, guide them toward a new perspective or solution. Let's explore the "Feel, Felt, Found" method, how it works, and provide practical examples of its application in various scenarios.

What is the "Feel, Felt, Found" Method?

The "Feel, Felt, Found" method is a persuasive communication technique used to connect with others by acknowledging their feelings, sharing a similar experience, and presenting a solution or a new perspective. It is particularly effective in situations where you want to offer support, convey empathy, or provide guidance without coming across as pushy or condescending.

How it Works

The "Feel, Felt, Found" method is structured in three distinct stages:

1. Feel: Begin by empathizing with the person you're communicating with. Acknowledge their feelings, emotions, or concerns. This step involves validating their emotions and demonstrating that you understand where they're coming from.

2. Felt: Share a personal or relatable experience that you or someone else has gone through. This experience should be similar to what the other person is currently facing. By doing this, you demonstrate that you, or someone you know, have been in their shoes and can relate to their situation.

3. Found: Finally, offer a solution, insight, or a new perspective that helped you or the person in the shared experience overcome a similar challenge. This step should gently guide the person toward considering an alternative viewpoint or solution without forcing it upon them.

Examples of the "Feel, Felt, Found" Method in Action

1. Scenario: Persuading a Colleague to Embrace a New Work Process

Feel: "I understand that you feel apprehensive about adopting this new work process. Change can be intimidating, and it's natural to have concerns."

Felt: "I've been there too. When we implemented a similar process in my previous team, I was initially skeptical. I felt like it would disrupt our workflow."

Found: "However, after some time, I found that the new process streamlined our tasks and improved our efficiency. It made our work more manageable and allowed us to focus on higher-value activities."

2. Scenario: Comforting a Friend Dealing with Loss

Feel: "I can't imagine how you must be feeling right now. Losing a loved one is incredibly painful, and the grief can be overwhelming."

Felt: "I remember when I lost my grandmother. I felt lost and heartbroken, like I would never heal from the pain."

Found: "But with time, I found that sharing my feelings with friends and family, and seeking support from a grief counselor, helped me cope and eventually find solace."

3. Scenario: Encouraging a Team Member to Take on a Challenging Project

Feel: "I can sense your apprehension about taking on this project. It's natural to feel a bit anxious when facing something new and challenging."

Felt: "I've been in your shoes before. When I was asked to lead a project of this scale, I felt overwhelmed and unsure of my abilities."

Found: "However, I found that with the support of the team, a clear plan, and by breaking the project into manageable tasks, it became a rewarding experience that helped me grow both personally and professionally."

Conclusion

The "Feel, Felt, Found" method is a potent tool for effective communication, allowing you to empathize with others, relate to their experiences, and gently guide them toward a solution or a new perspective. By following this method, you can foster understanding, build trust, and help others navigate challenges, making it an invaluable skill in both personal and professional interactions. Remember that the key to success with this method is authenticity and genuine empathy, as people are more likely to connect with you when they sense your sincerity.

The Power of Social Proof and Testimonials

Introduction

In today's digital age, consumers are more informed and discerning than ever before. They rely on the experiences and opinions of others to make informed decisions, whether it's purchasing a product, choosing a service provider, or even subscribing to a new streaming service. Social proof and testimonials play a pivotal role in shaping these decisions. This educational article will explore the significance of social proof and testimonials and provide insights into how you can effectively leverage them in your business or personal endeavors.

Understanding Social Proof

Social proof is a psychological phenomenon where individuals look to the actions and opinions of others to guide their own behavior and decisions. It stems from the innate human tendency to seek safety and validation through conformity. In the context of marketing and decision-making, social proof is a powerful tool that can influence people's choices.

Types of Social Proof

1. Expert Social Proof: When an authority or credible expert endorses a product, service, or idea, it carries weight. People are more likely to trust and adopt something when an authority figure supports it.

2. Celebrity Social Proof: The endorsement of a celebrity or well-known personality can significantly influence people's perceptions and decisions. Celebrities can lend their credibility to products or causes.

3. User Social Proof: This is based on the experiences and opinions of everyday consumers. User reviews, ratings, and testimonials from real customers carry a lot of weight, as they represent the firsthand experiences of people like the prospective buyer.

4. Wisdom of the Crowd: This type of social proof relies on numbers. When a significant number of people have already adopted a product or service, it implies its popularity and credibility, making it more appealing to others.

The Significance of Testimonials

Testimonials are a specific form of user social proof. They are written or spoken endorsements of a product, service, or experience by individuals who have had a positive interaction with it. Testimonials serve several crucial functions:

1. Credibility: Testimonials provide third-party validation, increasing the credibility of your product or service.

2. Relatability: Potential customers can identify with the experiences shared in testimonials, making them more relatable and convincing.

3. Emotional Appeal: Testimonials often include personal stories, emotions, and authentic expressions of satisfaction, which can strike a chord with potential customers.

4. Social Proof: Testimonials are a prime example of user social proof, reinforcing that others have benefited from your offering.

Utilizing Social Proof and Testimonials

1. Display Testimonials Strategically: On your website, marketing materials, or product listings, prominently display authentic, well-crafted testimonials. Ensure they are easily accessible to potential customers.

2. Use Rich Media: Whenever possible, incorporate videos, images, or audio recordings of satisfied customers giving their testimonials. Visual and auditory content can be even more persuasive than text alone.

3. Highlight Key Benefits: Encourage your satisfied customers to emphasize the specific benefits they received from your product or service in their testimonials.

4. Diversify Your Sources: Seek testimonials from a variety of customers, representing different demographics and experiences. This diversity can broaden your appeal.

5. Showcase Before-and-After Scenarios: If applicable, include testimonials that illustrate the transformation or positive change experienced by customers after using your product or service.

6. Address Objections: Use testimonials to counter common objections or concerns potential customers might have. For instance, if cost is a common objection, share testimonials that highlight the product's cost-effectiveness.

7. Request Permission: Always seek permission from customers before using their testimonials, respecting their privacy and ensuring legal compliance.

8. Monitor and Update: Regularly review and update your testimonials to keep the content fresh and relevant. Outdated testimonials can diminish their impact.

Conclusion

Social proof and testimonials are invaluable tools for building trust, credibility, and influence. By understanding the various forms of social proof, leveraging user experiences, and effectively utilizing testimonials, you can bolster your marketing efforts, increase customer trust, and make more persuasive, informed decisions in your personal and professional life. Ultimately, the combination of social proof and testimonials is a dynamic force that shapes the choices of individuals in today's information-rich world.

Tailored to Perfection: The Art of Offering Customized Solutions

Introduction

In a world where one-size-fits-all approaches have their limitations, offering customized solutions is a valuable skill in various professional and personal contexts. Whether you're in business, education, healthcare, or any other field, recognizing the unique needs and preferences of individuals or groups is key to achieving success. This educational article will explore the importance of offering customized solutions, how to create them, and the benefits they bring to the table.

The Significance of Customized Solutions

1. Addressing Diverse Needs: People have distinct preferences, requirements, and challenges. Customized solutions allow you to adapt your approach to meet these diverse needs effectively.

2. Enhancing Engagement: Tailored solutions are more engaging because they resonate with the specific interests and objectives of your audience. This higher level of engagement can lead to better outcomes.

3. Building Trust and Loyalty: When you provide customized solutions, it shows your commitment to understanding and meeting the needs of your clients or audience. This builds trust and fosters long-term loyalty.

4. Improving Efficiency: Tailoring solutions can lead to more efficient and effective results. You're not wasting resources on generic strategies that might not apply to the situation.

5. Solving Complex Problems: Some problems are intricate and cannot be solved with a one-size-fits-all approach. Customization allows you to dissect complex issues and provide targeted solutions.

Steps to Offering Customized Solutions

1. Gather Information: Start by gathering data and information about the individual or group you're working with. This includes their goals, challenges, preferences, and any other relevant details.

2. Analyze the Data: Once you have collected the necessary information, analyze it to identify patterns, trends, and unique needs. This analysis will form the basis for your customized solution.

3. Define Objectives: Clearly define the objectives of the customized solution. What do you aim to achieve? Make sure the objectives are specific, measurable, achievable, relevant, and time-bound (SMART).

4. Tailor Your Approach: Develop a tailored approach that aligns with the specific needs and objectives. This may involve adjusting strategies, content, or methods to suit the situation.

5. Seek Feedback: Throughout the implementation of the customized solution, seek feedback from your clients or audience. Their input can help fine-tune and improve the solution further.

6. Continuously Adapt: Be prepared to adapt and modify the customized solution as needed. Situations and needs change, so flexibility is essential.

Benefits of Offering Customized Solutions

1. Personalized Experiences: Customized solutions provide a more personalized and meaningful experience, which is appreciated by clients and audiences.

2. Higher Success Rates: Since these solutions are designed to meet specific needs, they are more likely to achieve the desired outcomes and, as a result, lead to higher success rates.

3. Competitive Advantage: Businesses and professionals who offer customized solutions gain a competitive edge by providing unique value that generic solutions cannot match.

4. Better Problem-Solving: Customization allows for more precise problem-solving, especially in complex or unique scenarios.

5. Enhanced Client Satisfaction: Tailored solutions result in happier clients and audiences, which can lead to repeat business and positive referrals.

Conclusion

The ability to offer customized solutions is a valuable skill that can be applied across numerous fields and industries. By recognizing the unique needs and preferences of your clients or audience, gathering and analyzing relevant information, and tailoring your approach accordingly, you can provide more personalized, effective, and engaging solutions. The benefits of customization, including enhanced satisfaction, loyalty, and better problem-solving, make it a worthwhile investment in both professional and personal endeavors. Customization is not a one-time process but an ongoing commitment to understanding and serving the specific needs of those you work with, ultimately leading to better outcomes and success.

Empowering Minds: Providing Education and Valuable Insights

Introduction

In today's information-driven world, providing education and valuable insights is a powerful way to foster personal growth, professional development, and the expansion of knowledge. Whether you're an educator, a mentor, or simply someone passionate about sharing information, the act of imparting knowledge and insights has a profound impact on individuals and society as a whole. This educational article explores the importance of providing education and valuable insights, how to effectively deliver them, and the enduring benefits of this practice.

The Importance of Providing Education and Valuable Insights

1. Promoting Lifelong Learning: Education and insights encourage individuals to become lifelong learners. The quest for knowledge becomes a constant and rewarding pursuit.

2. Nurturing Critical Thinking: Providing information and insights fosters critical thinking skills. Individuals learn to analyze, evaluate, and synthesize information, enhancing their problem-solving abilities.

3. Empowering Decision-Making: Valuable insights allow individuals to make informed decisions, whether in their personal lives or professional careers. Educated choices lead to better outcomes.

4. Fostering Innovation: A well-informed and insightful population is more likely to innovate and create new solutions to problems, driving progress and growth.

5. Strengthening Communities: Sharing education and insights within communities enhances social cohesion, cooperation, and mutual understanding.

Effectively Providing Education and Valuable Insights

1. Understand Your Audience: Tailor your education and insights to the specific needs, interests, and level of understanding of your audience. This ensures that your message resonates with them.

2. Deliver Information Clearly: Communicate information in a clear, organized, and accessible manner. Use visual aids, storytelling, and real-life examples to enhance understanding.

3. Encourage Critical Thinking: Instead of simply providing answers, encourage your audience to ask questions, think critically, and explore different perspectives.

4. Promote Active Learning: Engage your audience actively through discussions, group activities, and problem-solving exercises. This promotes retention and application of knowledge.

5. Stay Updated: Ensure that the information and insights you provide are accurate and up-to-date. Continuous learning keeps your knowledge current and reliable.

6. Provide Context: Place information and insights in context to help your audience better understand the relevance and significance of what they're learning.

Benefits of Providing Education and Valuable Insights

1. Personal Growth: Education and insights enable individuals to expand their knowledge, skills, and perspectives, contributing to personal growth and development.

2. Career Advancement: Well-informed individuals are better equipped to excel in their careers and seek new opportunities.

3. Empowerment: Access to education and valuable insights empowers individuals to make informed decisions about their lives, health, and well-being.

4. Innovation: A well-educated and insightful population is more likely to innovate, leading to societal progress and advancements.

5. Social Cohesion: Sharing knowledge and insights within communities fosters social cohesion, collaboration, and empathy.

Conclusion

Providing education and valuable insights is a noble endeavor with far-reaching benefits. By encouraging lifelong learning, critical thinking, and informed decision-making, you contribute to personal growth, professional development, and societal advancement. Remember to understand your audience, deliver information clearly, promote active learning, and stay updated to ensure the effectiveness of your educational efforts. Whether you're a formal educator, mentor, or a passionate advocate for knowledge sharing, your commitment to providing education and valuable insights enriches the lives of individuals and the broader community, leaving a lasting and positive impact.

The Pillars of Trust: Maintaining Honesty and Transparency

Introduction

Honesty and transparency are fundamental principles that underpin healthy relationships, effective communication, and ethical conduct in both personal and professional contexts. These values are the cornerstones of trust, and without trust, meaningful and successful interactions become challenging. This educational article delves into the significance of maintaining honesty and transparency, why they are vital, and how they can be incorporated into daily life.

The Importance of Honesty and Transparency

1. Building Trust: Trust is the bedrock of any strong relationship, be it personal or professional. Honesty and transparency are the surest ways to build and maintain trust over time.

2. Fostering Accountability: Honesty and transparency encourage individuals to take responsibility for their actions and decisions. When you're open about your intentions and outcomes, accountability naturally follows.

3. Effective Communication: Clear, honest, and transparent communication is more likely to be understood and well-received. This is crucial in resolving conflicts, making decisions, and conveying information.

4. Ethical Behavior: Upholding honesty and transparency is not only morally sound but also ensures that individuals and organizations adhere to ethical standards and legal requirements.

5. Strengthening Relationships: Authentic and honest interactions lead to deeper and more meaningful relationships with friends, family, colleagues, and clients.

Ways to Maintain Honesty and Transparency

1. Self-Reflection: Start by reflecting on your values and intentions. Recognize the importance of honesty and transparency in your life and how they contribute to your overall well-being and relationships.

2. Open Communication: Foster open and honest communication with others. Encourage dialogue, actively listen, and express yourself clearly and authentically.

3. Admit Mistakes: When you make a mistake, acknowledge it without hesitation. Taking responsibility for your errors is a sign of honesty and transparency.

4. Share Information: In both personal and professional settings, share relevant information with others. Be open about your plans, decisions, and any important changes.

5. Encourage Feedback: Create an environment where others feel comfortable providing feedback. Constructive criticism can help you identify areas where you need to be more honest and transparent.

6. Set Realistic Expectations: Manage expectations by being realistic about what you can and cannot do. Avoid making promises you can't keep, and be honest about your capabilities.

7. Avoid Deception: Avoid any form of deception, including lying, hiding information, or misrepresenting facts. These actions erode trust and hinder transparent communication.

8. Seek Guidance: If you're unsure about a situation, seek advice or guidance from someone you trust. Consulting with others can help you make more informed and honest decisions.

The Benefits of Honesty and Transparency

1. Stronger Trust: Maintaining honesty and transparency strengthens trust within your relationships, making them more resilient.

2. Improved Decision-Making: Open communication and honest feedback lead to better decision-making in personal and professional life.

3. Enhanced Reputation: Upholding honesty and transparency leads to a positive reputation, which can open doors to new opportunities.

4. Healthier Relationships: Authentic interactions built on these values result in healthier, more fulfilling relationships.

5. Greater Peace of Mind: Living with integrity brings peace of mind, as you're not burdened by the weight of deceit or hidden truths.

Conclusion

Honesty and transparency are essential components of ethical and effective communication. By embracing these values, individuals and organizations can build trust, enhance relationships, make better decisions, and maintain a positive reputation. Upholding these principles requires self-reflection, open communication, and a commitment to ethical behavior. By integrating honesty and transparency into your daily life, you contribute to a more open, honest, and trustworthy world.

Selling with Integrity: The Art of Avoiding High-Pressure Sales Tactics

Introduction

High-pressure sales tactics have long been a controversial and often criticized aspect of sales and marketing. These tactics rely on pressure, manipulation, and urgency to persuade potential customers to make quick decisions. While they may generate short-term results, high-pressure tactics can damage long-term relationships and tarnish a business's reputation. This educational article explores the importance of avoiding high-pressure sales tactics, why ethical sales methods are essential, and how you can build lasting customer relationships by selling with integrity.

The Consequences of High-Pressure Sales Tactics

1. Eroding Trust: High-pressure tactics can erode trust between the salesperson and the customer. When customers feel manipulated or coerced, they are less likely to trust the salesperson or the company in the future.

2. Damaging Reputation: Engaging in high-pressure sales tactics can harm a business's reputation. Negative reviews, customer complaints, and word-of-mouth can spread, deterring potential customers.

3. Short-Term Gains, Long-Term Losses: High-pressure tactics may lead to short-term sales, but they often result in high cancellation rates, returns, and customer dissatisfaction. In the long run, this can lead to financial losses.

4. Legal and Ethical Issues: In some cases, high-pressure sales tactics may cross ethical and even legal boundaries, resulting in legal repercussions and damage to a company's brand.

The Value of Ethical Sales Methods

1. Building Trust: Ethical sales methods build trust with customers. When you prioritize their needs and well-being, customers are more likely to trust your recommendations and return to you for future purchases.

2. Sustainable Business Growth: Fostering long-term relationships with customers leads to sustainable business growth. Loyal customers are not only repeat buyers but also advocates who refer others to your business.

3. Enhanced Reputation: An ethical sales approach enhances your reputation. It positions your business as one that cares about customers and is committed to their success.

4. Legal and Ethical Compliance: By adhering to ethical sales methods, you ensure compliance with legal and ethical standards, reducing the risk of legal issues and public backlash.

How to Avoid High-Pressure Sales Tactics

1. Listen Actively: Instead of pressuring customers, actively listen to their needs and concerns. Understand their motivations and preferences.

2. Educate and Inform: Provide customers with comprehensive information about your product or service. Transparency and education help them make informed decisions.

3. Avoid Manipulative Language: Steer clear of manipulative language or phrases designed to create a sense of urgency or fear. Instead, focus on positive and constructive messaging.

4. Be Patient: Allow customers the time they need to consider their options. Avoid rushing them into a decision and offer support for their decision-making process.

5. Offer Alternatives: Instead of pressuring customers into a single solution, offer them a range of alternatives that cater to their needs and budget.

6. Be Honest About Limitations: Clearly communicate any limitations or downsides of your product or service. Honesty and transparency build trust.

7. Provide a Cooling-Off Period: Allow customers a grace period to reconsider their purchase. This shows respect for their decision-making process.

Benefits of Avoiding High-Pressure Sales Tactics

1. Enhanced Customer Trust: Ethical sales methods build trust, leading to stronger customer relationships and loyalty.

2. Sustainable Growth: A customer-centric approach fosters sustainable business growth as loyal customers become advocates.

3. Positive Reputation: Ethical sales practices enhance your reputation and brand image.

4. Compliance and Legal Safety: Avoiding high-pressure tactics ensures that you remain compliant with legal and ethical standards.

Conclusion

High-pressure sales tactics may yield short-term gains, but they can damage trust, reputation, and long-term customer relationships. Ethical sales methods prioritize customer well-being and satisfaction, resulting in sustainable business growth, a positive reputation, and legal compliance. By selling with integrity and avoiding high-pressure tactics, you create a foundation for lasting success built on trust and genuine customer relationships.

Nurturing Forever Bonds: The Art of Establishing a Long-Term Relationship Mindset

Introduction

In our fast-paced world, the value of long-term relationships, whether personal or professional, cannot be overstated. These relationships provide stability, mutual support, and the potential for growth over time. To establish a long-term relationship mindset, it is crucial to prioritize qualities like patience, communication, trust, and mutual respect. This educational article explores the significance of adopting a long-term relationship mindset, its key components, and how to apply it in various areas of life.

The Significance of a Long-Term Relationship Mindset

1. Stability: Long-term relationships provide stability and a sense of security. They offer a foundation upon which individuals can build their lives and plans.

2. Mutual Growth: In long-term relationships, both parties have the opportunity to learn, grow, and adapt together. These relationships foster personal and collective development.

3. Emotional Support: Long-term relationships offer a reliable source of emotional support during challenging times. Knowing someone has your back can make a significant difference in overcoming obstacles.

4. Consistency: Long-term relationships are built on consistency and reliability. They provide a sense of predictability and trust.

5. Lasting Memories: These relationships create the opportunity to build a treasure trove of shared memories and experiences, contributing to a fulfilling and enriched life.

Key Components of a Long-Term Relationship Mindset

1. Patience: Patience is vital in any long-term relationship. It helps you navigate through rough patches, misunderstandings, and periods of change without making hasty decisions.

2. Communication: Effective communication is the foundation of any lasting relationship. It enables you to express your feelings, understand the other person's perspective, and resolve conflicts.

3. Trust: Trust is the linchpin of a long-term relationship. It is developed over time through consistency, reliability, and the absence of deceit.

4. Mutual Respect: Respect for each other's boundaries, opinions, and individuality is essential. It establishes a strong foundation for a long-term relationship.

5. Adaptability: The ability to adapt to changes and challenges is critical in long-term relationships. It allows both parties to evolve and grow together.

Applying a Long-Term Relationship Mindset

1. Personal Relationships: In personal relationships, such as marriage, friendships, or family bonds, prioritize communication, patience, and

understanding. Remember that building and maintaining a meaningful relationship takes time and effort.

2. Professional Relationships: In your career, focus on nurturing long-term relationships with colleagues, clients, and mentors. Offer support, maintain open communication, and always strive for mutual growth.

3. Community Involvement: Extend the long-term relationship mindset to your involvement in the community. Building enduring bonds with community members fosters cooperation, trust, and a sense of belonging.

4. Networking: In the professional world, networking is essential. Instead of focusing solely on immediate gains, approach networking with a long-term mindset, valuing relationships over transactions.

5. Personal Development: Invest in your personal growth by seeking out mentors and guides who can provide ongoing support and guidance throughout your journey.

Benefits of a Long-Term Relationship Mindset

1. Stability: Long-term relationships offer stability, a foundation upon which individuals can build their lives and plans.

2. Emotional Support: Knowing that someone has your back can provide a significant source of emotional support.

3. Mutual Growth: In long-term relationships, both parties have the opportunity to learn, grow, and adapt together.

4. Consistency: These relationships are built on consistency and reliability, providing a sense of predictability and trust.

5. Lasting Memories: Long-term relationships create the opportunity to build a treasure trove of shared memories and experiences, contributing to a fulfilling and enriched life.

Conclusion

A long-term relationship mindset is a valuable asset in personal, professional, and community endeavors. It fosters stability, mutual growth, emotional support, and lasting memories. To cultivate this mindset, prioritize qualities like patience, communication, trust, and mutual respect. Remember that building and maintaining meaningful relationships takes time and effort, but the rewards are enduring bonds that enrich your life and the lives of those around you.

The Power of Knowledge: Leveraging Content Marketing for Education

Introduction

In today's digital age, content marketing has evolved beyond mere promotion and branding. It has become a dynamic tool for educational institutions, educators, and organizations to disseminate knowledge and provide value to their target audiences. This educational article delves into the strategic application of content marketing for education, exploring its significance, best practices, and the benefits it offers to learners and institutions alike.

The Significance of Content Marketing for Education

1. Accessible Learning Resources: Content marketing provides an avenue to share educational materials, making learning resources more accessible to a broader audience.

2. Engagement and Interaction: Content marketing allows for interactive and engaging educational experiences, including videos, quizzes, webinars, and more.

3. Positioning as an Authority: Educational institutions and educators can use content marketing to establish themselves as authorities in their respective fields.

4. Building an Online Community: Content marketing fosters the creation of online communities where learners can connect, collaborate, and learn from one another.

5. Reaching a Global Audience: With the power of the internet, educational content can reach a global audience, transcending geographical limitations.

Best Practices for Leveraging Content Marketing in Education

1. Know Your Audience: Understand your target audience's needs, interests, and learning preferences. Tailor your content to cater to their specific requirements.

2. Create High-Quality Content: Strive for excellence in your content creation. Ensure that your content is accurate, well-researched, and engaging.

3. Use Various Formats: Diversify your content by using different formats such as articles, videos, podcasts, infographics, webinars, and interactive quizzes to cater to various learning styles.

4. Consistency Is Key: Maintain a consistent content schedule to keep your audience engaged and coming back for more.

5. Foster Interaction: Encourage learners to engage with your content through comments, discussions, or interactive elements. Create a sense of community around your educational content.

6. Optimize for SEO: Make your content discoverable by optimizing it for search engines. Use relevant keywords, meta descriptions, and alt text for images.

7. Offer Value: Prioritize value over promotion. Your content should solve problems, answer questions, and provide valuable insights to your audience.

Benefits of Leveraging Content Marketing for Education

1. Accessible Learning: Content marketing extends access to educational resources beyond traditional classrooms, making learning accessible to people of all ages and backgrounds.

2. Personalized Learning: Learners can choose content that aligns with their interests and pace, allowing for personalized learning experiences.

3. Cost-Efficiency: Content marketing reduces the cost of delivering education. It minimizes the need for physical infrastructure, textbooks, and printed materials.

4. Reach and Scalability: Educational content can reach a global audience, making it scalable for educational institutions and educators.

5. Improved Engagement: Interactive and engaging content leads to better learner engagement and retention.

6. Establishing Authority: Content marketing helps educational institutions and educators establish themselves as authoritative sources in their field.

Conclusion

Leveraging content marketing for education is a transformative approach that enables accessible, personalized, and engaging learning experiences. By understanding the needs and preferences of your audience, creating high-quality content, and fostering interaction and community, you can provide valuable educational resources to a global audience. Whether you're an educational institution, educator, or an organization with educational content to share, content marketing is a powerful tool for spreading knowledge and enriching the learning journey.

The Power of Follow-Up in Sales: Turning Leads into Loyal Customers

Introduction

In the world of sales, the journey from a lead to a loyal customer is not always a straight line. It often requires persistence, commitment, and the power of follow-up. Follow-up in sales is the process of maintaining contact with potential customers and nurturing the relationship from the initial interaction to the point of conversion. This educational article will delve into the significance of follow-up in sales, best practices for effective follow-up, and the benefits it offers in turning leads into loyal customers.

The Significance of Follow-Up in Sales

1. Building Trust: Consistent follow-up demonstrates your commitment and reliability. It fosters trust between you and the potential customer.

2. Addressing Concerns: Follow-up provides the opportunity to address any concerns, objections, or questions the potential customer may have, leading to better understanding and resolution.

3. Personalization: Follow-up allows you to personalize your interactions and tailor your sales approach to the specific needs and interests of the potential customer.

4. Staying Top of Mind: By maintaining regular contact, you ensure that your product or service remains top of mind, increasing the likelihood of conversion.

5. Maximizing Opportunities: Many potential customers may not be ready to make a decision during the initial interaction. Follow-up extends the opportunity to convert them at a later time.

Best Practices for Effective Follow-Up in Sales

1. Timeliness: Follow up promptly after the initial contact. This shows that you value the potential customer's time and interest.

2. Personalization: Tailor your follow-up messages to the specific needs and interests of the potential customer. Reference previous interactions and discussions to demonstrate your commitment to their unique requirements.

3. Provide Value: Offer something of value during each follow-up. Whether it's additional information, a resource, or an exclusive offer, providing value keeps the potential customer engaged.

4. Persistence with Respect: Be persistent but respect the potential customer's boundaries. If they indicate they are not interested, respect their decision and leave the door open for future communication.

5. Multiple Channels: Use a variety of communication channels, such as email, phone calls, and social media, to reach potential customers. Different people prefer different methods of communication.

6. Record and Track: Keep records of your interactions and track the potential customer's progress through the sales funnel. This data helps you tailor your follow-up approach.

The Benefits of Effective Follow-Up in Sales

1. Increased Conversion Rates: Consistent follow-up leads to higher conversion rates, as potential customers become more familiar and comfortable with your product or service.

2. Better Customer Understanding: Through follow-up, you gain a deeper understanding of the potential customer's needs, enabling you to offer more tailored solutions.

3. Enhanced Customer Loyalty: The relationships established through follow-up often result in loyal customers who return for repeat business and advocate for your products or services.

4. Competitive Advantage: Effective follow-up sets you apart from competitors who may neglect this critical aspect of sales.

5. Maximizing Opportunities: Follow-up ensures that you make the most of every sales opportunity, even with leads that were not initially ready to convert.

Conclusion

Follow-up in sales is a powerful tool for turning leads into loyal customers. It builds trust, addresses concerns, personalizes the sales process, and ensures that your product or service remains top of mind. By following best practices for effective follow-up and respecting potential customers' boundaries, you can increase conversion rates, foster customer loyalty, and gain a competitive advantage in the ever-evolving world of sales. Whether you're in B2B or B2C sales, the power of follow-up cannot be overstated in nurturing valuable, long-term customer relationships.

Building Authority and Expertise: Your Path to Recognition and Influence

Introduction

In a world filled with information and expertise, establishing yourself as an authority in your field is a powerful way to gain recognition, influence, and trust. Whether you're a professional, an entrepreneur, or an enthusiast in any domain, building authority and expertise can open doors to new opportunities and enhance your personal and professional growth. This educational article delves into the importance of building authority and expertise, strategies to achieve it, and the benefits it brings to individuals and organizations.

The Significance of Building Authority and Expertise

1. Trust and Credibility: Becoming an authority in your field lends credibility to your knowledge and skills. People are more likely to trust and seek advice from recognized experts.

2. Influence: Authority and expertise provide a platform for you to influence decisions, opinions, and trends in your area of knowledge.

3. Opportunities: Doors open to new opportunities, such as speaking engagements, collaborations, partnerships, and career advancements, when you're perceived as an expert.

4. Continuous Learning: Building expertise involves a commitment to continuous learning and self-improvement, which keeps you at the forefront of your field.

5. Contribution: As an authority, you have the opportunity to contribute positively to your field, impacting others and leaving a lasting legacy.

Strategies for Building Authority and Expertise

1. Choose Your Niche: Define a specific area within your field where you want to establish your authority. A focused niche allows you to dive deeper into your subject matter.

2. Educate Yourself: Invest time in continuous learning. Stay updated with the latest trends, research, and developments in your chosen field.

3. Share Your Knowledge: Actively share your expertise through various mediums such as blogs, podcasts, social media, webinars, workshops, and publications.

4. Networking: Build relationships with professionals, experts, and enthusiasts in your field. Networking provides opportunities to learn from others and share your knowledge.

5. Create Valuable Content: Produce high-quality content that addresses the needs and interests of your target audience. Solve problems, offer insights, and provide value.

6. Public Speaking: Present your expertise at conferences, webinars, or local events. Public speaking showcases your knowledge and positions you as an authority.

7. Writing: Publish articles, books, or research papers related to your field. Authorship establishes your authority and leaves a lasting record of your expertise.

8. Provide Solutions: Offer solutions and insights that can help others overcome challenges and improve their skills. Being helpful builds trust and authority.

Benefits of Building Authority and Expertise

1. Trust and Credibility: As an authority, you are perceived as a credible and trustworthy source of information or guidance.

2. Influence and Impact: Your expertise allows you to influence decisions, inspire others, and create positive change in your field.

3. Opportunities: Doors open to new career opportunities, partnerships, and collaborations when you're recognized as an expert.

4. Personal Growth: The journey of building expertise leads to personal growth, learning, and a deep understanding of your field.

5. Contribution: Being an authority enables you to contribute positively to your field, helping others and making a lasting impact.

Conclusion

Building authority and expertise is a journey that requires dedication, continuous learning, and a commitment to sharing knowledge with others. The benefits of becoming an authority in your field are far-reaching, including trust, credibility, influence, opportunities, personal growth, and the chance to make a meaningful contribution. Whether you're a professional, an entrepreneur, or an enthusiast, the path to becoming an authority is open to anyone willing to invest the time and effort required to become a recognized expert in their chosen domain.

Empowering Your Customers: The Value of Offering Free Resources

Introduction

In today's competitive business landscape, companies often seek to distinguish themselves by going the extra mile to assist their customers. One powerful way to do this is by offering free resources that provide value and support to the customer's needs. Whether you're a small business, a non-profit organization, or a large corporation, offering free resources can help you build trust, enhance customer relationships, and create a loyal customer base. This educational article explores the significance of offering free resources, strategies to provide value, and the benefits it brings to both businesses and customers.

The Significance of Offering Free Resources

1. Building Trust: Offering free resources is a genuine demonstration of your commitment to helping customers. It builds trust and fosters a positive brand image.

2. Customer Engagement: Free resources are a way to engage and retain customers. When they find value in your offerings, they're more likely to return and recommend your brand to others.

3. Demonstrating Expertise: By providing free resources, you showcase your expertise and establish your authority in your industry or field.

4. Generating Leads: Free resources can serve as lead magnets, attracting potential customers to your business and expanding your reach.

5. Solving Problems: These resources address common problems or questions that customers may have, providing practical solutions and guidance.

Strategies for Providing Value Through Free Resources

1. Identify Customer Needs: Understand your customer's pain points and challenges. Create free resources that directly address these needs.

2. Diversify Content: Offer a variety of free resources, such as eBooks, whitepapers, webinars, templates, guides, infographics, and how-to articles.

3. Personalize Content: Tailor your free resources to different customer segments or personas. Personalization enhances the relevance and effectiveness of your offerings.

4. Regular Updates: Keep your free resources up to date with the latest information, trends, and industry insights to maintain their value.

5. Provide Clear Access: Make it easy for customers to access and download your free resources. User-friendly interfaces and simple navigation are crucial.

6. Promote Effectively: Use your website, social media, email marketing, and other channels to promote your free resources to reach a wider audience.

Benefits of Offering Free Resources

1. Trust and Credibility: Offering free resources establishes trust and credibility, strengthening the customer's perception of your brand.

2. Customer Engagement: Engaged customers are more likely to return and make repeat purchases, contributing to your business's long-term success.

3. Expertise and Authority: Providing valuable resources positions you as an expert in your field, enhancing your authority.

4. Lead Generation: Free resources attract potential customers, expanding your reach and generating new leads for your business.

5. Problem Solving: Free resources offer practical solutions to customer problems, demonstrating your commitment to their success.

Conclusion

Offering free resources is a powerful way to assist your customers and build lasting relationships. It demonstrates your commitment to their needs, builds trust, enhances your brand's credibility, and positions you as an authority in your field. By identifying customer needs, diversifying your content, providing regular updates, and effectively promoting your resources, you can create a valuable resource ecosystem that benefits both your business and your customers. In the end, the value of offering free resources extends beyond immediate customer interactions, as it fosters loyalty, engagement, and mutual growth over time.

Mastering the Art of Nurturing Leads with Email Marketing

Introduction

In the dynamic world of marketing and sales, nurturing leads is a critical process for converting potential customers into loyal, paying clients. One of the most effective tools for lead nurturing is email marketing. With its ability to deliver personalized content and build relationships over time, email marketing is a powerful way to guide leads through the sales funnel. This educational article will explore the importance of email marketing in lead nurturing, best practices, and the benefits it offers to businesses looking to boost their conversion rates.

The Importance of Email Marketing for Nurturing Leads

1. Personalization: Email marketing allows businesses to send personalized and targeted messages to leads, addressing their specific needs and interests.

2. Relationship Building: Email communication builds a relationship with leads over time, increasing trust and familiarity with your brand.

3. Lead Scoring: Through email marketing, businesses can monitor lead engagement and adjust their communication strategies accordingly.

4. Content Delivery: Email is an effective medium for delivering valuable content, such as eBooks, whitepapers, and webinars, which help educate leads and position your business as an authority in the industry.

5. Conversion Path: Email marketing provides a clear path for leads to move from the awareness stage to the decision stage, ultimately leading to conversion.

Best Practices for Nurturing Leads with Email Marketing

1. Segment Your Email Lists: Divide your email lists into segments based on lead characteristics or behavior, allowing for more targeted and relevant communication.

2. Send Relevant Content: Provide leads with content that aligns with their interests and stage in the buying process. This keeps them engaged and moving down the sales funnel.

3. Create Drip Campaigns: Develop automated drip campaigns that send a series of emails at set intervals to educate and nurture leads.

4. Use Personalization: Address leads by their name and personalize content to make the emails feel more individualized.

5. Include a Clear Call to Action (CTA): Every email should have a clear and compelling CTA that guides leads to take the next step in the buying process.

6. Test and Optimize: Continuously test different email elements, such as subject lines, content, and send times, to optimize your email marketing strategy for maximum effectiveness.

7. Monitor Engagement: Keep an eye on how leads are engaging with your emails. Analyze open rates, click-through rates, and conversion rates to gauge performance.

Benefits of Nurturing Leads with Email Marketing

1. Improved Conversion Rates: Effective lead nurturing through email marketing can lead to higher conversion rates as leads progress through the sales funnel.

2. Cost-Efficient: Email marketing is a cost-effective method to reach leads compared to traditional advertising channels.

3. Relationship Building: Consistent, targeted communication fosters a relationship with leads, increasing trust and loyalty.

4. Data-Driven Insights: Email marketing provides valuable data on lead engagement and behavior, which can inform your marketing strategy.

5. Enhanced Brand Authority: By providing valuable content and addressing lead needs, your business is seen as an authority in your industry.

Conclusion

Nurturing leads through email marketing is an essential part of the sales and marketing process. By providing personalized, relevant content, building relationships, and guiding leads through the sales funnel, businesses can improve conversion rates, lower marketing costs, and establish themselves as trusted authorities in their industry. To succeed in lead nurturing with email marketing, it is crucial to segment email lists, send relevant content, create drip campaigns, personalize communication, and consistently test and optimize strategies. When done right, email marketing becomes a powerful tool for businesses to achieve long-term success and build lasting relationships with their leads.

Crafting Effective Sales Emails: A Guide to Persuasive Communication

Introduction

In the digital age, sales professionals and marketers rely heavily on email to reach potential customers and convert leads into clients. Crafting an effective sales email is a skill that can significantly impact your success in the world of sales and marketing. Well-crafted sales email not only catches the recipient's attention but also persuades them to take action. Let's explore the art of crafting effective sales emails, including key principles, best practices, and strategies for success.

The Key Principles of Effective Sales Emails

1. Personalization: Personalized emails that address the recipient by name and consider their individual needs are more likely to grab attention and engage the reader.

2. Clarity: A well-structured and clear email is more effective. Make your message concise and easy to understand.

3. Relevance: Tailor your email content to the recipient's interests, challenges, and preferences. Highlight the value your product or service offers to them.

4. Compelling Subject Lines: The subject line is the first thing your recipient sees. Craft a compelling subject line that entices them to open the email.

5. Call to Action (CTA): Every sales email should have a clear and compelling CTA that guides the recipient on the next steps they should take.

Best Practices for Crafting Effective Sales Emails

1. Know Your Audience: Understand the pain points, goals, and interests of your target audience. The more you know about them, the better you can tailor your email content.

2. Start with a Strong Subject Line: As mentioned earlier, a compelling subject line is crucial. It should be concise, relevant, and create curiosity or urgency.

3. Address the Recipient: Use the recipient's name to make the email more personal. A personalized greeting immediately grabs attention.

4. Offer Value: Clearly communicate the value of your product or service. Explain how it can solve the recipient's problem or enhance their life.

5. Keep it Concise: Brevity is key in email communication. Avoid lengthy paragraphs and get to the point quickly.

6. Use Visuals: Incorporate relevant visuals like images, infographics, or videos to break up text and make your message more engaging.

7. Customize Your CTA: Your call to action should be specific and relevant to the recipient's needs. Make it clear what you want them to do next.

Strategies for Success in Crafting Sales Emails

1. A/B Testing: Experiment with different subject lines, content, visuals, and CTAs to identify what resonates best with your audience. A/B testing can help you refine your email strategy.

2. Follow-Up: Don't be afraid to send follow-up emails. Sometimes, a prospect needs multiple touches to take action.

3. Timing: Consider the timing of your emails. Send them when your audience is most likely to check their inbox.

4. Mobile Optimization: Ensure that your emails are mobile-responsive, as many recipients read emails on their smartphones.

5. Segment Your List: Segment your email list based on different criteria such as interests, behavior, or demographics. This allows you to send highly targeted messages.

Benefits of Effective Sales Emails

1. Increased Conversions: Well-crafted sales emails can lead to higher conversion rates, turning leads into paying customers.

2. Time Efficiency: Email allows you to communicate with multiple leads simultaneously, saving time compared to one-on-one phone calls.

3. Scalability: Email marketing can be scaled to reach a large number of leads or customers with relatively low effort.

4. Data-Driven Insights: Email campaigns provide valuable data that can inform your sales and marketing strategies.

5. Cost-Effective: Compared to traditional marketing methods, email marketing is a cost-effective way to reach your target audience.

Conclusion

Crafting effective sales emails is both an art and a science. It requires understanding your audience, personalizing your message, and following best practices. When done right, sales emails can significantly increase your chances of converting leads into loyal customers. By focusing on clarity, relevance, and personalization, you can create emails that stand out in crowded inboxes and inspire your recipients to take action. Mastering the art of crafting effective sales emails is a valuable skill for anyone in sales and marketing, ultimately leading to better results and success in your endeavors.

Understanding the Buyer's Journey

Introduction

In the world of sales and marketing, understanding the buyer's journey is crucial for effectively connecting with potential customers and guiding them through the purchasing process. The buyer's journey represents the steps and stages that a consumer goes through when making a purchasing decision. By gaining insight into this journey, businesses can create more targeted and personalized marketing strategies, ultimately increasing their chances of converting prospects into loyal customers. This educational article will explore the buyer's journey, its key stages, and how to tailor your marketing efforts to meet the needs of consumers at each step.

The Three Key Stages of the Buyer's Journey

1. Awareness Stage:

At this stage, the buyer becomes aware of a problem, need, or opportunity. They are in the early stages of researching and identifying their pain points.

2. Consideration Stage:

In the consideration stage, the buyer is actively seeking solutions to their problem. They explore various options and gather information to evaluate which one best addresses their needs.

3. Decision Stage:

The decision stage is where the buyer has identified a solution and is ready to make a purchase. They are comparing specific products or services, looking at factors like pricing, features, and vendor reputation.

Understanding the Buyer's Journey

1. Awareness Stage:

At this stage, the buyer is looking for information and education. Your marketing efforts should focus on providing valuable, educational content that helps the buyer understand their problem or need better.

- Content Types: Blog posts, educational videos, eBooks, and infographics.
- Messaging: Address the buyer's pain points and provide educational information without pushing sales.

2. Consideration Stage:

During the consideration stage, the buyer is evaluating different options. Your marketing efforts should guide them through the evaluation process and provide them with valuable comparisons.

- Content Types: Comparative guides, case studies, product webinars, and expert reviews.
- Messaging: Focus on highlighting the unique features and benefits of your product or service.

3. Decision Stage:

In the decision stage, the buyer is ready to make a purchase. Your marketing efforts should aim to make the buying process as smooth and appealing as possible.

- Content Types: Product demonstrations, free trials, customer testimonials, and special offers.
- Messaging: Encourage the buyer to take action and emphasize what sets your solution apart.

Tailoring Your Marketing Efforts to the Buyer's Journey

1. Content Creation:

Develop content that caters to each stage of the buyer's journey. Offer educational content at the awareness stage, comparison content in the consideration stage, and persuasive content at the decision stage.

2. Lead Nurturing:

Implement a lead nurturing strategy using email marketing, targeted advertising, and personalized messaging to guide prospects through the buyer's journey.

3. Customer Personas:

Create detailed customer personas to better understand your target audience and their pain points. This will allow you to align your content and messaging with their specific needs.

4. Analytics:

Regularly analyze the data to understand how prospects are progressing through the buyer's journey. Adjust your strategies based on the insights gained from your analytics.

Benefits of Understanding the Buyer's Journey

1. More Effective Marketing: Tailoring your marketing efforts to each stage of the buyer's journey results in more effective and relevant communication with your target audience.

2. Higher Conversion Rates: By providing the right information at the right time, you increase the likelihood of converting leads into customers.

3. Improved Customer Satisfaction: Understanding the buyer's journey allows you to meet the expectations and needs of your customers, leading to greater satisfaction and loyalty.

4. Cost Efficiency: Targeted marketing reduces wasted resources, leading to a more cost-efficient marketing strategy.

Conclusion

Understanding the buyer's journey is a fundamental aspect of modern sales and marketing. It enables businesses to create more targeted, relevant, and effective strategies that cater to the specific needs and preferences of potential customers. By focusing on educational content at the awareness stage, comparison materials in the consideration stage, and persuasive messaging at the decision stage, you can guide prospects through their journey and increase your chances of converting them into loyal customers. The benefits of this approach include higher conversion rates, improved customer satisfaction, and cost efficiency, making it a crucial tool for any business seeking success in the competitive marketplace.

Building Business Success: A Comprehensive Guide to Implementing Referral Programs

Introduction

Referral programs have proven to be a highly effective strategy for businesses looking to expand their customer base, increase sales, and foster customer loyalty. These programs leverage the power of word-of-mouth marketing, turning satisfied customers and loyal advocates into brand ambassadors. This educational article explores the importance of implementing referral programs, strategies for creating successful programs, and the benefits they offer to businesses looking to grow through the power of referrals.

The Significance of Implementing Referral Programs

1. Cost-Effective Growth: Referral programs are cost-effective because they leverage the existing customer base to attract new customers, reducing acquisition costs.

2. Trust and Credibility: Referrals are a powerful form of advertising because they come from trusted sources—friends, family, or peers—building immediate credibility.

3. Higher Conversion Rates: Referred customers often have higher conversion rates and lifetime value, as they are pre-qualified by the referrer's endorsement.

4. Enhanced Customer Loyalty: Referral programs reward loyal customers, increasing their commitment to your brand and encouraging them to continue promoting it.

5. Measurable Results: Referral programs are highly trackable, allowing businesses to measure their success and identify areas for improvement.

Strategies for Successful Referral Programs

1. Clear Goals and Objectives: Define the purpose and goals of your referral program, whether it's to acquire new customers, increase sales, or boost brand awareness.

2. Incentives and Rewards: Determine what incentives and rewards you will offer to referrers and their friends. These can include discounts, cash rewards, free products, or exclusive access.

3. User-Friendly Process: Make the referral process as simple and user-friendly as possible. Use dedicated landing pages, email templates, or mobile apps to facilitate referrals.

4. Promotional Materials: Provide referrers with marketing materials like banners, buttons, and social media graphics that make it easy for them to share and promote your brand.

5. Targeted Outreach: Identify your most loyal customers and advocates, and reach out to them directly to encourage participation in the referral program.

6. Effective Tracking: Implement tracking mechanisms to monitor the success of your referral program, including referral sources, conversion rates, and reward distribution.

7. Communication and Transparency: Keep referrers and referees informed about the status of their referrals, rewards, and any program updates.

Benefits of Implementing Referral Programs

1. Increased Customer Acquisition: Referral programs attract new customers at a lower cost compared to traditional advertising and marketing efforts.

2. Enhanced Brand Awareness: Referral programs create brand advocates who spread the word about your business, boosting its visibility.

3. Higher Customer Loyalty: By rewarding loyal customers, referral programs encourage them to continue supporting your brand and advocating on your behalf.

4. Better Conversion Rates: Referred customers tend to have higher conversion rates and a longer customer lifetime value, leading to increased revenue.

5. Measurable Results: Referral programs provide clear metrics and insights that help businesses refine their marketing strategies and achieve growth.

Conclusion

Implementing a well-structured referral program is a valuable strategy for businesses looking to grow, increase customer loyalty, and expand their customer base. It leverages the trust and credibility of word-of-mouth marketing to acquire new customers cost-effectively. By setting clear goals, providing attractive incentives, simplifying the referral process, and maintaining transparent communication, businesses can create successful referral programs that yield measurable results. The benefits are numerous, including increased customer acquisition, enhanced brand awareness, higher customer loyalty, better conversion rates, and cost-efficient growth, making referral programs a valuable asset for any business seeking to achieve success and sustainable expansion.

Building a Loyal Customer Community: A Comprehensive Guide to Success

Introduction

In today's competitive business landscape, building a loyal customer community has become a fundamental strategy for fostering brand advocacy, long-term customer relationships, and sustainable growth. A loyal customer community is more than just a group of satisfied buyers; it's a network of advocates who share a deep connection with your brand. This educational article explores the significance of building a loyal customer community, strategies to cultivate such a community, and the benefits it offers to businesses looking to thrive in the digital age.

The Importance of Building a Loyal Customer Community

1. Advocacy and Word-of-Mouth Marketing: Loyal customer communities are a source of powerful advocates who share their positive experiences, driving word-of-mouth marketing and referrals.

2. Feedback and Improvement: Engaging with a community allows businesses to gather valuable feedback and insights, enabling them to continuously improve their products and services.

3. Customer Retention: A loyal customer community helps retain existing customers by creating a sense of belonging and shared values, making them less likely to switch to competitors.

4. Brand Loyalty: A strong community fosters brand loyalty, encouraging customers to choose your products or services over alternatives.

5. Competitive Advantage: Businesses with loyal customer communities have a distinct advantage over competitors, as community members are less susceptible to marketing from other brands.

Strategies for Building a Loyal Customer Community

1. Define Your Brand Values:

Articulate your brand's core values, mission, and purpose. These principles will form the foundation for your community.

2. Provide Exceptional Customer Service:

Outstanding customer service is a key driver of loyalty. Be responsive, empathetic, and attentive to customer needs and concerns.

3. Create an Online Space:

Establish an online platform, such as a private forum, social media group, or community website, where customers can connect and engage.

4. Engage in Conversations:

Actively participate in conversations within your community. Respond to questions, provide support, and join discussions related to your brand.

5. Foster User-Generated Content:

Encourage members to share their experiences, stories, and content related to your products or services. Celebrate user-generated content as a testament to your community's value.

6. Exclusive Rewards:

Offer exclusive rewards, discounts, or access to community members as a token of appreciation for their loyalty.

7. Regular Communication:

Keep the community informed with regular updates, newsletters, and announcements. Share news, product launches, and relevant content.

8. Events and Meetups:

Organize virtual or in-person events and meetups where members can connect, learn, and bond with one another and your brand.

Benefits of Building a Loyal Customer Community

1. Brand Advocacy: Loyal community members become enthusiastic brand advocates who promote your products or services to their networks.

2. Customer Retention: A sense of belonging and shared values within the community contributes to customer retention and reduces churn.

3. Valuable Feedback: Your community provides valuable insights and feedback that can drive product improvements and innovations.

4. Enhanced Brand Loyalty: A strong community fosters deeper brand loyalty and trust among customers.

5. Competitive Edge: Businesses with loyal customer communities have a significant competitive advantage in the marketplace.

Conclusion

Building a loyal customer community is a strategic imperative for businesses seeking long-term success and growth. Such communities go beyond mere customer satisfaction, creating a network of advocates who share values, engage in conversations, and promote your brand. By defining brand values, providing exceptional customer service, creating an online space, fostering user-generated content, offering exclusive rewards, maintaining regular communication, and organizing events, businesses can cultivate a thriving community that offers numerous benefits.

The advantages include brand advocacy, enhanced customer retention, valuable feedback, increased brand loyalty, and a competitive edge in a crowded marketplace. Building a loyal customer community is an investment in the future that pays dividends in brand recognition, customer loyalty, and long-term profitability.

The Power of Social Listening: How to Engage Actively and Gain Insights

Introduction

In today's digitally connected world, social media has become a vital platform for communication and interaction. Businesses, brands, and individuals alike leverage social media to engage with their audience. But it's not just about talking to your audience; it's about listening actively to what they have to say. This practice, known as social listening, offers valuable insights, fosters relationships, and enhances brand reputation. Let's explore the importance of social listening, strategies to engage in active social listening, and the benefits it offers in the age of social media.

The Significance of Social Listening

1. Customer Insights: Social listening provides real-time access to customer opinions, feedback, and sentiments, helping businesses better understand their audience.

2. Competitive Analysis: Monitoring competitors' social media activity can reveal trends, strategies, and gaps to leverage for your own success.

3. Crisis Management: Detecting potential issues early on allows businesses to respond proactively and mitigate reputation-damaging situations.

4. Content Ideas: Social listening can inspire content creation by identifying trending topics, questions, and discussions within your niche.

5. Relationship Building: Engaging with your audience demonstrates a commitment to customer satisfaction and community building.

Strategies for Active Social Listening

1. Choose the Right Tools:

Select social listening tools that suit your needs. Tools like Mention, Hootsuite, and Brandwatch help you track brand mentions, keywords, and industry trends.

2. Define Your Objectives:

Clearly define your social listening objectives. Are you seeking customer feedback, monitoring your brand reputation, or tracking industry trends?

3. Monitor Multiple Platforms:

Engage across multiple social media platforms. Monitor not only your own channels but also popular forums, blogs, and other online communities.

4. Set Up Alerts:

Use alert systems to receive notifications when specific keywords, mentions, or conversations relevant to your brand or industry arise.

5. Analyze Data:

Regularly analyze the data you collect, identifying trends, sentiments, and areas that require attention or action.

6. Respond Appropriately:

Engage with your audience by responding to comments, questions, and mentions. Be proactive in addressing both positive and negative feedback.

7. Track Competitors:

Monitor the social media activity of your competitors to stay informed about their strategies and identify opportunities.

Benefits of Active Social Listening

1. Enhanced Customer Understanding: Social listening provides valuable insights into customer behavior, preferences, and pain points.

2. Improved Brand Reputation: By addressing issues and responding to feedback, you can enhance your brand's reputation and credibility.

3. Competitive Advantage: Staying informed about industry trends and competitors' activities allows you to make informed decisions and gain a competitive edge.

4. Content Inspiration: Social listening inspires content creation by identifying trending topics, questions, and discussions that your audience is interested in.

5. Crisis Prevention: Detecting potential issues early on enables you to proactively manage crises and minimize damage to your brand.

Conclusion

In the age of social media, engaging in active social listening is a vital practice for businesses, brands, and individuals. It provides valuable insights into customer opinions, competitor activities, and industry trends. By choosing the right tools, defining clear objectives, monitoring multiple platforms, setting up alerts, analyzing data, responding appropriately, and tracking competitors, you can effectively leverage social listening to your advantage. The benefits include improved customer understanding, enhanced brand reputation, a competitive advantage, content inspiration, and crisis prevention.

In a world where conversations and opinions are shared openly on social media, active social listening is a powerful tool that can lead to more informed decisions and long-term success.

Building Lasting Connections: How to Leverage Social Media for Relationship-Building

Introduction

In today's digital age, social media has evolved beyond a mere communication tool; it has become a powerful platform for fostering and nurturing relationships. Whether you are an individual, a business, or an organization, leveraging social media for relationship-building can lead to increased engagement, brand loyalty, and long-lasting connections. This educational article explores the importance of using social media for relationship-building, strategies to connect authentically with your audience, and the benefits it offers in the realm of digital interactions.

The Significance of Leveraging Social Media for Relationship-Building

1. Authentic Engagement: Social media enables authentic two-way conversations, creating a sense of closeness and trust with your audience.

2. Increased Brand Loyalty: Building relationships on social media fosters brand loyalty, as customers and followers feel a personal connection with your brand.

3. Personalized Communication: Social media allows for personalized interactions, tailoring messages and content to individual preferences and needs.

4. Customer Insights: Engaging with your audience on social media provides valuable insights into their opinions, feedback, and pain points.

5. Reputation Management: Actively managing your social media presence helps maintain a positive brand reputation and address potential issues swiftly.

Strategies for Leveraging Social Media for Relationship-Building

1. Authentic Engagement:

- Be genuinely interested in your audience's needs and opinions.
- Respond promptly and meaningfully to comments, messages, and feedback.
- Use conversational language that encourages interaction and connection.

2. Storytelling:

- Share personal stories, anecdotes, and experiences to create a more human connection with your audience.
- Use stories to highlight your brand's values and mission.

3. Personalization:

- Address individuals by their names in messages and comments.
- Segment your audience and tailor content to specific interests or demographics.

4. Active Listening:

- Pay attention to what your audience is saying and respond thoughtfully.
- Use social listening tools to monitor mentions and keywords relevant to your brand.

5. User-Generated Content:

- Encourage users to create and share content related to your brand.
- Showcase user-generated content as a way to celebrate your community.

6. Consistency:

- Maintain a consistent presence on social media by posting regularly.
- Set a posting schedule that aligns with your audience's active times.

7. Behind-the-Scenes Content:

- Share behind-the-scenes glimpses of your brand, products, or services.
- This transparency builds trust and makes your audience feel like insiders.

Benefits of Leveraging Social Media for Relationship-Building

1. Authentic Connections: Leveraging social media for relationship-building fosters authentic, meaningful connections with your audience.

2. Increased Brand Loyalty: Engaging with your audience on a personal level leads to greater brand loyalty and customer retention.

3. Personalized Communication: Personalizing interactions enhances customer experiences and strengthens relationships.

4. Valuable Insights: Active engagement on social media provides insights into customer opinions, feedback, and market trends.

5. Reputation Management: Actively managing your social media presence allows for effective reputation management, addressing potential issues and building a positive brand image.

Conclusion

Leveraging social media for relationship-building is a strategic approach that can yield numerous benefits for individuals and businesses alike. By authentically engaging with your audience, sharing personal stories, using personalization, practicing active listening, encouraging user-generated content, maintaining consistency, and offering behind-the-scenes glimpses, you can foster genuine connections with your followers. The advantages of these efforts include authentic connections, increased brand loyalty, personalized communication, valuable insights, and effective reputation management. In a digital landscape where relationships matter, leveraging social media for relationship-building is a powerful tool for creating lasting connections that can drive your personal or business success.

Hosting Webinars for Education and Connection

Introduction

Webinars have emerged as a powerful tool for facilitating education and establishing connections with a global audience. Whether you are an educator, a business professional, or a non-profit organization, hosting webinars can provide a platform to share knowledge, engage your audience, and build meaningful relationships. Let's explore the significance of hosting webinars for education and connection, strategies for successful webinars, and the benefits they offer in the realm of online learning and collaboration.

The Significance of Hosting Webinars for Education and Connection

1. Interactive Learning: Webinars offer an interactive format that allows educators to engage with learners, answer questions, and provide real-time feedback.

2. Global Reach: Webinars have a vast reach, making it possible to connect with individuals from all around the world, transcending geographical boundaries.

3. Cost-Effective Education: Hosting webinars can be a cost-effective alternative to in-person training or seminars, reducing travel and venue expenses.

4. Building Relationships: Webinars foster connections and relationships with your audience, be it students, customers, or members of your community.

5. Versatile Content: Webinars can cover a wide range of topics, from educational lectures to product demonstrations, and can be tailored to diverse audiences.

Strategies for Successful Webinars

1. Define Your Objectives:

Clearly define the goals and objectives of your webinar. What do you want participants to learn, achieve, or take away from the session?

2. Engaging Content:

Create engaging, informative, and visually appealing content. Use a mix of visuals, slides, and multimedia to keep participants interested.

3. Interactive Features:

Incorporate interactive features like polls, Q&A sessions, and chat functions to encourage active participation.

4. Tech and Equipment:

Invest in good quality audio and video equipment to ensure clear communication. Use reliable webinar platforms like Zoom, GoToWebinar, or Webex.

5. Promote in Advance:

Promote your webinar well in advance through various channels such as email, social media, and your website to maximize attendance.

6. Engage Participants:

Encourage active participation by asking questions, involving participants in discussions, and creating a friendly, inclusive environment.

7. Provide Resources:

Offer supplementary resources, such as downloadable materials, reading lists, or post-webinar follow-ups, to support learning.

8. Test and Prepare:

Conduct thorough testing of your equipment, software, and presentation to avoid technical glitches during the webinar.

Benefits of Hosting Webinars for Education and Connection

1. Interactive Learning: Webinars facilitate interactive learning, allowing educators to engage with learners and provide immediate feedback.

2. Global Reach: Hosting webinars transcends geographical boundaries, enabling connections with a worldwide audience.

3. Cost-Efficiency: Webinars are cost-effective, eliminating the need for travel and venue expenses associated with in-person events.

4. Relationship Building: Webinars foster relationships with your audience, whether they are students, customers, or community members.

5. Versatile Content: Webinars cover a wide range of topics and can be tailored to suit various audiences and educational needs.

Conclusion

Hosting webinars for education and connection is a versatile and valuable tool for educators, businesses, and organizations alike. The interactive learning format, global reach, cost-efficiency, relationship-building potential, and versatile content make webinars a compelling choice for those seeking to connect, educate, and engage with a diverse audience. By defining clear objectives, creating engaging content, using interactive features, promoting in advance, engaging participants, providing resources, and thorough preparation, you can ensure successful webinars that yield numerous benefits. In an era where online education and remote collaboration are increasingly important, webinars have emerged as an effective means of achieving educational and connection goals while overcoming geographical barriers.

Leveraging Chatbots for Instant Support

Introduction

In the fast-paced digital age, customer support and communication have evolved significantly. Businesses, whether large or small, are constantly seeking ways to provide quick and efficient support to their customers. Chatbots have emerged as a powerful solution for delivering instant support, answering common queries, and enhancing the overall customer experience. Let's explore the importance of using chatbots for instant support, strategies for implementing them effectively, and the benefits they offer in the realm of customer service and engagement.

The Significance of Using Chatbots for Instant Support

1. Immediate Response: Chatbots offer 24/7 availability, ensuring customers receive quick responses to their queries and issues at any time.

2. Enhanced Efficiency: By automating repetitive tasks and queries, chatbots free up human agents to focus on more complex and meaningful interactions.

3. Cost-Effective: Chatbots are a cost-efficient solution, reducing the need for a large customer support team and minimizing operational expenses.

4. Scalability: Chatbots can handle a high volume of queries simultaneously, making them ideal for businesses experiencing growth.

5. Consistency: Chatbots provide consistent responses, ensuring customers receive uniform and accurate information.

Strategies for Implementing Chatbots for Instant Support

1. Define Objectives:

Clearly define the goals and objectives of your chatbot, such as the types of queries it will handle, response times, and customer satisfaction benchmarks.

2. Develop a Knowledge Base:

Equip your chatbot with a robust knowledge base that includes frequently asked questions, product information, troubleshooting guides, and other relevant data.

3. Natural Language Processing (NLP):

Implement Natural Language Processing to enable your chatbot to understand and respond to natural language queries effectively.

4. Escalation to Human Agents:

Set up a seamless handoff process from the chatbot to human agents when queries are too complex or require personalized attention.

5. Continuous Learning:

Use machine learning to train your chatbot based on historical interactions, enabling it to improve its responses over time.

6. Multichannel Integration:

Integrate your chatbot with various communication channels, including your website, mobile apps, and messaging platforms, to offer a consistent support experience.

7. User Feedback:

Collect and analyze user feedback to fine-tune your chatbot's performance and enhance its capabilities.

Benefits of Using Chatbots for Instant Support

1. Immediate Response: Chatbots provide instant support and 24/7 availability, meeting customer needs at any time.

2. Enhanced Efficiency: By automating repetitive tasks and queries, chatbots improve efficiency and reduce the workload on human agents.

3. Cost-Effective: Chatbots are a cost-efficient support solution, reducing the need for a large customer support team and operational expenses.

4. Scalability: Chatbots can handle a high volume of queries simultaneously, making them ideal for growing businesses.

5. Consistency: Chatbots offer consistent and accurate responses, ensuring customers receive uniform information.

Conclusion

Leveraging chatbots for instant support is a strategic move that enhances the customer support experience while improving efficiency and reducing operational costs. With the ability to provide immediate responses, handle a high volume of queries, and ensure consistency in communication, chatbots are increasingly valuable in the realm of customer service and engagement. By defining clear objectives, developing a knowledge base, implementing NLP, enabling escalation to human agents, facilitating continuous learning, integrating with multiple channels, and collecting user feedback, businesses can successfully implement chatbots to meet customer needs effectively.

Providing Exceptional Customer Service

Introduction

Exceptional customer service is the cornerstone of a successful business. It's not just about resolving issues but also about creating memorable experiences that keep customers coming back. In this educational article, we'll explore the significance of providing exceptional customer service, the key principles, and the strategies to ensure that every customer interaction is a positive one.

The Significance of Providing Exceptional Customer Service

1. Customer Loyalty: Exceptional service builds trust and fosters loyalty, turning one-time buyers into repeat customers.

2. Positive Reputation: Satisfied customers become advocates, sharing their positive experiences, and enhancing your brand's reputation.

3. Competitive Advantage: Exceptional service sets your business apart from competitors who offer only standard customer support.

4. Increased Revenue: Loyal customers are more likely to make larger and more frequent purchases, boosting your bottom line.

5. Problem Resolution: Outstanding service resolves issues effectively, preventing negative reviews and complaints from escalating.

Key Principles of Exceptional Customer Service

1. Active Listening:

Listen attentively to your customers, ask clarifying questions, and show empathy. Let them know you genuinely care about their concerns.

2. Empowerment:

Empower your employees to make decisions and solve problems on the spot without needing multiple layers of approval.

3. Personalization:

Treat customers as individuals, remembering their preferences and past interactions to create a more personalized experience.

4. Timeliness:

Respond promptly to customer inquiries or issues. Quick responses signal your commitment to their needs.

5. Transparency:

Be honest with your customers. If you make a mistake, admit it and work to make it right. Transparency builds trust.

6. Consistency:

Ensure that the quality of your service remains consistent across all channels and touchpoints.

Strategies for Providing Exceptional Customer Service

1. Invest in Training:

Provide ongoing training for your employees, emphasizing the importance of exceptional service and giving them the tools and knowledge to deliver it.

2. Develop Clear Guidelines:

Create clear customer service guidelines and standards, including response times, problem-solving processes, and communication etiquette.

3. Encourage Feedback:

Actively seek feedback from your customers through surveys, reviews, and direct inquiries. Use this input to make improvements.

4. Leverage Technology:

Implement customer relationship management (CRM) software and service platforms to streamline support processes and manage customer interactions more efficiently.

5. Empower Your Team:

Empower your employees to make decisions and resolve issues on the spot. Avoid rigid, scripted responses.

6. Anticipate Needs:

Proactively address customer needs, often before they realize they have them. Offer recommendations, assistance, and proactive communication.

Benefits of Providing Exceptional Customer Service

1. Customer Loyalty: Exceptional service builds customer loyalty and keeps them coming back.

2. Positive Reputation: Satisfied customers share their experiences, enhancing your brand's reputation.

3. Competitive Advantage: Outstanding service sets your business apart from competitors.

4. Increased Revenue: Loyal customers make larger and more frequent purchases, boosting revenue.

5. Problem Resolution: Exceptional service resolves issues effectively, preventing negative reviews and complaints.

Conclusion

Providing exceptional customer service is not only good for your customers but also good for your business. It builds customer loyalty, enhances your brand's reputation, provides a competitive advantage, increases revenue, and resolves issues effectively. By actively listening, empowering your team, personalizing interactions, being timely and transparent, and maintaining consistency, you can deliver memorable experiences that keep customers coming back for more. In an age where customer experience is paramount, providing exceptional service is a strategic imperative for businesses that aspire to long-term success and growth.

Responding to Customer Feedback with Gratitude

Introduction

Customer feedback is an invaluable resource that provides businesses with insights, suggestions, and the opportunity for improvement. How you respond to customer feedback, whether positive or negative, plays a crucial role in shaping your brand's reputation and customer relationships. Let's explore the importance of responding to customer feedback with gratitude, strategies for doing so effectively, and the benefits it brings in terms of customer satisfaction and loyalty.

The Significance of Responding to Customer Feedback with Gratitude

1. Acknowledging Value: Expressing gratitude when responding to feedback demonstrates that you value your customers' opinions and contributions.

2. Building Relationships: Gratitude in responses fosters a sense of connection and builds trust, strengthening the customer-business relationship.

3. Encouraging Feedback: When customers see that their feedback is appreciated, they are more likely to continue providing input, helping you make necessary improvements.

4. Positive Reputation: Demonstrating gratitude in responses enhances your brand's reputation as a customer-centric and appreciative company.

5. Customer Loyalty: Acknowledging feedback with gratitude shows your commitment to providing the best possible experience, encouraging customer loyalty.

Strategies for Responding to Customer Feedback with Gratitude

1. Timeliness:

Respond promptly to customer feedback, whether it's a glowing review, a suggestion, or a complaint. This shows that you value their input.

2. Personalization:

Personalize your responses by addressing the customer by name and referring to specific details from their feedback.

3. Express Sincere Gratitude:

Begin your response by thanking the customer for taking the time to share their feedback. Use words that convey genuine appreciation.

4. Acknowledge Feedback:

Acknowledge the specific feedback the customer provided, whether it's praise, a suggestion, or a concern. Show that you've read and understood their input.

5. Take Responsibility:

If the feedback is about an issue or problem, take responsibility for it and express your commitment to addressing and resolving the matter.

6. Offer Solutions:

When addressing negative feedback, offer solutions or actions you plan to take to rectify the situation. This shows that you're committed to improving.

7. Encourage Further Engagement:

Invite customers to reach out if they have any more feedback or questions. This encourages ongoing dialogue.

8. Maintain Positivity:

Keep your tone positive and respectful, even when addressing negative feedback. Avoid becoming defensive or confrontational.

Benefits of Responding to Customer Feedback with Gratitude

1. Enhanced Customer Relationships: Gratitude in responses fosters a sense of connection, trust, and respect, leading to stronger customer relationships.

2. Increased Customer Satisfaction: Acknowledging feedback and expressing gratitude shows your commitment to addressing concerns, ultimately increasing customer satisfaction.

3. Brand Loyalty: Gratitude encourages customer loyalty as it demonstrates your dedication to providing a positive customer experience.

4. Positive Reputation: Responding to feedback with gratitude enhances your brand's reputation as a customer-centric and appreciative business.

5. Continuous Improvement: Valuing feedback and expressing gratitude encourages ongoing customer engagement, helping you make necessary improvements.

Conclusion

Responding to customer feedback with gratitude is not only a matter of courtesy but also a strategic choice for fostering customer loyalty and building a positive brand reputation. By acknowledging the value of feedback, expressing sincere gratitude, taking responsibility, offering solutions, encouraging further engagement, and maintaining a positive tone, you can demonstrate your commitment to customer satisfaction and ongoing improvement. In an era where customer experience is pivotal, showing gratitude in your responses is an essential practice for businesses that prioritize building meaningful and lasting customer relationships.

Hosting Exclusive Customer Appreciation Events

Introduction

Customer appreciation events are an invaluable opportunity for businesses to express gratitude and strengthen relationships with their most loyal clients. These exclusive gatherings allow you to connect with your customers on a personal level, show your appreciation for their support, and foster a sense of community. Let's explore the significance of hosting exclusive customer appreciation events, strategies for planning and executing them effectively, and the benefits they offer in terms of customer loyalty and brand reputation.

The Significance of Hosting Exclusive Customer Appreciation Events

1. Customer Loyalty: Customer appreciation events reinforce the bond between your business and your loyal clients, leading to increased customer loyalty.

2. Positive Brand Perception: Such events enhance your brand's image, showing that you value and care for your customers.

3. Referral Opportunities: Satisfied and appreciated customers are more likely to refer others to your business, contributing to organic growth.

4. Enhanced Relationships: Hosting these events provides an opportunity for face-to-face interaction, helping you build stronger and more meaningful relationships.

5. Competitive Advantage: Customer appreciation events set your business apart from competitors and demonstrate your commitment to customer satisfaction.

Strategies for Hosting Exclusive Customer Appreciation Events

1. Define Objectives:

Clearly define the goals and objectives of your customer appreciation event. What message do you want to convey, and what outcomes are you aiming for?

2. Guest List:

Create a list of your most loyal customers or clients who will be invited to the event. This should include individuals who have consistently supported your business.

3. Personalized Invitations:

Send personalized invitations that express your gratitude and make attendees feel valued. Consider handwritten notes for a personal touch.

4. Event Venue:

Select a suitable venue that reflects your brand's image and accommodates the number of guests comfortably.

5. Event Format:

Decide on the format of the event, which can range from informal gatherings to more structured affairs, such as cocktail parties or luncheons.

6. Entertainment and Activities:

Incorporate entertainment and activities that match your guests' interests and preferences. This could include live music, games, or interactive sessions.

7. Giveaways and Swag:

Provide guests with branded giveaways and swag items as tokens of appreciation.

8. Engage with Attendees:

Take time to personally connect with your guests, express gratitude, and listen to their feedback and suggestions.

Benefits of Hosting Exclusive Customer Appreciation Events

1. Customer Loyalty: Hosting exclusive events deepens customer loyalty and strengthens the customer-business relationship.

2. Positive Brand Perception: Customer appreciation events enhance your brand's image as one that cares about its customers.

3. Referral Opportunities: Satisfied and appreciated customers are more likely to refer others to your business.

4. Enhanced Relationships: Face-to-face interactions allow you to build stronger, more meaningful relationships with your customers.

5. Competitive Advantage: Customer appreciation events set your business apart from competitors and demonstrate your commitment to customer satisfaction.

Conclusion

Hosting exclusive customer appreciation events is a strategic initiative that can lead to increased customer loyalty, positive brand perception, referral opportunities, enhanced relationships, and a competitive advantage in the marketplace. By clearly defining your objectives, curating a guest list of loyal customers, sending personalized invitations, selecting an appropriate venue, planning engaging activities, providing giveaways, and personally engaging with attendees, you can create memorable events that strengthen your customer relationships. In an age where customer engagement and loyalty are paramount, customer appreciation events are a powerful tool for demonstrating your commitment to your most valued clients and building lasting connections.

Recognizing and Rewarding Customer Loyalty

Introduction

Customer loyalty is the cornerstone of a successful business. Loyal customers not only provide consistent revenue but also act as brand advocates, helping attract new customers. Recognizing and rewarding customer loyalty is a strategic approach that fosters lasting relationships, enhances brand reputation, and drives long-term growth. Let's explore the significance of recognizing and rewarding customer loyalty, strategies for implementing loyalty programs effectively, and the benefits they offer to businesses and their loyal customers.

The Significance of Recognizing and Rewarding Customer Loyalty

1. Customer Retention: Recognizing and rewarding customer loyalty helps retain existing customers, reducing the need for costly acquisition of new ones.

2. Positive Brand Image: Loyalty programs enhance your brand's image by demonstrating your commitment to customer satisfaction and appreciation.

3. Word-of-Mouth Marketing: Loyal customers become brand advocates, sharing their positive experiences with others and contributing to organic growth.

4. Competitive Advantage: Businesses with effective loyalty programs have a competitive edge in the marketplace.

5. Increased Revenue: Loyal customers make larger and more frequent purchases, increasing your revenue and profitability.

Strategies for Recognizing and Rewarding Customer Loyalty

1. Create a Loyalty Program:

Develop a structured loyalty program that provides incentives and rewards for repeat purchases. This can include point-based systems, tiers, or exclusive offers.

2. Personalization:

Personalize your communication with loyal customers by addressing them by name and sending tailored offers that match their preferences.

3. Exclusive Benefits:

Offer exclusive benefits such as early access to sales, personalized recommendations, and invitations to VIP events.

4. Surprise and Delight:

Occasionally surprise loyal customers with unexpected gifts, discounts, or personalized thank-you notes.

5. Acknowledge Milestones:

Recognize and celebrate milestones in the customer's journey, such as their first purchase anniversary or reaching a certain spending threshold.

6. Gather Feedback:

Seek feedback from your loyal customers to continually improve your products, services, and loyalty program.

7. Communicate Gratitude:

Express your gratitude for their loyalty through personalized messages and gestures, making them feel appreciated.

Benefits of Recognizing and Rewarding Customer Loyalty

1. Customer Retention: Recognizing and rewarding loyalty helps retain existing customers, reducing the need for costly customer acquisition.

2. Positive Brand Image: Loyalty programs enhance your brand's image by demonstrating your commitment to customer satisfaction and appreciation.

3. Word-of-Mouth Marketing: Loyal customers become brand advocates, contributing to organic growth through positive word-of-mouth.

4. Competitive Advantage: Businesses with effective loyalty programs have a competitive edge in the marketplace.

5. Increased Revenue: Loyal customers make larger and more frequent purchases, leading to increased revenue and profitability.

Conclusion

Recognizing and rewarding customer loyalty is a strategic initiative that results in increased customer retention, a positive brand image, word-of-mouth marketing, a competitive advantage, and higher revenue. By creating a structured loyalty program, offering personalized incentives, providing exclusive benefits, occasionally surprising and delighting customers, acknowledging milestones, gathering feedback, and communicating gratitude, businesses can demonstrate their commitment to customer satisfaction and appreciation. In an era where customer experience and loyalty are pivotal, recognizing and rewarding customer loyalty is a powerful tool for building lasting customer relationships, enhancing brand reputation, and achieving sustainable growth.

Building a Brand Ambassador Program

Introduction

A brand ambassador program is a strategic initiative that leverages the power of passionate and loyal customers or fans to represent and promote your brand. These individuals, known as brand ambassadors, play a crucial role in building brand awareness, trust, and engagement. Let's explore the importance of building a brand ambassador program, the key steps to create an effective program, and the benefits it offers to businesses seeking to expand their reach and influence.

The Significance of Building a Brand Ambassador Program

1. Authentic Advocacy: Brand ambassadors are authentic advocates who genuinely love your brand, making their recommendations and endorsements more trusted by others.

2. Word-of-Mouth Marketing: Ambassadors actively spread the word about your brand, contributing to positive word-of-mouth marketing and organic growth.

3. Expanded Reach: Leveraging ambassadors extends your brand's reach to new audiences and demographics you may not have reached otherwise.

4. Community Building: A brand ambassador program helps build a community of like-minded individuals who share a passion for your brand.

5. Content Creation: Ambassadors often create user-generated content that can be repurposed for marketing campaigns, providing fresh and authentic content.

Key Steps for Building a Brand Ambassador Program

1. Define Objectives:

Clearly define the goals and objectives of your brand ambassador program. What do you want to achieve? Increased brand awareness, more sales, or something else?

2. Identify Your Ambassadors:

Identify individuals who are already passionate and engaged with your brand. They may be customers, employees, or social media followers.

3. Create an Application Process:

Develop an application process for prospective brand ambassadors. Ask them to explain why they want to represent your brand and what they can bring to the program.

4. Offer Perks and Incentives:

Provide perks and incentives, such as discounts, exclusive access, or branded merchandise, to motivate and reward your ambassadors.

5. Provide Training:

Offer training and guidance to your brand ambassadors, ensuring they understand your brand's values, products, and messaging.

6. Encourage Authenticity:

Encourage your ambassadors to share their honest experiences and opinions about your brand. Authenticity is key to building trust.

7. Create Exclusive Content:

Generate exclusive content, such as promotional materials or social media templates, to make it easier for your ambassadors to promote your brand.

8. Monitor and Support:

Regularly monitor your ambassador program, offer ongoing support, and maintain open communication channels to address questions or concerns.

Benefits of Building a Brand Ambassador Program

1. Authentic Advocacy: Brand ambassadors offer authentic advocacy that is trusted by others.

2. Word-of-Mouth Marketing: Ambassadors contribute to positive word-of-mouth marketing and organic growth.

3. Expanded Reach: Ambassadors extend your brand's reach to new audiences and demographics.

4. Community Building: A brand ambassador program helps build a community of like-minded brand enthusiasts.

5. Content Creation: Ambassadors often create user-generated content that can be repurposed for marketing campaigns.

Conclusion

Building a brand ambassador program is a strategic approach that can lead to authentic advocacy, word-of-mouth marketing, expanded reach, community building, and valuable user-generated content. By clearly defining your objectives, identifying ambassadors, creating an application process, offering incentives, providing training, encouraging authenticity, creating exclusive content, and offering support, businesses can tap into the passion and loyalty of their customers and fans. In an age where trust and authentic recommendations are pivotal, a brand ambassador program is a powerful tool for expanding your brand's influence and building a loyal and engaged community of advocates.

Encouraging Customer Reviews and Referrals

Introduction

Customer reviews and referrals are potent tools in building trust, boosting brand reputation, and expanding your customer base. They serve as genuine endorsements of your products or services, influencing potential buyers and facilitating organic growth. Let's explore the significance of encouraging customer reviews and referrals, effective strategies for implementing these initiatives, and the benefits they offer to businesses aiming to enhance their credibility and reach.

The Significance of Encouraging Customer Reviews and Referrals

1. Trust and Credibility: Positive reviews and referrals from satisfied customers build trust and credibility for your brand.

2. Word-of-Mouth Marketing: Reviews and referrals serve as word-of-mouth marketing, as people trust recommendations from friends, family, or peers.

3. Increased Sales: Customers are more likely to make purchases when they see favorable reviews and recommendations from others.

4. Brand Reputation: Encouraging reviews and referrals enhances your brand's reputation and visibility in the marketplace.

5. Cost-Effective Growth: Reviews and referrals are cost-effective ways to attract new customers, reducing acquisition costs.

Effective Strategies for Encouraging Customer Reviews and Referrals

1. Outstanding Customer Experience:

Provide an exceptional customer experience, ensuring customers are happy with your products or services.

2. Request Feedback:

Proactively ask customers for their feedback and reviews, making it easy for them to share their opinions.

3. Offer Incentives:

Provide incentives for customers to leave reviews or make referrals, such as discounts, exclusive access, or loyalty points.

4. Simplify the Process:

Make the process of leaving reviews and referring others simple and user-friendly. Provide direct links and clear instructions.

5. Timing Matters:

Request reviews and referrals at the right moment, typically after a successful transaction or when customers express satisfaction.

6. Personalize Requests:

Personalize your requests by addressing customers by their names and mentioning specific interactions or purchases.

7. Utilize Multiple Channels:

Request reviews and referrals through various channels, including email, social media, and your website.

8. Show Gratitude:

Express your gratitude to customers who leave reviews or make referrals, making them feel appreciated.

Benefits of Encouraging Customer Reviews and Referrals

1. Trust and Credibility: Positive reviews and referrals build trust and credibility for your brand.

2. Word-of-Mouth Marketing: Reviews and referrals serve as effective word-of-mouth marketing.

3. Increased Sales: Favorable reviews and recommendations influence potential buyers to make purchases.

4. Brand Reputation: Encouraging reviews and referrals enhances your brand's reputation and visibility.

5. Cost-Effective Growth: Reviews and referrals are cost-effective tools for attracting new customers.

Conclusion

Encouraging customer reviews and referrals is a strategic approach that can lead to enhanced trust, word-of-mouth marketing, increased sales, brand reputation, and cost-effective growth. By providing an outstanding customer experience, requesting feedback, offering incentives, simplifying the process, timing your requests, personalizing requests, utilizing multiple channels, and showing gratitude, businesses can leverage the voice of satisfied customers to influence potential buyers. In an era where trust and recommendations are pivotal, encouraging customer reviews and referrals is a powerful tool for building credibility, attracting new customers, and enhancing your brand's reach and reputation.

Using Feedback to Continuously Improve

Introduction

Feedback is a valuable resource that can drive growth, enhance quality, and improve overall performance in various aspects of life, from personal development to business success. Let's explore the significance of using feedback to continuously improve, strategies for gathering and analyzing feedback effectively, and the benefits it offers to individuals and organizations seeking to achieve continuous progress.

The Significance of Using Feedback to Continuously Improve

1. Quality Enhancement: Feedback highlights areas that require improvement, leading to the enhancement of products, services, and processes.

2. Problem Identification: Constructive feedback uncovers issues or challenges that may have gone unnoticed, enabling their timely resolution.

3. Learning and Growth: Feedback provides opportunities for learning and personal or professional growth.

4. Stakeholder Satisfaction: Using feedback to improve fosters satisfaction among customers, employees, and stakeholders.

5. Competitive Advantage: Organizations that actively use feedback to improve gain a competitive edge in the marketplace.

Strategies for Using Feedback to Continuously Improve

1. Establish a Feedback Culture:

Promote a culture of open and honest feedback within your organization, encouraging stakeholders to share their thoughts and ideas.

2. Solicit Feedback:

Actively seek feedback from customers, employees, and other stakeholders using surveys, suggestion boxes, and open communication channels.

3. Analyze Data:

Collect and analyze feedback data, identifying trends, common themes, and areas that require attention.

4. Set Objectives:

Based on the feedback analysis, set specific objectives and improvement goals. What do you want to achieve or change?

5. Develop Action Plans:

Create detailed action plans that outline steps, responsibilities, and timelines for implementing improvements.

6. Implement Changes:

Execute the action plans, making necessary improvements, and monitoring progress.

7. Communicate Progress:

Keep stakeholders informed about the progress of improvements and their impact on the organization.

8. Evaluate Results:

Regularly assess the results of the improvements and gather additional feedback to ensure continued progress.

Benefits of Using Feedback to Continuously Improve

1. Quality Enhancement: Feedback leads to the improvement of products, services, and processes.

2. Problem Identification: Feedback uncovers issues or challenges, enabling their timely resolution.

3. Learning and Growth: Feedback provides opportunities for learning and personal or professional growth.

4. Stakeholder Satisfaction: Using feedback to improve fosters satisfaction among customers, employees, and stakeholders.

5. Competitive Advantage: Organizations that actively use feedback to improve gain a competitive edge in the marketplace.

Conclusion

Using feedback to continuously improve is not just a best practice but a strategic approach that leads to enhanced quality, problem resolution, learning and growth, stakeholder satisfaction, and competitive advantage. By establishing a feedback culture, soliciting feedback, analyzing data, setting objectives, developing action plans, implementing changes, communicating progress, and evaluating results, individuals and organizations can harness the power of feedback to drive progress and success. In a world where adaptation and innovation are crucial, feedback is an invaluable tool for achieving continuous improvement and excellence.

Staying Adaptable in a Changing Market

Introduction

In today's dynamic business landscape, the ability to adapt and thrive in a changing market is critical for individuals and organizations. Markets continuously evolve due to technological advancements, shifting consumer preferences, economic fluctuations, and unforeseen global events. Let's explore the significance of staying adaptable in a changing market, strategies for building and maintaining adaptability, and the benefits it offers to those who seek to navigate uncertainty with resilience and success.

The Significance of Staying Adaptable in a Changing Market

1. Survival and Sustainability: Adaptability is essential for survival and long-term sustainability in a dynamic market.

2. Competitive Advantage: Businesses that adapt effectively gain a competitive edge by responding to emerging opportunities and challenges.

3. Innovation and Growth: Adaptability fosters innovation, leading to growth and expansion in new and emerging markets.

4. Customer Satisfaction: Adapting to changing consumer preferences ensures continued customer satisfaction and loyalty.

5. Resilience: Adaptability is a key component of resilience, enabling businesses and individuals to bounce back from setbacks.

Strategies for Staying Adaptable in a Changing Market

1. Continuous Learning:

Embrace a mindset of continuous learning and curiosity. Stay informed about market trends, emerging technologies, and consumer behavior.

2. Flexibility:

Cultivate a flexible approach to change, be open to new ideas, and encourage innovative thinking within your organization.

3. Market Research:

Invest in thorough market research to understand evolving customer needs, preferences, and emerging opportunities.

4. Scenario Planning:

Anticipate potential scenarios and develop strategies to respond to various market conditions and uncertainties.

5. Diversification:

Diversify your product or service offerings to reduce risk and adapt to market shifts.

6. Agile Decision-Making:

Develop an agile decision-making process that allows for quick and effective responses to market changes.

7. Technology Adoption:

Embrace technological advancements that can streamline processes, enhance customer experiences, and improve your market position.

8. Collaborative Networking:

Build strong networks and partnerships with industry peers to share knowledge and insights and stay informed about market developments.

Benefits of Staying Adaptable in a Changing Market

1. Survival and Sustainability: Adaptability ensures survival and long-term sustainability in a dynamic market.

2. Competitive Advantage: Effective adaptability provides a competitive edge by responding to opportunities and challenges.

3. Innovation and Growth: Adaptability fosters innovation, leading to growth and expansion in new markets.

4. Customer Satisfaction: Adapting to changing consumer preferences ensures continued customer satisfaction and loyalty.

5. Resilience: Adaptability is a key component of resilience, enabling businesses and individuals to bounce back from setbacks.

Conclusion

Staying adaptable in a changing market is a fundamental requirement for success and survival. It offers a competitive advantage, drives innovation and growth, ensures customer satisfaction, and fosters resilience. By embracing continuous learning, flexibility, market research, scenario planning, diversification, agile decision-making, technology adoption, and collaborative networking, individuals and organizations can navigate market uncertainties with confidence and resilience. In an ever-evolving business landscape, adaptability is not merely a valuable skill; it is a strategic imperative for those seeking long-term success and sustained growth.

Measuring Customer Satisfaction and Loyalty

Introduction

In today's highly competitive business landscape, understanding and measuring customer satisfaction and loyalty are vital for maintaining and growing a successful enterprise. Satisfied and loyal customers are more likely to make repeat purchases, refer others, and become advocates for your brand. Let's explore the significance of measuring customer satisfaction and loyalty, methods and metrics for doing so effectively, and the benefits it offers to businesses aiming to enhance customer relationships and drive long-term success.

The Significance of Measuring Customer Satisfaction and Loyalty

1. Customer Retention: Understanding satisfaction and loyalty helps in retaining existing customers, reducing the need for costly customer acquisition.

2. Positive Brand Image: High levels of satisfaction and loyalty contribute to a positive brand image, reinforcing trust and reputation.

3. Word-of-Mouth Marketing: Satisfied and loyal customers become brand advocates, influencing potential buyers through positive word-of-mouth.

4. Competitive Advantage: Businesses that measure and act on customer feedback gain a competitive edge in the marketplace.

5. Continuous Improvement: Measuring customer satisfaction and loyalty provides insights for continuous product and service enhancement.

Methods and Metrics for Measuring Customer Satisfaction and Loyalty

1. Surveys:

Conduct customer satisfaction surveys that include Net Promoter Score (NPS) questions, Customer Satisfaction Score (CSAT) questions, and open-ended questions to gather detailed feedback.

2. Customer Feedback:

Regularly collect and analyze customer feedback through various channels, such as emails, social media, and customer service interactions.

3. Customer Lifetime Value (CLV):

Calculate CLV to determine the total value of a customer's relationship with your business, providing insights into long-term loyalty.

4. Repeat Purchase Rate:

Measure how frequently customers make repeat purchases from your business.

5. Customer Churn Rate:

Calculate the churn rate by determining how many customers you lose over a specific period, providing insight into customer loyalty.

6. Customer Referrals:

Monitor the number of referrals your loyal customers generate, as this is a sign of high satisfaction and loyalty.

7. Online Reviews and Ratings:

Keep an eye on online reviews and ratings on platforms like Yelp, Google, or industry-specific websites.

8. Social Media Monitoring:

Monitor social media mentions and interactions to gauge customer sentiment and satisfaction.

Benefits of Measuring Customer Satisfaction and Loyalty

1. Customer Retention: Understanding satisfaction and loyalty helps in retaining existing customers, reducing the need for costly customer acquisition.

2. Positive Brand Image: High levels of satisfaction and loyalty contribute to a positive brand image, reinforcing trust and reputation.

3. Word-of-Mouth Marketing: Satisfied and loyal customers become brand advocates, influencing potential buyers through positive word-of-mouth.

4. Competitive Advantage: Businesses that measure and act on customer feedback gain a competitive edge in the marketplace.

5. Continuous Improvement: Measuring customer satisfaction and loyalty provides insights for continuous product and service enhancement.

Conclusion

Measuring customer satisfaction and loyalty is not just good practice; it is a strategic imperative for maintaining a successful business. It leads to customer retention, a positive brand image, word-of-mouth marketing, competitive advantage, and continuous improvement. By employing methods such as surveys, feedback collection, CLV analysis, repeat purchase rate measurement, customer churn rate calculation, customer referrals tracking, online review monitoring, and social media sentiment analysis, businesses can gain insights that drive customer relationships and long-term success. In an era where customer experience is pivotal, measuring customer satisfaction and loyalty is a powerful tool for building lasting customer relationships and achieving sustained growth.

Demonstrating Authenticity and Integrity

Introduction

In an era where trust is paramount, authenticity and integrity are virtues that not only define an individual's character but also shape the reputation of businesses and organizations. Demonstrating authenticity and integrity is not only a moral imperative but also a strategic one. Let's explore the significance of demonstrating authenticity and integrity, strategies for embodying these qualities, and the benefits they offer to individuals and businesses striving to build trust and establish credibility.

The Significance of Demonstrating Authenticity and Integrity

1. Building Trust: Authenticity and integrity are the foundation of trust, both on an individual and organizational level.

2. Positive Reputation: Demonstrating these qualities leads to a positive reputation, enhancing credibility and respect.

3. Long-term Success: Authenticity and integrity are keys to building lasting relationships, both personal and professional.

4. Attracting Like-minded Individuals: Authenticity attracts like-minded individuals who share similar values, fostering deeper and more meaningful connections.

5. Ethical Decision-Making: Demonstrating authenticity and integrity guides ethical decision-making, ensuring you make choices aligned with your values.

Strategies for Demonstrating Authenticity and Integrity

1. Know Your Values:

Identify your core values and principles. Understanding what you stand for is the first step in demonstrating authenticity and integrity.

2. Consistency:

Consistently align your actions, decisions, and communication with your values and principles.

3. Open and Honest Communication:

Foster open and honest communication by being transparent about your intentions and decisions.

4. Admit Mistakes:

Acknowledge and take responsibility for your mistakes. Authenticity includes owning up to your errors.

5. Show Empathy:

Empathize with others, understand their perspectives, and actively listen to their concerns.

6. Be Genuine:

Be yourself. Authenticity is about embracing your true self rather than adopting a façade.

7. Ethical Decision-Making:

Prioritize ethical decision-making, even when faced with challenging choices.

8. Build Trust:

Consistently act in ways that build trust, whether it's by meeting commitments, honoring agreements, or being reliable.

Benefits of Demonstrating Authenticity and Integrity

1. Building Trust: Authenticity and integrity are the foundation of trust, both on an individual and organizational level.

2. Positive Reputation: Demonstrating these qualities leads to a positive reputation, enhancing credibility and respect.

3. Long-term Success: Authenticity and integrity are keys to building lasting relationships, both personal and professional.

4. Attracting Like-minded Individuals: Authenticity attracts like-minded individuals who share similar values, fostering deeper and more meaningful connections.

5. Ethical Decision-Making: Demonstrating authenticity and integrity guides ethical decision-making, ensuring you make choices aligned with your values.

Conclusion

Demonstrating authenticity and integrity is not merely a matter of ethical virtue but also a strategic choice for individuals and businesses alike. These qualities underpin trust, reputation, lasting relationships, and ethical decision-making. By knowing your values, maintaining consistency, communicating openly and honestly, admitting mistakes, showing empathy, being genuine, prioritizing ethical decision-making, and consistently building trust, you can foster an environment of trust, respect, and credibility. In an age where authenticity and integrity are highly valued, demonstrating these qualities is a powerful means of building meaningful relationships and achieving long-term success.

Becoming a Trusted Advisor to Your Customers

Introduction

In a business world where trust is the currency that underpins successful relationships, becoming a trusted advisor to your customers is invaluable. Trusted advisors are not just salespeople but partners who offer valuable insights, solutions, and support. Let's explore the significance of becoming a trusted advisor, strategies for achieving this status, and the benefits it brings to businesses and individuals striving to build strong, lasting customer relationships.

The Significance of Becoming a Trusted Advisor to Your Customers

1. Deepened Customer Relationships: Trusted advisors cultivate deeper, more meaningful relationships with their customers, resulting in long-term partnerships.

2. Enhanced Credibility: Trusted advisors are considered credible experts in their field, leading to greater customer trust and respect.

3. Increased Sales and Loyalty: Customers who view you as a trusted advisor are more likely to make repeat purchases and remain loyal.

4. Competitive Advantage: Becoming a trusted advisor sets you apart from competitors who are merely transactional in their approach.

5. Consultative Approach: Trusted advisors offer a consultative, problem-solving approach that adds significant value to the customer.

Strategies for Becoming a Trusted Advisor to Your Customers

1. Understand Your Customers:

Take the time to understand your customers' needs, goals, and challenges. You can do this through in-depth research and active listening.

2. Offer Solutions, Not Just Products:

Move beyond pushing products and instead offer solutions that genuinely address your customers' needs and challenges.

3. Consistent Communication:

Maintain open and consistent communication with your customers, providing updates, insights, and relevant information.

4. Be a Knowledge Resource:

Position yourself as a knowledge resource by staying updated on industry trends, best practices, and innovations.

5. Tailor Your Approach:

Tailor your recommendations and solutions to meet the specific needs and circumstances of each customer.

6. Provide Exceptional Service:

Offer exceptional customer service by responding promptly to inquiries, addressing concerns, and ensuring a smooth customer experience.

7. Anticipate Needs:

Anticipate your customers' future needs and proactively suggest solutions or strategies to address them.

8. Offer Insights:

Share valuable insights, thought leadership, and educational content with your customers to help them make informed decisions.

Benefits of Becoming a Trusted Advisor to Your Customers

1. Deepened Customer Relationships: Trusted advisors cultivate deeper, more meaningful relationships with their customers, resulting in long-term partnerships.

2. Enhanced Credibility: Trusted advisors are considered credible experts in their field, leading to greater customer trust and respect.

3. Increased Sales and Loyalty: Customers who view you as a trusted advisor are more likely to make repeat purchases and remain loyal.

4. Competitive Advantage: Becoming a trusted advisor sets you apart from competitors who are merely transactional in their approach.

5. Consultative Approach: Trusted advisors offer a consultative, problem-solving approach that adds significant value to the customer.

Conclusion

Becoming a trusted advisor to your customers is not just about selling products or services; it's about building deep, enduring relationships. It results in enhanced credibility, increased sales and customer loyalty, and a competitive advantage in the market. By understanding your customers, offering solutions, maintaining consistent communication, being a knowledge resource, tailoring your approach, providing exceptional service, anticipating needs, and offering valuable insights, you can establish yourself as a trusted advisor who offers meaningful value to your customers. In an environment where trust and relationship-building are paramount, becoming a trusted advisor is a powerful strategy for achieving long-term success and strong, lasting customer relationships.

Building a Reputation for Exceptional Service

Introduction

In today's competitive business landscape, providing exceptional service is more than just good practice; it's a strategic imperative. Building a reputation for exceptional service can set you apart from competitors, enhance brand loyalty, and drive business growth. Let's explore the significance of building a reputation for exceptional service, strategies for achieving this reputation, and the benefits it offers to businesses and individuals aiming to deliver unparalleled customer experiences.

The Significance of Building a Reputation for Exceptional Service

1. Customer Loyalty: Exceptional service fosters customer loyalty, resulting in repeat business and long-term relationships.

2. Positive Brand Image: A reputation for exceptional service enhances your brand's image and credibility.

3. Word-of-Mouth Marketing: Satisfied customers become brand advocates, leading to positive word-of-mouth marketing.

4. Competitive Advantage: Businesses known for exceptional service gain a competitive edge in the marketplace.

5. Customer Retention: Exceptional service reduces customer churn, as satisfied customers are less likely to switch to competitors.

Strategies for Building a Reputation for Exceptional Service

1. Define Service Standards:

Establish clear service standards and guidelines that set the expectations for your team's performance.

2. Train and Empower Your Team:

Invest in ongoing training to ensure your team has the necessary skills and knowledge to provide exceptional service. Empower them to make decisions that benefit customers.

3. Personalize the Experience:

Treat each customer as an individual. Learn their preferences, use their names, and tailor your service to their unique needs.

4. Active Listening:

Practice active listening to fully understand and address customer concerns and needs.

5. Swift Problem Resolution:

Resolve customer issues and problems swiftly, ensuring a smooth and hassle-free experience.

6. Regular Feedback Collection:

Collect feedback from customers to understand their experiences and identify areas for improvement.

7. Consistent Quality Control:

Maintain consistent quality control to ensure that your service meets or exceeds established standards.

8. Anticipate Customer Needs:

Proactively anticipate customer needs and offer solutions before customers even realize they require assistance.

Benefits of Building a Reputation for Exceptional Service

1. Customer Loyalty: Exceptional service fosters customer loyalty, resulting in repeat business and long-term relationships.

2. Positive Brand Image: A reputation for exceptional service enhances your brand's image and credibility.

3. Word-of-Mouth Marketing: Satisfied customers become brand advocates, leading to positive word-of-mouth marketing.

4. Competitive Advantage: Businesses known for exceptional service gain a competitive edge in the marketplace.

5. Customer Retention: Exceptional service reduces customer churn, as satisfied customers are less likely to switch to competitors.

Conclusion

Building a reputation for exceptional service is not just a matter of good practice; it's a strategic choice that leads to customer loyalty, a positive brand image, word-of-mouth marketing, competitive advantage, and high customer retention. By defining service standards, training and empowering your team, personalizing the customer experience, practicing active listening, offering swift problem resolution, collecting regular feedback, maintaining quality control, and anticipating customer needs, you can set your business or brand apart in a competitive market. In an environment where customer experience is pivotal, building a reputation for exceptional service is a powerful strategy for achieving long-term success and creating a loyal customer base.

Celebrating Customer Success Stories

Introduction

In the world of business, success stories not only validate the value of products or services but also inspire confidence and trust in potential customers. Celebrating customer success stories is a powerful way to showcase the real-world impact of your offerings and build credibility. Let's explore the significance of celebrating customer success stories, strategies for doing so effectively, and the benefits it offers to businesses and individuals aiming to attract, retain, and engage their customers.

The Significance of Celebrating Customer Success Stories

1. Building Trust: Success stories provide tangible evidence of your products or services' effectiveness, building trust among potential customers.

2. Credibility: Success stories demonstrate that your offerings are tried, tested, and reliable, enhancing your brand's credibility.

3. Inspiring Confidence: Success stories inspire confidence and motivate potential customers to take action.

4. Human Connection: Sharing success stories humanizes your brand, making it relatable and resonant with your target audience.

5. Marketing Tool: Success stories serve as a potent marketing tool, helping you stand out in a competitive landscape.

Strategies for Celebrating Customer Success Stories

1. Identify Compelling Stories:

Identify customers who have achieved remarkable results with your products or services. Seek out stories that are compelling and relatable.

2. Request Permission:

Before sharing a customer's success story, obtain their explicit permission. Ensure they are comfortable with you sharing their experience.

3. Craft a Story:

Craft the customer's success story into a compelling narrative. Highlight their journey, challenges, solutions, and outcomes.

4. Use Various Media:

Leverage various media formats, such as written case studies, video testimonials, infographics, or podcasts, to showcase success stories.

5. Share on Multiple Platforms:

Distribute success stories across multiple platforms, including your website, social media, email newsletters, and marketing collateral.

6. Customer Interviews:

Conduct interviews with customers to get firsthand accounts of their experiences and record their voices and emotions.

7. Highlight Specific Outcomes:

Focus on the specific outcomes and benefits your customers have achieved. Use data and statistics when applicable.

8. Use Visuals:

Incorporate visuals, such as before-and-after photos, charts, or graphics, to enhance the storytelling.

Benefits of Celebrating Customer Success Stories

1. Building Trust: Success stories provide tangible evidence of your products or services' effectiveness, building trust among potential customers.

2. Credibility: Success stories demonstrate that your offerings are tried, tested, and reliable, enhancing your brand's credibility.

3. Inspiring Confidence: Success stories inspire confidence and motivate potential customers to take action.

4. Human Connection: Sharing success stories humanizes your brand, making it relatable and resonant with your target audience.

5. Marketing Tool: Success stories serve as a potent marketing tool, helping you stand out in a competitive landscape.

Conclusion

Celebrating customer success stories is not just a means of showcasing accomplishments; it is a strategic approach to building trust, credibility, and confidence among potential customers. Success stories provide social proof, humanize your brand, and serve as powerful marketing tools. By identifying compelling stories, requesting permission, crafting narratives, using various media, sharing on multiple platforms, conducting customer interviews, highlighting specific outcomes, and using visuals, you can effectively leverage success stories to attract, retain, and engage your audience. In a competitive market where trust and credibility are pivotal, celebrating customer success stories is a powerful strategy for achieving business growth and building a loyal customer base.

About the Author

Sydney Brown has spent over thirty-five years in the business world and later in the corporate world. She has learned what works and what doesn't when the goal is to get out of the stale, vanilla world of the generations before us.

She believes that each person has at least one successful business, one book, and one grand adventure in them, but most people don't know how to figure out their best fit, so they stay where they are.

She is a best-selling author, speaker, and coach, helping people reach out of their current situation and reinvent themselves so they can do more than exist and survive while in this great space.

Personally, she's a mom of two adulting children and proudly owns the title of "Crazy Cat Lady" among her friends. After too many years of avoiding living life, she is on a mission to help others identify and begin their own "Great Ascension."

Let's Connect

If you've enjoyed this book, you'll love what else is ahead!
Start out at https://beyourownsolution.com/ and see what you can look forward to.
We have courses, certifications, and life and business focused free groups!

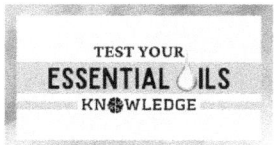

Free Essential Oil Quiz

Aromatherapy Alchemy: Gateway to Wellness

Project Flow Mastery: Universal Laws at Work

Life in Flow: Path Toward Personal Wellness

The Inner Circle

Free Groups:
https://www.facebook.com/groups/fundsfriendsfutures
https://www.facebook.com/groups/shifttimes

Also From TLM Publishing House

FICTION –
Sydney Brown Presents Series
https://www.amazon.com/dp/B0BSBT36HN
The Mall Cadet Series
https://www.amazon.com/gp/product/B0B66MDK3T
All In or Nothing Series
https://www.amazon.com/dp/B0B7FW9W8M
The 7 Wishes Series
https://www.amazon.com/dp/B0B62XJY59
The Deception Series
https://www.amazon.com/dp/B0B5RNQMF1
The Forbidden Love Series (18+)
https://www.amazon.com/dp/B0B5SX24SX

NONFICTION –
How to Start It Series
https://www.amazon.com/dp/B09Y2QHDPM
Aromatherapy Alchemy
https://www.amazon.com/dp/B0CJ5DD5C1

www.ingramcontent.com/pod-product-compliance
Lightning Source LLC
Chambersburg PA
CBHW060227240426
43671CB00016B/2877